SEX AND GOD

The Editor

Linda Hurcombe teaches writing and literature at the American School in London. She lives in the East End of London with her husband, an Anglican priest, and their two children. She is an active supporter of peace and ecology issues, and is co-author (with Susan Dowell) of *Dispossessed Daughters of Eve* (SCM Press, 1981).

A heart pierced by an arrow. Everybody has seen it, sprayed on a wall with other graffiti, carved in a tree trunk, perhaps used as a 'valentine'. It is a sentimental vestige of a powerful archaic perception: androgyny. It is not particularly difficult to look at. Yet most androgynous images are. At least I am uneasy looking at them, and I suspect most people are too.

Any picture of half a woman side to side with half a man meant to represent a total human being at once fascinates, yet repels, depicting as it does something unnatural, indeed impossible, an aberration. What then fascinates? Why do we stare at and investigate such images? Bacause the sign of androgyny shows us something which we feel is true but cannot comprehend or experience. What we gaze at is an artist's attempt at visualizing a mystery: the *coniunctio oppositorum*, the integration of duality.

The symbolic dual being in whom the opposing energies are united is a sign of Divine creative life, the energy born 'in the mind' and 'in the body' of a Divine bi-unity. Each of us experiences this sexual polarity in striving for our own completeness and harmony. It is the sign of the Mother-Father creative spirit within, and in each soul these energies are uniquely reconciled.

The painting on the cover of *Sex and God* visualizes this double birth: the bodily birth (God as Mother of the entire fabric of creation) and the mental birth (God as Father of the creative mind which must be 'spoken' for ideas to be born). Moon and sun, earth and sky, and the tree which lives at both ends, take part in this image about the mystery of wholeness.

Meinrad Craighead

SEX AND GOD

SOME VARIETIES OF
WOMEN'S RELIGIOUS EXPERIENCE

Edited by
Linda Hurcombe

*'The erotic is the realm in which the spiritual, the political
and the personal come together.'*

Starhawk

Routledge & Kegan Paul
New York and London

First published in 1987 by
Routledge & Kegan Paul Inc.
in association with Methuen Inc.
29 West 35th Street, New York, NY 10001

Published in Great Britain by
Routledge & Kegan Paul Ltd
11 New Fetter Lane, London EC4P 4EE

Set in 10/12pt Baskerville.
by Inforum Ltd, Portsmouth
and printed in Great Britain
by the Guernsey Press Co Ltd,
Guernsey, Channel Islands

Library of Congress Cataloging in Publication Data

Sex and God.

Includes index.
1. Women and religion. I. Hurcombe, Linda.
BL458.S47   1987   200'.88042   86–29846

British Library CIP Data also available
ISBN 0-7102-0945-2

Dedication

This one is to your memory,
Rosalie Virginia Williams Gould (mom),
and to my dear friends in Tower Hamlets
Women's Peace Group, especially
Helen Griffiths

The sweet soul is sexual we say
lost in each other, what he called
the id is so much more and
no object in the universe travels faster
than the speed of light, we whisper,
love this motion of light
does not change, I see it
in the saying of it to you,
I hear in your hearing
your hands find me saying
yes, how everything
I could die, fits together,
and the sweet soul
is so large, so large, and hold
me so that bone bursts upon bone
and this is the bone of your face
I say astonished and let me be
possessed by astonishment
of you, your being and the history
of your bright speech breaking in me
as light on every distant feeling
the story of how you came here
evokes to fullness in me, taste
and take you into your mouth, love, this sweetness
your sweetness you made in me
we say, shuddering, delight.

Susan Griffin

CONTENTS

ACKNOWLEDGMENTS

The following friends and colleagues are only the tip of a veritable 'peopleberg' of help and inspiration for this book: Linda Keister for her encouragement not only of yours truly but of many other women writers; Sally Dowell, Judith Jenner and Elaine Willis for helping me assemble my thoughts in the early days; Lindsay Turner for wisdom; Sheelagh Robinson and Polly Blue for making several transatlantic phone calls and thus assuaging my uninteresting neurosis about phoning people; Bernadette Moloney for tracing Jenjoy's flower and walking the dogs; John Moran, Kathy and Merlin Jones for the loan of a wonderful electronic typewriter with a memory and a featherlight touch; Tree Sarasunflower for nursing my occasional despair; Bryony Dahl for venery and sloe gin and Scrabble; Susan Dowell for her front room in Clun and Special Brew and Scrabble; the poets (Lauren Liebling, Bryony Dahl, Mykel Johnson, Polly Blue) who generously offered contributions for the collection; Maggie and Jane at the American School in London for providing sanctuary at my worst points of exhaustion; Linda McKeen for mug shots, and all the McKeens for Caitlin's fun weekends; my children Sean and Caitlin for enduring Mum's primadonna-ish demands for solitude; Tom, my husband, for decorating the bathroom and bedroom, and for enduring my primadonna-ish, etc., etc.; Germaine Greer for raggedy ham and pease pudding and a pleasant afternoon in the country; and finally my editor Eileen Campbell for supporting encouragement from the very beginning and spot-on, no-nonsense editing.

The editor and publishers are grateful to the following for permission to reproduce some of the poetry quoted in this book: Beacon Press, for 'The Woman Dance Naked in Jail' from *Dreaming the Dark* by Starhawk, copyright © 1982 by Miriam Simos; for Alla Bozarth-Campbell's 'Water Women'; *Christian Action Journal* for Polly Blue's 'performance' first published Spring 1982; Persephone Press for the poem 'Some Unsaid Things' by Joan Larkin quoted in the contribution of Elaine Willis; *Women for Life on Earth* for Linda Hurcombe's 'Goddess', first published Spring 1983. The photograph on p. 200 is copyright © Raissa Page.

NOTES ON CONTRIBUTORS

POLLY BLUE is the only child of a Rural Dean and a schoolteacher, was born in North Wales in 1952, and is now not only an alcoholic Aquarian lesbian poet but also an office manager in part of the Methodist church. She has been involved in different bits of the Women's Movement since about 1971, and currently enjoys living in East London and hanging around with Tower Hamlets Women for Peace. At the moment she no longer considers herself either celibate or Christian. However, she is notoriously indecisive, and will probably change her mind again sooner or later. For four years she lived in the same house as Linda Hurcombe as well as several other people, but has just started living alone again. She may soon decide she needs a cat.

SHEILA BRIGGS is a black Roman Catholic from Scunthorpe, England. At present, she is Assistant Professor of Systematic and Historical Theology at the University of Southern California. She studied history and theology at the universities of Cambridge and Tübingen in West Germany. She was a Visiting Lecturer in Women's Studies in Religion at the Harvard Divinity School. Her hobbies are computers, cooking and suing the Protestant Faculty of the University of Tübingen for the doctoral degree it refused her on the grounds of her being Roman Catholic. Much of her research is devoted to obscure German theologians of the nineteenth century, the study of which she attempts to enliven by introducing the perspectives and questions of contemporary liberation movements among women, blacks and gays.

LÉONIE CALDECOTT   I was born in London in 1956. Until recently, I worked as a freelance journalist, with a special interest in the arts, the social impact of technology, women's issues, ecology, psychology and religion. I was also active, to a small extent, in the women's peace movement and eco-feminism. I co-edited a book, *Reclaim the Earth*, contributed to several others, and wrote one of my own, *Women of Our Century*, commissioned by the BBC to accompany the TV series of the same name. Back in 1981 I started researching a book on women and Christianity. The book as originally planned never got written, but it led me into friendships with many interesting women, and to a long process of reflection and change, culminating in my conversion to the Roman Catholic Church in 1983. The focus of my activities since then has gradually shifted away from the political dimension, as I have become more and more aware of the need for personal conversion as the basis for lasting change. The belief that the church is an oppressive patriarchal institution, which originally informed my spiritual journey, no longer seems tenable to me in the light of my personal experience of the faith. My writing these days is very much concerned with trying to express this experience and deepen it, and tends to be more in the form of autobiography, poetry and fiction, though I am also working on a book about St Teresa of Avila. I currently live in London with my husband and small daughter.

JENJOY SILVERBIRCH STRONGBODY CLEVERMIND, wise woman, writer, broadcaster, healer, dancer, Greenham woman, mother of two children, died on Valentine's Day 1986. Linda and Polly edited some of her uncompleted chapter from her notes. Many of us first knew her as one of the most creative members of the Christian Feminist network in this country, though her spirituality later blossomed in other directions. Her first battle with cancer led to radical mastectomy in 1979, and in the last few years of her life she dealt with cancer reappearing throughout her body, and with the possibilities of both dying and living, with great clarity, twice bringing herself back from the edge of death. She founded a support group for women with cancer and a women's writing group; was loving, honest, intelligent and funny; and inspired many people in an enormous number of ways.

SUSAN DOWELL is a true daughter of Eve – and of Fred the fireman, both from the Forest of Dean, where Susan was not, alas, born, but likes to pretend she was. In 1964, she followed her university chaplain to Ethiopia (he had invited her) and married him three days later. There for three and a half years she worked with handicapped children, taught, and gave birth to Clare and Dominic. After a two-year stay in Zambia the family moved to London, where they have worked since 1970 – Susan teaching, writing, acting, working in the peace movement and having twins Ben and Barnaby. She wrote *Dispossessed Daughters of Eve* with Linda Hurcombe in 1981.

HEATHER FORMAINI was born in Melbourne in January 1943.

She grew up for the first two years in an all-female society and became accustomed more and more to the company of women – for seventeen years she was the eldest of four daughters, until a brother was born. She received a BA Hons (History of Art) from the University of London, and is at present completing an MPhil, in women's studies from the University of Western Australia.

Determined from an early age (was it seven?) never to marry, she has pursued a number of professional paths including art, publishing, broadcasting and therapy. Nowadays she works full-time in broadcasting and in therapy with a number of people, mostly women.

Heather Formaini lived in London for fourteen years and returned to Australia at the end of 1984. Every day she remembers the women she left behind.

SUSAN GRIFFIN is the author of *Women and Nature: The Roaring Inside Her; Pornography and Silence: Culture's Revenge Against Nature; Made From This Earth*; the play *Voices*; and she has also published several volumes of poetry. She is currently working on a book on nuclear war called *The First and the Last: A Woman Thinks About War*. She is 43, and lives in Berkeley, California, where she meditates each day, so don't try to phone her before 10.00 a.m. her time.

MARY E. HUNT received her doctorate from the Graduate Theological Union. Over the years she has been active in the development of women's base communities in Latin America, and she is a founder of WATER, the Women's Alliance for Theology, Ethics, and Ritual. The year 1986 marked the publication of *Fierce Tenderness* (Seabury), a book on 'the politics of friendship'.

UNA KROLL is a Christian feminist. She is a school doctor who specializes in the care of handicapped children and socially deprived families. Her work with disadvantaged women has brought her into conflict with church and state. She is the author of five books on different subjects but considers she only writes about various aspects of reconciliation as she has experienced it in her own personality and life. She is a keen supporter of women's ordination in the Church of England, and is also active in the healing ministries of her church.

AILEEN LA TOURETTE   Fast approaching forty, which is no less astonishing than the fact that my oldest son will be fifteen this month, or for that matter that the younger one is eleven. Enough numerology. I enjoy most of what I do at the moment, wish I were a somewhat less anxious mother, am working on it. My second novel, *Cry Wolf*, published by Virago (1986), represents a big step forward for me, and I am happy about it, not complacent at all, but happy. Just finished a collection of poems, *Grit for Icy Roads*, with photographs by Philippa Nice. I like collaboration, shudder at collectivity. My hobby is heresy.

SARA MAITLAND is a feminist writer. Her books include two novels, two volumes of short stories, and two works on feminist theology – despite which she remains a trinitarian. Much of her writing, including her most recent novel *Virgin Territory*, explores the connections between religion and the erotic, so she is now working on a book about women saints. She lives in an East End Victorian Gothic vicarage with its vicar and their two children.

ROSEMARY RADFORD RUETHER is Georgia Harkness Professor of Applied Theology at Garrett Evangelical Theological Seminary in Evanston, Illinois, and faculty member in the joint doctoral programme at Northwestern University. She has been active in the civil rights and peace movements since the early 1960s and has worked to integrate feminism with issues of racism, peace and global economic justice. A specialist in ancient history and Christian origins, Ruether is contributing editor to several Christian publications and the author of eighteen books including *New Woman, New Earth*, *Religion and Sexism*, *Sexism and God Talk*, *Mary, the Feminine Face of the Church*, *Womanguides: Readings toward a Feminist Theology*, and most recently, *Women-Church: Theology and Practice of Feminist Liturgical Communities* (1986).

STARHAWK is a writer, feminist, peace activist, and author of two books, *The Spiral Dance: Rebirth of the Ancient Religion of the Great Goddess*, and *Dreaming the Dark: Magic, Sex and Politics*. She teaches a Women's Studies programme at Antioch West in San Francisco and at Holy Name College, Oakland, and lives with eight other people and two dogs in a collective house in San Francisco. She's very involved in political organization and direct action around militarism and peace. She travels a lot doing talks and lectures and workshops. Starhawk is a priestess of the Religion of the Goddess, also known as witchcraft. Currently she is working on her third book, called *Truth or Dare: An Encounter of Power, Authority and Mystery*, to be published in 1987 by Harper & Row.

HANNAH WARD CSF   After briefly trying my hand at teaching and some exhilarating postgraduate work in Religious Studies, I opted after six years chronic indecision to join a franciscan community. I continue to ask whether that particular lifestyle best expresses who I am. I enjoy the opportunity to do lots of different things with my time and the freedom to experiment. During the last seven years I have lived in London and in Somerset – I love the city and fantasize about living alone in the depths of the country. Right now I value most the warmth and fun of those I live with and the friends who are so much part of my journey.

ELAINE WILLIS   Although born in London I do not seem to have lived in the same place for more than two or three years since my student days. Nowadays when I telephone friends, conversations are prefaced with the question 'Where are you?' and I have learned to take this more as a comment on their lifestyle than my own. I'm currently in the process of moving more permanently into London to live on my own and of disengaging from involvement in formal lesbian and women's organizations in order to give more time to myself and my friends.

INTRODUCTION

This morning a presenter on BBC radio arrests my attention. She reminds her audience that 1985 marks the end of a decade designated the UN Decade for Women. She is interviewing a woman just elected 'Most Feminine Woman of the Year'; this woman is vociferous in her defence of traditional female roles. Although in the past she had been a member of the Alliance of Radical Midwives, she now considers the mothering of her young children her unique, specific full-time preoccupation, and perceives herself as a pioneer traditionalist in a world already sadly won over by 'those feminists'.

'My husband makes the important decisions in our life together; I am in charge of the children and the domestic realm. It is natural for men to dominate. It is *not* natural for women not to want children.' Etcetera. There is a man on the programme, a well-known humorist; he takes Feminine Woman of the Year at her word and gruffly tells her to shut up when she tries to interrupt him. It is his birthday, and as he sips his breakfast champagne, he describes his own chaotically egalitarian domestic life, where the woman he lives with and loves takes full responsibility with him in organizing their lives.

Listening to this exchange I begin to explore my own rejection of this reassertion of traditional values. I scramble in my files for a fragment of a sermon preached in 1884 at Oxford University, a time when the doctrine of natural rights and political democracy fed into women's longing for justice and a public role in the course of society:

> Home is clearly Woman's intended place; and the duties which belong to Home are Woman's peculiar province. The primaeval decree will never lose its force while sun and moon endure, that woman is designed to Man's help. And it is in the sweet sanctities of domestic life, in home duties, in whatever belongs to and makes the happiness of the Home that Woman is taught by the Spirit to find scope for her activity, to recognise her most appropriate sphere of service. To be a keeper at home.

Etcetera. Service, silence, submission.

The Feminine Woman of the Year reveals that she is a Creationist, and I again recognize a person I once was: created by a male deity, formed from a man's rib, destined to be the cause of the fall from grace and innocence because I am curious. The patriarchal myth which undergirds our culture. And although patriarchy is not very old at all

1

when measured against the long sweep of human history, these assumptions die hard. But having grasped the immense damage caused to women by this view of our nature; having grasped, as a student of religion and literature, the immense implications of this truth – that patriarchy is about the domination of both creation and procreation – I come to see that this woman's decision for domesticity as the full meaning of her life comes from fear of change, fear perhaps of a loss of clarity:

> Our fear of change intersects with a fear that lucidity and love cannot co-exist, that political awareness and personal intensity are contradictions, that consciousness must dissolve tenderness, intimacy and loyalty.[1]

Yet despite this predictable backlash, the second wave of the women's liberation movement has birthed immense changes in our perception of what is 'natural' for women. Those of us interested in the spiritual dimension have begun to perceive God from our own experience as women. The personal is political is spiritual.

A wonderful example of woman-defined God talk occurs in Alice Walker's *The Color Purple*.[2] Celie, the main character, has stopped writing letters to God because she's discovered that He's 'trifling, forgitful and lowdown', like all the real men in her life. Celie's friend Shug Avery has different ideas:

> God ain't a he or a she, but a It. Don't look like nothing, she say. It ain't a picture show. It ain't something you can look at apart from anything else, including yourself. I believe God is everything, say Shug. Everything that is or ever was or ever will be. And when you feel that, and be happy to feel that, you've found it . . . She say, My first step from the old white man was trees. Then air. Then birds. Then other people. But one day when I was sitting quiet and feeling like a motherless child, which I was, it come to me: that feeling of being part of everything, not separate at all. I knew that if I cut a tree, my arm would bleed. And I laughed and I cried and I run all around the house. I knew just what it was. In fact, when it happen, you can't miss it. It sort of like you know what, she say grinning and rubbing high up on my thigh.
>
> *Shug*! I say.
>
> Oh, she say. God love all them feelings. That's some of the best stuff God did. And when you know God loves 'em you enjoys 'em a lot more. You can just relax, go with everything that's going, and praise God by liking what you like.
>
> God don't think it dirty? I ast.
>
> Naw, she say. God made it. Listen, God love everything you love – and a mess of stuff you don't . . .

> Well, us talk and talk about God, but I'm still adrift. Trying to chase that old white man out of my head . . . it is like Shug say, You have to git man off your eyeball, before you can see anything a'tall.

Chasing the old white man out of our heads. Engaged in the journey towards a self-defined spirituality we are no longer satisfied with the crudeness of a theology which neglects or excludes the 'she-ness' or 'it-ness' or immanence of the divine, which all too often describes sexual ecstasy as evil. We begin to envisage other possibilities:

> A true transformation of our culture would require reclaiming the erotic as power-from-within, as empowerment. The erotic can become the bridge that connects feeling with doing; it can infuse our sense of mastery and control with emotion so that it becomes life-serving instead of destructive. In the dialectic of merging and separating, the erotic can confirm our uniqueness while affirming our deep oneness with all being. It is the realm in which the spiritual, the political, and the personal come together.[3]

Not that everything is sexual, but that the sexual is an expression of the creative activity which permeates everything and gives it life. This connectedness is a central observation of feminist spirituality:

> Our sexuality is intended to be diffused throughout the entire body. The body as a whole should be the source of sexual pleasure – in responsiveness, feeling, giving, and receiving. Under the pressure of the performance principle, however, our sexuality becomes genitalized, identified with specific 'sex acts'.[4]

Alienation from one's own sexuality and from society go hand in hand. So before I take the Feminine Woman of the Year seriously and scoot back to the comfort of the patriarchal pyramid, I take stock of the cost of Father rule – the poisoned planet, the ravaged ocean, the arms race (whose arms? racing towards what?), millions of women mutilated to make suitable candidates for marriage. The list could be very long. We may have to stay in the wilderness for a while, but we shall not be returning to Egypt.

The journey is not easy. Society protects its deity and The Family with great zeal. Two incidents will illustrate my point. A few years ago, the now-defunct *Gay News* published a poem, part of which praised the image of the crucified Jesus having an erection and rousing the passion of the centurion who was looking after his body. It is a *very* bad poem, written in a style I can only describe as torrid public schoolboy lavatory language. I will not inflict the entire poem on you, but quote one of the less-than-eloquent verses:

3

As they took him from the cross
I, the centurion, took him in my arms –
the tough, lean body
of a man no longer young,
beardless, breathless,
but well hung.

The poem sparked off the first invoking of England's blasphemy law in fifty-five years. In spite of more recent efforts to remove the blasphemy law from the statute books, a novel called *The Wild Girl* by Michèle Roberts (Women's Press, 1985) was published; the author explores fictionally Mary Magdalene's sexual relationship with Jesus. The Attorney General's threat to prosecute sent sales of the book soaring. (How, I wonder, did Robert Graves escape public opprobrium when he wrote *King Jesus* in 1946? In Graves's account Jesus is married.) It occurs to me at this writing that although we have no scriptural record of Jesus' sex life, it is also true that there is no proclamation of his continence, simply that he was 'without sin'. The notion of his celibate state is not the product of the apostolic age, but most likely grew out of Christianity's later contact with Hellenistic dualism.

Paradoxically, while we fervently maintain that our God is not sexual, i.e., that even the incarnate God did not rub genitals, we remain a society obsessed with the exploitation and commercialization of sex. Perhaps we have simply swapped places with our Victorian ancestors of whom it is said that the ultimate social taboo was sex and the ultimate social obsession death, whilst our ultimate taboo today is death and our ultimate obsession sex – sex as religion:

The new opiate of the people, like all religions, has its ritual observance. The discipline imposed is the discipline of the orgasm, not just any orgasm, but the perfect orgasm, regular, spontaneous, potent and reliable. The cathartic function of sex has replaced all other rituals of purification. The blessed are laid-back, into their bodies, in touch with themselves. They shrink from no penetration, they feel no invasion of self, they fear nothing and regret nothing, they defy jealousy. The regular recurrence of orgasm provides the proof that they are in the state of grace. To object that orgasm is itself inadequate to this high purpose is to expose oneself as orgiastically impotent, for sex religion, like all others, relies upon self-fulfilling prophecies. To the faithful, who believe that orgasm will release tension, make all potentialities accessible, dissipate discontent and aggression and stabilize the ego in its right relation to the world, all these are achieved when the sacred duty is discharged. (*sic*)[5]

.

Greer goes on to describe sex as a

> magical, suggestive and utterly indefinable idea. It includes gender, eroticism, genitality, mystery, prurience, fertility, virility, titillation, neurology, psychopathology, hygiene, pornography and sin, all hovering about actual experiences of the most intractable subjectivity, and therefore an ideal focus for religion.[6]

Unfortunately, Greer's eloquent put-down of religion (and sex) does no more than Marx or Freud to illuminate the longing within people who speak of spiritual need, and her description of our culture obsessed with orgasm should more correctly be qualified as a culture obsessed with *male* orgasm and definitions of the erotic.

Although historically women have tended to defer to whatever model of their sexuality offered them by men, we have seen radical changes across the spectrum of the women's movement. Sex may not for much longer be the new opiate of the people. The implications of this self-defined erotic spirituality are far-reaching. All the contributors in this collection repudiate the dominating idol of patriarchy. We make connections between women's spiritual power and her absence from altar and place of blessing, as well as exploring more woman-centred ideas which are the fruit of the second wave of the women's movement. Although its brief is limited to my own background in Judeo-Christian culture, my hunch is that were I to include women of other religious traditions there would be more similarities than differences in our described experience.

The contributors to this book also have these things in common: we love other women; we are enriched by and like to think we enrich women's culture; we are passionately committed to it. We are strong but we are not afraid to cry. We are committed to the survival of the human race, women and men, and working on this one is not easy because we are afraid we may have waited too long to find our voices. We believe that our sexuality and our spirituality are organically related, and when understood will make all our lives more liveable. The religious part of our nature is not a sexual neurosis or an overload of certain hormones; it is fundamental to our longing for human wholeness, a terrible wanting anchoring us together in this treacherous world.

An important difference between this collection and others on feminist spirituality is the inclusion of women who can be described as 'reformist'. By and large, those in the intellectual vanguard of radical feminism believe that equal rights movements within patriarchal religious structures can only go so far in critiquing these traditions. Main energy has therefore focused on feminist witchcraft and Goddess worship, woman-identified culture, and woman-identified chronicles, philosophy and theory.

I have come to believe fervently that, while exploring our own perspectives with passion and discipline, we need to continue to listen to each other. Yes, we all have our limits, and in this case my editor and I create them. I've no desire to drag the sisters back kicking and screaming to Daddy's arms; on the other hand I fail to see what is so odious about the word 'reform', which after all is about making anew what is defective, vicious, corrupt and depraved. We are all connected.

Another important aspect of this collection is that we focus on sex as our starting point precisely because, having come to an understanding of the bankruptcy of phallocentric religion, we still see the need to look at our own perspectives on sexual and spiritual energy. Like life, sexual desire is richer than the order that 'socializes' it; so we explore the spiritual aspects of the erotic. The contributions cluster around the following topics: monogamy; sex and politics; childbirth; healing, sex and dying; feminist sexual psychology; lesbian identity; feminist 'body theology'; and historical perspectives on asceticism and masochism.

The *Shorter Oxford English Dictionary* defines 'sex' thus:

> 1) Either of the two divisions of organic beings distinguished as male and female respectively; the males or the females (esp. of the human race) viewed collectively . . . 3) The sum of those differences in the structure and function of the reproductive organs . . . and of the other physiological differences consequent on these; . . . (examples:) the fair sex, the gentle sex, the softer sex, the weaker sex, the devout sex, the second sex, the female sex . . .

Sex redefined is 'a biologically based need oriented not only toward procreation but toward pleasure and release of tension. It involves varieties of genital and erogenous activities, possibly but not necessarily including orgasm. While sex is usually infused with a variety of human and religious meanings, the focus is upon erotic phenomena of a largely genital nature (a form, according to my friend Bryony, of venery, from Venus; Practice or pursuit of sexual pleasure; indulgence of sexual desire; fig: a source of great enjoyment).

Sexuality is a more diffuse and symbolic term. It both includes and transcends biological organ states. It is a basic dimension of our personhood. It permeates and affects all our feelings, thoughts and actions. It is our self-understanding and way of being in the world as female. Sexuality involves much more than what we do with our genitals. It is 'who we are as body selves who experience the emotional, cognitive, physical, and spiritual need for intimate communion, human and divine.'[7] It is clear that an understanding of women's sexuality is essential to a full understanding of what it means to be made in God's image.

Recently I was talking to some of my students about language and clarity. I asked, 'Do you think with your mind or with your body?'

Reply in chorus: 'Mind.'

'Is your mind part of your body?'

'Yes. But what the mind *produces* is not the body.'

'So,' I asked. 'What do your instructors mean when they ask you to "Use your mind"?'

'They want us to be logical and objective. Facts which are proven and not necessarily related to us or to our own experience. Connected to information gleaned from research into expert opinion.'

'OK, in what way do you participate in this production?'

'We organize the thoughts of others, because teachers want facts.'

'Tell me which of the following statements is factual: (1) Ten new nuclear weapons are being built per day even though there are already four tons of explosives for each person on this planet. (2) We want our children to grow up in a world free from the politics of terror.'

The first statement was clear favourite, the second less acceptable as logical because it involves desire, feelings. Platonic dualism dies hard.

It seems light years ago (it was 1976) that Adrienne Rich made this comment on new ways of thinking:

> I am really asking whether or not women cannot begin at last to think through the body, to connect what has been so cruelly disorganized – our great mental capacities, hardly used; our highly developed tactile sense, our genius for close observation; our complicated, pain-enduring, multi-pleasured physicality. There is for the first time a possibility of converting our physicality into both knowledge and power.[8]

Is there indeed a way of thinking through the body and allowing language to express this connection? I think yes. I am told I think this way because I am female. Susan Griffin expands on this idea of the flesh become word, in my terms a kind of body theology:

Erotic[9] feeling brings one back to this state of innocence before culture teaches us to forget the knowledge of the body. To make love is to become like this infant again. We grope with our mouths toward the body of another being, whom we trust, who takes us in her arms. We rock together with this loved one. We move beyond speech. Our bodies move past all the controls we have learned. We cry out in ecstasy, in feeling. We are back in a natural world before culture tried to erase our experience of nature. In this world, to touch another is to express love; there is no idea apart from feeling and no feeling which does not ring through our bodies and our souls at once.[10]

Sadly, at this writing, the dualistic notion of separate body-mind patterns persists even amongst feminists. Discussion of the term 'spiritual' can release negative feelings. Most of us would agree that there remain huge gaps in feminist analysis, especially in religion, where the direction of western society has led for various reasons either to an intellectual dismissal of religion *per se*, or a transformation of spiritual consciousness into other secularized forms. Until quite recently the history of women and religion has tended to be a neglected area among academic feminists.

An anecdote. During the summer of 1984 I was invited with two other women to address the plenary of the History Workshop Conference at University of London. The convergence of recently researched history on women and religion excited and stimulated me. However, when discussion time rolled round, the organizers of the conference were quite roundly condemned for inviting women who were still 'inside' belief systems (us), whose analysis derived from a position of faith. One of us was a Roman Catholic feminist member of the Communist Party, one a Methodist minister, one a maverick socialist Christian feminist. Even amongst fine feminist historians the notion persists that only from the outside can history be understood. I point this out not as a complaint but as a plea that we respectively recognize the value of what we are doing.

The gaps in our knowledge remain formidable, but we are beginning to recover the 'old' feminism and the new as a single historical process. This time round our words are here to stay, first, because we are now doing our own publishing. Astonishingly, in less than two decades we have evolved from the inky smudges of the mimeograph machine to feminist publishing houses of international repute whose only serious competitor is the floppy disk. Second, we are spinning a worldwide web of women working against oppression, whether it be racial/ethnic, classist, militarist. We will continue to point out the symbolic bases of patriarchy to reclaim rights (and rites) over our own bodies, our society, and our own souls. The personal is sexual is political is spiritual.

I doodle the phrase on a piece of scratch paper. I like the poem that surfaces:

> The.............................Attention
> Personal.....................I
>   is............................being
> Sexual........................desire
>   is............................being
> Political ....we
>   is...........................being
> Spiritual ....love life

There is nothing natural about patriarchy, nor is transcendence summed up by it. We begin to birth ourselves, pushing toward a spirituality which recognizes the need for sexual wholeness. We move from re-membering to invention.

Linda Hurcombe

NOTES

1 Adrienne Rich, 'Husband Right and Father Right', *On Lies, Secrets, and Silence*, New York, Norton, 1979, p. 216.
2 Alice Walker, *The Color Purple*, London, Women's Press, 1983, pp. 166 ff.
3 Starhawk, *Dreaming the Dark; Magic, Sex and Politics*, Boston, Beacon Press, 1982, p. 138.
4 Quoted in James Nelson, *Embodiment: An Approach to Sexuality and Christian Theology*, London, SPCK, 1979, pp. 167 ff.
5 Germaine Greer, *Sex and Destiny*, London, Secker & Warburg, 1984, p. 199.
6 *Ibid.*
7 Nelson, *op. cit.*, p. 18.
8 Adrienne Rich, *Of Woman Born*, New York, Norton, 1976, p. 284.
9 'Eros' is defined as the aggregate of pleasure-directed life instincts whose energy is derived from libido. 'Libido' derives from the Latin for desire, lust, from 'libere', to please – emotional or psychic energy derived from biological urges, and usually goal-directed – sexual desire. Greer comments that 'Human libido is the only force which could renew the world' (*Sex and Destiny*, p. 217).

10 Susan Griffin, 'Pornography and Silence', *Made from this Earth*, London, Women's Press, 1982, p. 160.

I

HERESIES

GODDESS
Towards a Liturgy for Survival

Quite likely you will discover her squatting comfortably
  in your kitchen
  or perhaps
in the night time hallway by the narrow stair.
Quite likely she will arrive at a time
  of quiet futility.
The contours of her body may surprise you –
  ancient pagan circumference, small
  compact, her belly firmly round
  as if it has birthed more than once –
  her breasts large and generous
  as if nuzzled and butted hungrily.
    Wide hips, warm thighs.
Her hands, lithe and lightly strong
  move untrembling sure and travelled,
And her voice evokes the intimacy of stirring sheets.
Something in her eyes
  belies the impression of homely roundness
  – a mingling of impassivity and carnality.
She enters your domain simply equipped.
  A soft chemise, a candle, incense, music,
    one arrow.

Ask her for a map –
  she will not give it you.
She is the fierce archangel of unmarked travel
  from the places where dark and light
  become fused with the lost map of her journey.

Should you deceive her
  she will not return your lie
  with one of her own.
  The lie is not her province.
    She will be silent.
    Hear her silence carefully.

Also you know that you must not
    make an idol of her.

She is the image breaker,
     iconoclast of the simple solution
     of woman fear lived too long.

Already you may have been touched by her visitation
But there is an element of luck, even cunning
     in this discovery.
I am hopeful that you may find her soon.
Attend to the possible moments of her arriving –
     kitchen, narrow stair, quiet despair.

One whispered warning:
do not take her arrival lightly
for it may kill you both.

When you embrace her in the fire warm
  comfort of your bedded dreamtime
    (yes you must)
  you will begin to perceive
  the becoming word of woman
  groaning toward utterance –
  something to move towards.
One flame tongued word forming the firehills
  of your awesome longing
  the conceiving of a liturgy for survival.
  Having attended, you will never be the same.

Linda Hurcombe

THE WOMEN DANCE NAKED IN JAIL

Starhawk

The women arrested at the Diablo Canyon Nuclear Power Plant blockade are detained in an old gym at the California Men's Colony, a prison. We are watched, day and night, by male as well as female guards. The guards sit in the corners, looking over the floor of wall-to-wall mats. The women must undress in front of male eyes. There are no screens, no doors to shut. Late at night, guards walk up and down the rows, shining flashlights onto the faces and bodies of the women, who lie cold under the one blanket which has been provided. It is a situation of deliberate humiliation, a small, calculated harassment, part of the punishment inflicted by the state for challenging its authority with our women's bodies.

Outside is a small exercise yard. The central California sun is hot. And we begin to take off our shirts to lie in the sun bare-breasted. Some of the woman decide to wash their clothes; they wrap themselves in towels, or wear nothing. We feel good about our bodies; we enjoy looking at each other. In that setting of corrugated iron and concrete, we are soft and alive and beautiful.

'I never knew how many shapes and sizes women come in,' says a friend, whose life has not previously allowed her to hang out in the company of two hundred naked women. 'And we're all beautiful. Look at that woman there. She's like a sculpture – like a Venus of Willendorf, a Goddess.'

We are all the Goddess in her multitude of forms: an Aphrodite, an Artemis, a Maiden, a Mother, a Crone. We are all Persephone, dragged into the underworld by the authorities of patriarchy. But our living bodies transform hell. The situation is pornography brought to life, a constant humiliation that enacts a classic sadomasochistic guard/prisoner fantasy. Yet it is transformed by the presence of the erotic. We are connected with each other, and in our love for each other there is no footing for shame.

It is the guards who must adjust to us. Some are embarrassed; some delighted. Some deliberately feed us false information; some are genuinely friendly. They have no vested interest in the nuclear power plant. They have been transferred from San Quentin and Soledad prisons; for them this is a paid holiday. No one has asked them whether men should guard women, whether we should be given extra blankets, hot food or toothbrushes. Most of the women are white and middle-class; the guards are working-class, black, Latino. They have come to this particular job because it was the best of the choices their lives presented to them; as we have come to the blockade for the same reason. In that sense, none of us is free. None of us has the power, except as we demand it and take it, to determine what choices we are offered.

The women discuss the issue of bare breasts. Some feel it undermines the seriousness of our action, that it will look bad to the media. But we choose not to impose a restriction on each other.

At night we dance naked in jail. One woman plays the single guitar they have allowed in. We beat on tin cans; the corrugated iron walls become a drum. We clap our hands; we sing 'Jailhouse Rock'. We paint tuxedos on our bodies and make corsages out of waste paper. We pretend we are having a prom. The music rises and the rhythm rises; we sweat together, the room is filled with the odour of two hundred women. And we dance, knowing that we are allowed this as a privilege; knowing that women who are in a jail alone, who are not white, who do not have a movement, a legal team behind them, whose stories are not of interest to the newspapers, cannot dance, cannot go naked, may be raped and brutalized – not smiled at – by the guards.

Yet we dance, because this is, after all, what we are fighting for: this life, these bodies, breasts, wombs, this smell of flesh; this joy; this freedom – that it continue, that it prevail.

INNER LANDSCAPE: OUTER LANDSCAPE
To My Lady Wisdom

Heather Formaini

'I think it's time for some other tree of knowledge'.[1]

Everything in the world is connected.

Often I wonder whether life isn't just a matter of hermeneutics, a subtle question of interpretation. If that is true, then I'd like to be able to re-trace some of my steps and return to that point in my life where I felt that the world was all right as it was, a safe place for me. Is that what I thought?

Nowadays I'm uncomfortable with the knowledge I have. I wake every morning to the rising sun, the sky lovely with the pink trails of the sky-snails, as though captured by Schiavone or another of the sixteenth-century Venetianists. This, I say, is heaven. And this is earth. Thank you goddess/god. This is your imaging, your imagining, and I am empowered by your beauty. Here I belong.

Travel with me to my office, ten miles from the Australian seaport where I live. I always go on the river route. It surpasses all other beauty I know, and as I travel I talk to it, with it; I see myself reflected in its depths, its ripples my daily turmoils, its currents my conflicts. At this moment I am the river, the river is me. Shading the banks in part are my dear friends, the old wise ones, the eucalyptus immense in their knowledge, compassionate in all their undertakings. We understand each other. For some time after I first arrived here they kept me alive, throwing me lifelines of scented childhood memories, and gum-nuts for my table.

Six or so miles along we cross the bridge. Crossings are important I reflect, especially important in dreams. And this is the part where I would love to spend my day, for here are the pelicans, the herons, and the tiny islands which they call home.

A few minutes later I arrive, breathless with the knowledge of the morning, overwhelmed by the ideas that have flooded me over the distance of the journey, fed to me by my conversations with the water, the trees, and the birds.

Half an hour passes in the office. The Inspector of the World is about to pay us a visit. Again? He's been here every day, he's always here, watch him as he steps out of the lift. The Inspector comes from the World of Reality. He keeps custody of the eyes because he doesn't know about the goddess/god, he has never seen the water, the pelicans, and he's colourblind. But he's an expert on things that matter in the World of Reality. Take, for example, job descriptions, duty statements, time sheets, the reasons women make good secretaries – this is where he is at home.

Part of the problem is I'm not a secretary. And I can see it's a concern for him. I observe this in the way he looks at me (though his theological position requires him to go on keeping custody of the eyes – all the world's beauty is for God alone), the authority he uses with me, the way he doubles up in pain whenever I question the ways of the World of Reality. I'd like to be able to help the Inspector. But he only speaks about helping me. I know what would give him comfort. If I were to return to being the person I once was, all his problems would be over. Should I do it?

As I said, it seems to be a matter of hermeneutics. The world into which I was born had its own. Everything was interpreted from the perspective of the Church. I learned this well, I embraced it, longed to be able to make sense of it. This was, I know now, the World of Reality, of Inspectors. It was also the world at war (this was 1943) where men were men and women supported them. The God of our Fathers and the Church of England protected some of them and sent my father home to us.

That beginning shaped my entire life, and continues to shape it. My life was circumscribed by everything the Church taught, down to fish on Fridays, days of abstinence and fasting. It encompassed my clothes, my education (not for women, lest they get uppity and deny their true calling), my possibilities, all my expectations. I had none.

1970: London, twenty-seven years old, newly arrived from Australia, in love, about to marry (halt!) still practising member of the Church of England, book editor (I know, not a secretary), no revolutionary ideas, never heard of feminism, never heard of goddess, colour purple doesn't exist, acute pain all over, inside and outside. Up to now life, the life I might even have called my own, had been a strange ill-fitting garment not of my choosing. But I couldn't afford to question how it was that I came to be wearing such an unsuitable model. To have removed it would have been to leave me naked and I might then have been destroyed. I had to wait. My centre was still too soft, a raspberry pink cream, a liquid caramel.

I was at that time a true Daughter of Eve. For all the world's ills I took full responsibility, whispered *mea culpa* all the day long. I knew they were all my fault; I had successfully internalized all the theology of the World of Reality. God was God, the Church his mediator, all the laws and commandments had been created for women to preserve us from repeating what had given us that fatal flaw. Greatest amongst all the reasons for my existence was my imitation of the Virgin Mary. I almost succeeded and became a true imitation, a plastic Virgin awash with blue, asexual and unknowing.

It seems to me now that life always presents us with what we need if we have the eyes to see. I had gone to London to marry, but things weren't going well and I was thinking seriously about whether I could go through with it. A friend suggested an analyst to help sort things out. There was a wonderful old woman nearby and she had trained with Jung.

People ask what difference analysis makes. Does it change you? Does it provide a cure? Is one still the same person at the end? I am never able to answer these questions but what I do know is that it was crucial to be able to tell my own story, and to discover that I had a story to tell. If there were a story, there might be a me.

It was long, my story, and extended back in time over thousands of years. For it turned out to be not just my personal story, but that of all my sisters. And in the end it was the story of the way the world has been from the beginning. All this I found inside myself. I could have stopped when I got to the point, 'and this was how God's Spirit, Wisdom, brought the creation to being', or 'and then the Fathers, seeing that it would rob them of their power, decided to falsify the accounts of women's lives', or 'and this is why all women must love and serve a man – so that she can be true to her nature'. I discovered two stories in my inner world, that knotted across the horizon and blurred a vision of delight. One story was true, the other a fabrication. How was I to determine which was which? One represented (I discovered later) the story of the patriarchs – the inner view – while the other was a little-known story-dance which resonated with every movement in my body.

19

In my analysis I climbed many mountains, spent many freezing nights clinging to the rock face, torn and often bleeding. I was in the wilderness day after night recounting the tales of guilt, hurt and horror. At times I plunged to the depths of the ocean in search of the lost fragments of my past. (Remember the time when you see just two and you decided to sail away and were found pushing out the boat on the seashore . . .). It was beautiful, it was painful, it was hell, it was salvation. I glimpsed in my dreams sights of such splendour that nothing could have persuaded me to give up the journey until I knew that I had reached the end, or at least the part where I knew I could continue on alone in safety.

Stone by stone, the old building which had been my home, even me, was dismantled. Today I am using those old stones to build my new place. I have bought a piece of land on a hill and from there I can look back to where I have come from, see the mountains, cast my eyes to the wilderness, and gaze out to sea. Fresh crystal air will breeze through my house and the windows will bear coloured glass to cast reflections on walls of white.

This land, those stones, that mountain, are no longer just the places I have come from. They are me. In them I find the fullest expression of my sexuality. All that is the world of goddess/nature, I know now also as myself. In and with the world I have my unity. No longer is my hope of unity, or wholeness, predicated on the notion 'and when there will be another, and in twoness we will be united'.

Discovering, remembering and reclaiming are the daily exercises of the therapeutic process. With these practices come the removal of layers of armour. For me it was also the putting aside of all perspectives and points of interpretation that had been inherited and which I could not embrace as holding my values and my meaning. By letting go of the past and the collective values the real person buried beneath came into view.

I first let go of the Church. For years I had been sure that even to entertain the ideas of not participating fully in all that it stood for I'd be dumped into hell, if not for my action then at least for my thoughts. Every Sunday I returned from mass with a silent scream lodged in my throat. The more I acknowledged the truth of my own story the more I was offended by the denials of the church. How could the world be denied (the body of the goddess/god?) and cast out life in its denial? How could I continue to associate with it? But, worst, the church denied spirituality, a spirituality for which I would have given everything. I left. I left though fearful that the hand of the God of the Fathers and Inspector of the World would grip my shoulders and cast me back. It didn't happen. And I passed through the door marked Discover the World, Discover Life.

It was for me a new beginning. At this time my point of interpretation changed again. I travelled on, lighter, freer, but not altogether out of the darkness. And then a couple of years later I heard myself articulating an extraordinary notion. I realized finally something I had always felt in a distant sense, which like a thin veil had covered me since the time I was born. Over the years I had drawn nearer to its meaning until one day I discovered that I had always felt guilty. It was like touching the hidden recesses in myself. From that dark place I dredged up the feelings of unworthiness and recognized that I carried within me the guilt of all-woman. My guilt was attached not to any wrong-doing, but simply to having been born into a world which valued men and hated women. From the earliest times I had known that on a crowded planet it was wrong for me to take up the space that rightfully belonged to a man. That was why I was always starving myself to get small; that was my reason for working hard to be beautiful; that was why I cleaned ceaselessly.

If I were small they might not see me, if I were beautiful they might forgive me; if I were clean they might not find any trace of me. When the Inspector of the World came along he could vouch for that.

At first I thought I had found only *my* guilt, my personal guilt. Not long after though I realized, when I began to talk to my women friends, that we all felt the same way. Since then in my work with women I have found that they each carry a huge weight of guilt, the kind which often threatens to reduce them to nothing but obsessiveness. I begin to wonder how many women commit suicide because of this guilt.

So completely had I internalized patriarchal values, even before I was born, that I was prepared to accept my guilt as justifiable and take full responsibility for it. See then the number of falsehoods on which my life had been founded. I could not be happy with this knowledge nor could I possibly hope to understand why so much energy had gone to construct so much untruth. It made me question what else there was to discover that had been so cleverly hidden by those who have so much to fear. The sub-text, the sub-plot:

> A strong woman is a woman in whose head
> a voice is repeating. I told you so,

ugly, bad girl, bitch, bag, shrill, witch,
ballbuster, nobody will ever love you back,
   why aren't you feminine, why aren't
   you soft, why aren't you quiet, why
      aren't you dead?[2]

The two stories once entangled in my unconscious became with the passage of time disentwined: one I claimed to be true, the other false: one based on love; the other on power. The story of truth had come from the dark hidden places of the unconscious and from the collective knowledge to which we all have access. The story of power was that based on patriarchal notions which were constructed in the dark past and which we have carried within us, not through any choice of our own, but simply by being born into a world of patriarchal values.

At the end of my journey I found an ordinary woman who was also beautiful, passionate, desperate, and longing for a world where she could live fully in her knowledge.

Many friends have asked me how it is that a feminist has been able to find a meeting place in Jungian psychology. This is something I am less and less able to understand myself. It is quite true that Jung's psychology was helpful to me over many years and it is often still helpful (I am a therapist now) but it would be foolish to deny that Jung's psychology is not part of the patriarchal establishment. My quarrels with Jungian psychology become more vigorous the more I see the patriarchal basis of mythology, fairy tales and the other buttresses of male dominance. But the concept in Jung's psychology which is most damaging – as damaging I believe as the claims that woman was responsible for the fall – is the notion of the inner contrasexual partner. Although there is something very attractive about the idea of 'inner partner', or even 'inner marriage', there is a sense in which this concept is an extension of the theology which states that woman beguiled innocent man.

And just as the doctrine of the fall has kept the church ever vigilant that women maintain their invisibility from every task of importance, so the concept of the *animus* (the inner, male partner in a woman) has kept women silent in Jungian circles. The practice of the theory (of *anima* and *animus*) reinforces and perpetuates all the old ways of enhancing the lives of men while diminishing not only the lives but the true power of women. The *animus* in women is in my view the voice of the patriarchs, of the Inspector of the World.

A strong woman is a woman in whose head
   a voice is repeating. I told you so,
ugly, bad girl, bitch, bag, shrill, witch,
ballbuster, nobody will ever love you back,
    why aren't you feminine, why aren't
    you soft, why aren't you quiet, why
      aren't you dead?[3]

In his analytic practice Jung formed the opinion that most of the people who came to see him were out of touch with a religious attitude that would give them meaning in life. By religious attitude he meant a deep reverence for life. He saw the task of analysis as putting the person back in touch with that religious impulse. But as in most of his formulation of the concepts, he took as the starting point his own life and lives of other men. From there he assumed the women must be the same – just 'opposite'. What he saw to be the religious process for men he assumed was the same for women. What he failed to do was to grasp the roots of patriarchal culture and religion and see the great damage they had done to women (and men).

Jung not only failed to critique patriarchal models but he also was split in his personal attitude to women and for many years of his life had a companion/lover outside his marriage. This is not to point the finger moralistically but rather to question the nature of his control over two women who in the narrow Swiss society early this century must both have suffered acutely because of his actions – not to say his theories. Jung's personal division of women into mother (wife) and lover seems to be the very split between spirit and matter, the very nature of life itself. The splitting of spirit and matter has its roots in the story of falsehood I found within myself and rejected in favour of the ancient truth.

How much then are 'theories' also constructs with a mandate to control? Perhaps part of the way Jung justified his involvement with two women was through his theory of the *anima*. Jung described the *anima* as the 'compensating feminine element in a man' and went on to say that since there was this aspect to a man's inner world there must be an equivalent part in a woman. This was the *animus*. Whilst the concept momentarily appears to be a concept of equality, in practice it leads to the same inequalities found in any male-dominated system. For women the *animus* has been the instrument of the denial of their power and the means of maintaining their invisibility. And although Jung trained women as analysts and clearly respected many of his women colleagues, one suspects that he didn't easily give up his early opinion that women could love men (only men?) and not much besides. Within the circles of Jungian psychology the terms 'strong animus woman' and 'animus-ridden woman' linger. These are applied to any woman who speaks up for herself or has her own ideas. Women in these groups are paralysed. So it is men who are given positions of control and leadership, unless of course a woman has swallowed so completely the theories that she can be trusted not to speak up on her own behalf. Concepts such as *anima* and *animus* have an extraordinary mystifying power and for years I was convinced that it was my own stupidity which prevented me from understanding their true meaning. For how could anyone, especially a woman, believe something so demeaning, given that we were all born in the image of the goddess/god? If the world which is the image and body of the goddess/god is so beautiful might not also the same beauty be reflected in us? And if the world which is so beautiful is ravaged and plundered daily by the powerful and greedy might not we also be ravaged and plundered by the theories of those who have not examined carefully the substance from which we are made? The more feminist I become the more I feel the damaging nature of such theories. Given Jung's background – born into a late nineteenth-century Protestant family – it is almost possible to forgive him his chauvinism. What is much more difficult to understand is why so many thousands of his followers, many of them analysts, have adhered so rigidly to the tradition

Fortunately, a number of analysts are now revising Jung's concepts, and particularly the *anima* and *animus*. Edward Whitmont, in his book *The Return of the Goddess*, discusses it at some length, and I summarize briefly here:

> We have grown accustomed to reserving the terms *animus* and *anima* for contrasexual drive elements, male traits in women and female traits in men. Yet neither the qualities they represent, nor their specific *animus-anima* compulsivity, nor their capacity of relating us to the Self is limited to either sex . . . In the original Latin the two terms were used synonymously, with some preference given to *anima* in poetic usage. They both cover a wide spectrum of sentiment, affection, disposition, courage, spirit, pride, arrogance, desire, will, purpose, resolve, inclination, pleasure. Jung tended at times to define *animus* in terms of or equivalent to spirit, and *anima* as instinct or soul. Yet as instinct, soul, or spirit they pertain to both sexes equally. The notion of spirituality as a predominant male characteristic

24

and soul as a female property is heirloom of nineteenth-century romanticism. Dominant in Jung's day, it is no longer valid for our generation.[4]

Jung claimed that the quality of Eros (the male god!) belonged to women whilst the prerogative of men was Logos, or thinking. Looking a little more closely at the meaning behind this claim it is possible to see that Jung was claiming something noble for men when in fact he may have been seeking to justify what we know today to be men's separation (from life). By delegating Eros to women he may have been referring to the connectedness on which women's lives are based.

In her study at Harvard University Carol Gilligan found that for women and men there appear to be different systems of moral and psychological development. Gilligan found in her study that from early infancy and childhood girls connect whilst by the time boys are three or even younger they have already made a separation from their mothers and from female values. From these bases the patterns of relatedness and separation extend for women and men throughout life. So it is that in later life a man will describe himself in terms of the kind of work he does, whether he plays sport well, and how he sorts out the finances. 'Wives' are seen as one of the items that make life more or less satisfactory but not as central. A woman, on the other hand, describes her life through her relationships whether or not she is a doctor, a professor, a factory worker, or a full-time mother.[5]

In Jung's system it is because women are connected (Eros-related) that they can only be this. It is as though there is just so much relatedness available in the world and so much Logos – so women get one and men the other (and much more besides). Perhaps it would be more true to say that because women's lives are so based on relationship, they are therefore much more able to relate not only to others but to the world of ideas and creativity. Separation does not enhance life, but fragments it. Only lives bounded by such a sense could make decisions which wipe out whole communities of people; only those guided by separation can construct theories which uphold the need for war; only separateness can move Aboriginal people from the land they have lived in for forty thousand years for the sake of gold or diamonds. Only a man who lives in separation can force separation on his wife and children and never make provision for any of their needs. But in our world it is the separated ones who have the power.

Anne Wilson Schaef exposes the way the powerful separated ones deal with their power. She discusses the differences in the way women and men see love, power, and friendship:

> In the White Male System, power is conceived of in zero-sum fashion. In the Female System, power is seen as limitless. The White Male System assumes that if one has, say, twenty units of power and gives twelve of them away, he had only eight units of power left. The more one shares power or gives it up to others, the less one has for himself. There is only so much power available, and one had better scramble for it and hoard it. This concept of power is based on a scarcity model. In the Female System, power is viewed in much the same way as love. It is limitless, and when it is shared it regenerates and expands. There is no need to hoard it because it only increases when it is given away.[6]

Given, then, that the White Male System as Schaef describes it is based on the scarcity model when it comes to power, love and friendship, does this help to understand what Jung was doing when he theorized about *anima* and *animus*? Was Jung working from the basis of separation and with the notion that the world contained only so much love and so much ability?

Though Jung described the *animus* in the narrowest terms and with such negative implications for women, I believe that if we were to reconstruct the theory we would rename it *Sophia*, Wisdom. For what Jung called *animus* (or 'spirit') I call the Wisdom which for thousands of years has been repressed. She was our beginning and She will be our end, though in the world which *is* She, She has no place. Only lift away the word *animus* and find beneath it the world of Wisdom; find also the truth of women's psychology. I have a plan for women to discover this together. I am looking for an island somewhere in the Mediterranean, the women's island. There we will discover what it is to be women and we will spend long periods together, caring for each other as sisters, tending the earth as mother. Perhaps too (it is my hope) we will discover the truth of our sexuality living in the fullness of each other and the beauty of our island. The flowering gums bloom here. Neither the world nor I will ever be the same.

POSTSCRIPT

As for the Inspector of the World (commonly called the *animus*), I have a plan for him. I shall send him on a wonderful voyage on a ship bound for another island in the Mediterranean. We will fill his cabin with delicacies such as he has never known, remove the custody from his eyes, and allow him the merest glimpse of the women's island. He will be filled with wonder, and repent.

NOTES

1 Edward Whitmont, *The Return of the Goddess*, London, Routledge & Kegan Paul, 1982. The question arises for any woman contemplating analysis of whether it is possible to be analysed by a man. Do men encourage their women clients to their own male values or is the analytic process open enough to allow women to see their own way through and find their own truth? If a male analyst has not recognized the differences between women's truth and patriarchal system the damage to the woman may be immense.
2 Marge Piercy, 'For Strong Women', *The Moon is Always Female*, New York, Alfred Knopf, 1980.
3 *Ibid*.
4 Whitmont, *op. cit.*, p. 142.
5 Carol Gilligan, *In a Different Voice*, Boston, Harvard University Press, 1982, pp. 151–74.
6 Anne Wilson Schaef, *Women's Reality: an Emerging Female System in the White Male Society*, Minneapolis, Winston Press, 1981, pp. 124–5.

4

ESPRIT DE CORPS

Aileen La Tourette

We are the Church of the Valley. We thought of using 'Temple'. But the word made us giggle.

'Your bodies are the temple of the Holy Ghost.' Nuns said it. Priests said it. Parents didn't say it, but they were embarrassed by both bodies and temples, and didn't really like to hear the Holy Ghost mentioned. Especially my father, who was Protestant.

'Holy Ghost,' he echoed, frowning. 'What's that?'

'The third Person of the Blessed Trinity,' I'd recite. 'You know. The Holy Ghost. The one your body is a temple of.'

His frown deepened till his face looked dented. It was kinder to keep quiet and leave him to his heresy, even if it meant a long hitch in purgatory. The rest of us could smile and wave, from heaven.

Unless it meant hell. Father Leonard Feeney, SJ, said, 'Outside the Church there is no salvation,' and meant it. But he was a heretic too, or at least he was a bit confused. You probably couldn't be a Catholic heretic. What he meant was, if you knew the true church was the true church and you still refused to join up, you were damned. Only he thought everybody did know, really, deep down inside. Was his name Feeney, or was that another Jesuit? I forget.

Our church is different. Our way of talking about it is different. We are all epistle writers, evangelists, and we tend to talk a lot about ourselves in the course of our writings. It would be a definite help if other religious texts and letters were a little fuller, a little chattier. It would be nice to know some details. How long was Mary in labour? There must have been another woman present, a midwife, whether amateur or professional. Why do we never hear of her, but only of shepherds and kings and apocryphal little drummer boys? Did she ever write about the event? 'She brought forth her firstborn son and laid him in a manger' is a little cryptic, a little squeamish. Like the delicate

28

'The time for her to be delivered was fulfilled.' Yes, but what of the delivery?

Other items are conspicuous by their absence. What really went on at Cana? 'Woman, what have I to do with thee?' And, I suspect, she gaveth him a look of great witheringness and said in an undertone, 'Son, dost thou know about the birds and bees, or wouldst thou like me to explain, again?' So that he did what was required, pronto.

But I was speaking of the word 'church' and why we preferred it to 'temple'. Our bodies were temples of the Holy Ghost we were told. And where was this dovecote located? It wasn't hard to figure out. Where was there space in your flesh, for a bird to roost? Lots of space, so much you couldn't track it to its boundaries with your exploring fingers? You didn't feel the dove there, either, but it was a ghost, so that was all right. Ears, mouth, nose, all other orifices were less satisfying Holy Ghost sanctuaries. Too small or slimy or waxy. Not that the other place didn't have its own humidity. But the ghost wouldn't be bothered by that. A ghost wouldn't mind the dimensions or the precipitations of the other places either. Still, you knew where its temple was. You just knew. It was the way they said 'body'. Your *body* was the temple of the Holy Ghost. And your body began below the waist. Once you grew tits it began below the neck. It stopped at the knees. Arms, legs (from the knees down), necks, heads, chests (while they were flat), were all innocent and boring, neither sacred nor profane. Your *body* was both.

The Holy Ghost was something alive, hidden at the centre of this taboo region. You never thought where it was in men. You couldn't ask Daddy because he was a Protestant and didn't even know he was a temple. If he was.

Something alive, hidden at the centre, fluttering and fanning out in all directions, more like your brain than your brain. They didn't say much about brains. All the tremors and pulses and hummings you felt along internal wires, were the Ghost in the temple. It was an active familiar. Sometimes you wished you could see it. But there were so many pictures of the first two Persons of the Trinity and the hordes of saints and angels, statues and medals and Hummels, that it was rather satisfying not to know what this poor relation, this Third Person, looked like. There were a few ideas around, the dove and a sort of flashlight beam and tongues of fire, that gave your imagination lots of room. That was the thing about the Holy Ghost. It was closer than the other two, and it gave you lots of room.

The Ghost was nocturnal. As you drifted towards sleep, it woke up and stretched its wings inside you. In daylight, certain things could draw it out of its slumbers without warning. It liked water. It loved swinging on swings. Maybe it got a rush of fresh air when you lifted your legs to pump. Or maybe it liked the sensation of flying. Sometimes its wings seemed to rise up inside you and sweep you away, though you stayed in place.

It loved processions. Processions were probably its favourite. After all, it was a *holy* ghost. You'd dress in your white dress and veil, as if to match it. You were a bit of a ghost too, on those days. And the nuns gave you a basket, painted silver, though it had been green, you could see the green paint underneath, a silver basket heaped with rose petals and snapdragon heads. You followed the monstrance, a long line of white dresses and white veils, with silver baskets. The monstrance was a gold thing with a glass eye at the centre. A consecrated host fit in the glass eye and there were gold spikes around it like rays. The priest held it up, and two altar boys walked backwards in front of it swinging censers of incense. The censers made a ticking noise, like metronomes. You could hear it clearly in the pause between verses of hymns. The altar boys walking backwards through the smoke and the thick, thick fumes were hypnotic, like acrobats. They swung the censers on chains and it seemed, as the church blurred and spun, that they themselves swung, on trapezes, which somehow were mixed up with the swings outside in the playground that you swung on. The feeling was the same, when you closed your eyes. You had to pick up a rose petal or a snapdragon, put it to your lips, and drop it down on the floor of the aisle before the monstrance. Your fingers smelled of incense and roses. The snapdragons didn't smell much. Incense was the Second Person of the Blessed Trinity's favourite smell.

The Second Person was more respectable than the Third. More straightforward, more cleancut, despite the beard. The Third Person was a little shady, a little shifty. It didn't even have a sex. And its favourite smell – well, you knew what that was.

The First Person was the Father, the Old Testament God. His favourite smell was fear. You didn't like him at all, whatever they said. He was nasty, petulant, spoilt and shallow. Actually you were sometimes afraid it was Him, First Person, up there in the monstrance. It was so grand and the spikes so forbidding, Ego and Id. If you wanted to. But I must speak of this word, temple. We decided not to use it not so much because of the giggles, but because of what the giggles were about. It had stuck. Our bodies were, are, temples of the Holy Ghost. The dubious Third Person of ambivalent gender identification had stayed with us. It had remained incarnate in us, far more completely than the Second Person ever had been.

Temple is about time. We didn't know that we wished that emphasis. It's about houses of the Lord. I might go so far (I'm not sure all the others would) as to say we don't want the Lord in our house. He has plenty of houses. Ours are houses of the Holy Ghost. Without monstrances. We want tongues of fire, not sticky wafers.

We do appreciate that we can't live by tongues of fire alone. We have bread, and wine. We don't hocus pocus the latter. It hocus pocuses us.

Sounds like sour grapes. Perhaps it is. 'Going into a trance with Jesus' – that was my secret description of Communion, as a child. Behind your hands, your mind leapt and ran, flashed and then was still. When you dropped your hands, you blinked. The priest was putting the leftovers away in the tabernacle, like food wrapped in foil into the fridge.

It worked because you made it work. You knew you were doing it. Though you might have burnt at the stake rather than admit it. Saint Imelda died of joy at her First Communion. Someone gave me a book about her. It made me so nervous I ate the margins. There were vividly realistic drawings of this little nun (she joined the convent when she was nine) on her knees in rapture. When she was ten she communicated and died, on her knees in rapture. A smell of lilies filled the convent chapel; obviously a Second Person's person all the way.

But you couldn't have died if you'd wanted to, when First Communion rolled around. Getting dressed was much more thrilling and even holier. Putting on your scapular and medals. When the priest put sticky Jesus on your tongue and He immediately stuck, stubbornly, to the roof of your mouth, you could only concentrate on trying to ignore Him, and pray. He tasted a little bit like the margins of the Saint Imelda book.

After that you faked it. Squinched your eyes shut, held your breath, let images and colours roll. Produced, directed, and waited for the Second Person to star in, a strange waking dream. And did he? Well, no. Except that something happened, if you squeezed your eyeballs hard enough.

Church, not temple. Church comes from *cavus*: cave or hollow. And from *cawr*, giant. And from *sura*: strong giant hollow. Or, strong hollow giant.

We had all concluded that we could not afford to carry around the superego and ego allotted us by the church – by any church. They obliterated us. The superego speaks for itself. Usually in words of one syllable. True, He inspired a lot of poetry in His day. But He does not inspire us, and His day is past.

The ego. The Son. I know all this Freudian stuff is somewhat tedious and also reductive, but it is also very persuasive and interesting. If you think about it. What more perfect male phantasy could you design than an identification with the only son of a virgin mother? Of course, they don't want women priests. That's not what the whole thing is for. The only son of a virgin mother who is also God, so that he created her – no wonder they don't describe the labour! Or mention the midwife. It's perfect as it is. Perfect, because it excludes us completely, and I believe, though I know others do not, that that is its entire purpose, its providence. The exclusion is embedded in the mythology, not superimposed. It is the *raison d'être* of that mythology.

So I believe. With regret for the messianic beatnik of my adolescence. But then he, like so many others, preferred his women veiled. If you can't beat 'em, leave 'em, seemed to me a better way. And I don't seem to have lost all that much – at least, not now.

But the festivals, I hear someone say. The great cycles of anticipation and celebration. We have these! The Holy Ghost was there all along. The Holy Ghost was present at the Solstice long before Christ Mass came along. The trees danced with lights and reflectors to trap the colours we all hungered for. The sun returned and was welcomed. We have simply removed the scaffolding.

Ah, yes, you say, but you cannot remove the scaffold. Or the blood-thirsty First Person; they are there in you still. We know. But we do not centralize either.

We have the fertility festival, the time of resurrection. We have our resurrections of the body, while we live. And our eternal moments. Beyond that – we meditate, but we do not plan. We do not make death cosy with family reunions. Those are not usually cosy, anyway.

The Valley – sounds like depression, perhaps? We thought of that. But you see, we are committed to the Holy Ghost, both more known to us, now, and more mysterious, and to the old dovecote, the stirrings there – in that we never ceased to identify with the Spirit, even as we own them and acknowledge them as our own. We are committed to

ESPRIT DE CORPS

the valley, the space, the depression, if you like. To all spaces, where spirits dwell. We are pagan, you might say. We always were.

But what do we do, you ask. Come and visit us. We are a sisterhood. We struggle to unite virgin, whore, mother, prophet – all the titles, all the roles, always with the blessed reassurance that we escape them all, that the spirit is silent, is empty, and it is the spirit we seek. Be more definite, you say. I will. We struggle each to sustain herself in that integrity for which virginity is a metaphor; and we are open, promiscuous. Any women can come to us. We will look you in the eye, if you charge us with injustice in this, but say nothing.

Women come and stay for as long as they can or will, and they pay the same. Some cannot pay. All work with us, as well. Temple prostitution is an old, ennobled calling and we have revived it. It is an exorcism, a catharsis, a sacrament. There is terror in the touch of a stranger. There is pity for the pain of a stranger. There is tenderness, and sometimes harshness, too. We look always towards the great release of energy that is grace, the great release of warping tension, and we are patient, or we try to be. If we are impatient, we try to use that, too, to help us bring about the miracle.

Miracle! It is, and healing, laying on of hands, breathing in of life, sucking out of venom, soreness and pain and frustration, that blunt-toothed bite. Both before and after the lovemaking, there is a bath in the courtyard. It is always quiet there, however many bathe. Some are languid with satisfaction, some hunched with anticipation.

There is rest, or food, or talk. A visit to the library, or some few moments in the church itself, though we do not insist. We have never had anyone come to us who has not gone to the church, the dome. It is stained with colours sometimes, and sometimes, especially at night, it is transparent, and sometimes when it is warm we stand in the spot without it and still feel its shelter. It is a very high very spacious dome, I hasten to add. We are not trying to reproduce the stooped claustrophobia of the womb. Only to engage in a fantasy of it, as the cathedrals do.

But wait, you say, let's go back to this temple prostitution. Is it legal?

Probably not. We've never asked anyone.

But what if two of you – or one of you and a customer – want to go off together?

We do.

Or settle down together?

33

We do.

But you – they – must leave?

Oh no. They can stay. They can both act as temple prostitutes, yes I know it's confusing since we're a church, but that's the technical term – or one, or neither, if they like. We always have quite enough.

And if they don't – do that?

They do something else. There's plenty of other work. None of us are full-time prostitutes. It's too tiring. Our prostitution is part-time privileged. It is stressful, too. We couldn't manage it all the time.

But how does it work?

I will tell you. I will tell you the story of my yesterday. I am Isabelle, by the way. I wanted a liquid, a lubricious name.

You change your names when you – enter?

Shh. Sometimes. If we wish. I wished. I had a very plain, straight name. Isabella. I go to the house with four sides around a central courtyard. No one lives in this house. It is not a home. It has a kitchen, however, and food. It houses our library. It contains our bedrooms, in which we do not sleep; or at least, not much. The fact that it is not a home reminds us that we have no permanent home on earth. Which is not to say we have one elsewhere.

I have changed the way I dress. Not as you might think. I do not wear flowing togas or crepey Greek dresses. I do not rouge my nipples or put flowers in my hair. My Isabelle is a tailored courtesan in a suit. Grey, blue, black. Very severe, pencil skirts or pleated ones, one with the pleats low down, in the front, which makes me feel like a mermaid. A severe sort of mermaid. A bit of a teacher, yes, that's the idea. With my hair up, and the merest trace of makeup. Man-tailored shirts.

My women like this outfit. I could be a tour guide or the curator of a museum. I feel like both. Many who come to me feel their bodies hold wonders, but hold them aloof, behind glass, untouchable. Many who come feel their bodies are exotic countries, but faraway, inaccessible. We all live in ourselves like thieves in museums, on tiptoe, like tourists, inquisitive, intrusive; but we of the valley seek release from these estrangements. It is the Holy Ghost we seek to liberate in us. We wish the spirit to have full use of our flesh. Not only the space between our legs but the whole aviary, veins, arteries, organs. We wish to be alive.

A woman came to me as I lounged and read, in the garden. Only certain kinds of books are good to read while you wait for customers. Poems – because they are telegrammatic and make you alert. They do not whisk you away into themselves, as novels do. It is too distracting, too removing to read novels while you wait. I think so; some do not. It is not something we make rules about. We make relatively few rules.

One is this. You must ask the customer what she wants of you, not a metaphysical question; a physical one. She must choose her own act, her own carnal form.

Once, a woman wished me to take the basket of eggs she had brought over her arm, break the eggs and spread them, wipe the yolks and the whites, all over her, all over, muttering the words of the Latin consecration as I did so, *Hic est corpus mea, Hoc est sanguinis mea*, hocus pocus for sure –

And I did. We talked it through first, discussing every aspect of this act. The waste of food. She would make a donation to Oxfam. She must perform this act, she said, rather I must perform it for her. It had begun to obsess her.

We discussed the likely coldness of the eggstuff on her skin. I informed her she would have to shower it off before she bathed in the common pool. We agreed we were not certain what would happen after the last egg was broken and smoothed against her skin. We would wait and see.

We laughed, wondering if soft feathered chicks would be hatched from our mating, if we mated. We wondered whether her fixation dated from the dovecote days, the temple of the Holy Ghost turned henhouse. Then we were ready.

The eggs were slick as snakeskin, dry, not slimy. Their texture was so elastic, I bounced them between my fingers, the yolks that is, before I broke them. She lay golden as the heroine of Goldfinger, without the threat of suffocation.

We lay on the shells and scrunched them under us, as we rolled over and over, making love. The eggs clung to us both and we stood together under the shower, washing them off. Then we bathed.

We talked, but we did not analyse or interpret. She came back to see me, a week later. The obsession had gone, she said, the fantasy receded. In its place had come a memory. She had been remembering our afternoon together when – quite spontaneously – she found herself in the midst of another afternoon. She was small, and she stood at her mother's side as her mother mixed a cake for her birthday. Her mother cracked an egg into the mixing bowl and she, the woman I had loved, was lifted up onto the Formica and allowed to dab her finger in and feel the funny, runny texture of the egg. Her mother did the same,

35

and their fingers met in the bowl, as they laughed over the strange silk texture of the white, the velvet texture of the yolk. Then they held their fingers under the tap to wash it off, and the water was yet another texture. And then it was her birthday, with more texture and tastes. And before the next birthday, her mother was gone.

She was sad in the possession of her memory, but she would not have had it removed again, replaced by obsession and fantasy. She could make love without the intervention of eggs, which after all was quite handy.

You see what our work is like. Not all compulsions yield, of course. Sometimes there isn't the readiness. But when they do, there is a free flow again, and a chance to risk intimacy, beyond the barrier the compulsion has erected against it, and against the pain of the trapped memory. We work with all wishes, all desires, though we do not always fulfill them to the letter. We have women coming to us seeking death, seeking mutilation, seeking pain. We spend much time on this, discussing what it would do to us to administer these things. Often the talking is itself relaxing, and arousing. We are not afraid of a little pain, in the end, if that remains a craving; but there is a condition, another of our few rules. Those who wish to receive pain must also inflict it, in the same degree, on us. Therefore we have to negotiate a tolerable level. Those who wish to inflict pain have likewise to receive. This is the only way the experience is beneficial. Some who come resent this rule. But they must experience both sides of their own sado-masochism, for that is what it is, of course, and it is always double-edged. We will not do it one way round.

This is one of our discoveries. We are not here to collude with someone in being stuck, however fearful it may be to move on. One must become a child to enter the kingdom of heaven, or as a child, which is what the masochist fervently believes, and so she seeks to be reduced to a child. But she must be the adult as well, to make the experience real, the spanking or scolding or food-withholding or otherwise disciplining adult.

Sometimes people say they will abide by this flipping-over, as it were, and then refuse. We shrug; they have cheated themselves, not us. Very often these people return, wanting to complete the process they have begun. Sometimes we insist they perform their preferred action the other way first. This is not always practical; they may need the arousal value of their chosen role.

I can look like a schoolgirl, of course, as well as a teacher. Two sides of a coin. I can look like a doctor, a nurse, a social worker, a secretary. I have had women who wanted me to be their secretaries as I seduced them. Oh, dear, I mean as they seduced me, of course.

I can be a grey church lady. A nun in modern garb. Improvisation is everything – we are all actresses. But I was going to tell you about my yesterday.

'Grey,' said my customer, eyeing my suit. 'You don't have a brown suit, I don't suppose?'

'Y-es,' I said cautiously, 'but why – ?'

'I want you to look like a robin,' she said cheerfully.

'A – ?'

'I know all about the dovecote – only to me, the spirit is a robin. There's a robin in my garden, you see, ever so tame. And I wish – '

'But can't you just love this robin,' I began, feeling a bit RSPCA-ish about it, 'without – '

'Yes,' she nodded, 'I have no need to violate the actual robin. But a human robin – a full-grown robin – '

'Hence the brown suit.'

'Yes.'

I changed. I even wore a red bra, for all that it's the male robin who sports a red breast. I was going to this party as the Holy Ghost, and I could mix my genders like cocktails.

The spirit rose in us, all right. Stretched and uncoiled like the kundalini from the base of the spine, elevated like the phoenix from the fires, whatever image you like. It was there, we were it, dangerous, destructive, creative, constructive. I thought of the other woman, the egg woman, and it seemed to me her symbolism, too, had another level, the level of breaking free the *shekina*, the glory of God, from the shells that surrounded it, just as her own spirit was reborn from the shell her mother cracked for her birthday cake, and from the shells we cracked, forty of them, I forgot to say, because she was forty.

I thought of all these things as I heaved with the robin woman. I played the part of the spirit redbreast and I made her play the robin to me. It was too much power, it had to be felt to be believed. It was all right for me to be God to her if she would do the same. If and only if, *Iff*, as they said in geometry, a subject I once failed but could now pass with flying colours, I do believe.

It was strange and lovely. Embodied God. Dressed as God embodied and Undressed by God embodied. My arms fluttered around her. I was the Holy Ghost in her temple, and then I was there before

she was born, before she was constructed. I can't explain, and then I –
but there are no words, and there was no 'I'. Myself, without the 'my'?
Words come out bland, melodramatic, pornographic, all at once.
There is no formula, there are no words. Afterwards, I felt the Holy
Ghost brooding over the world with my ah! bright wings.

No words. That's one of the best things of the Valley – and one of
the hardest. The Father is words – Ten Commandments, for a start –
or one, in Genesis, multiplying rapidly as the Testament goes on till
there are more commandments, rules, regulations and dietary laws
than time to break them. The Son is a great talker. Parables maybe,
but plenty of words from the Word made flesh.

The Spirit is different. It is not about words. This, too, may be part
of the Third Person era. It sounds really suspect, like the (groan) Age
of Aquarius all over again. But even that was a good idea, really; to
replace the old Piscean age, so torturous to skin and bone.

The Holy Ghost, paradoxically, is at home in the flesh, is of it and in
it. We have to go on breaking the shells never mind splitting the atom,
breaking the shells and liberating glory, energy and grace. And pain,
and rage. That's what we're about, and the best way we know is sex.
There are others, and we use them, too.

Will there be a third testament, you ask. An old new testament or a
new old one. There will, we are writing it now. We love stories, you
know. Of course you know. I will tell you one, if you will tell me one
after. Bedtime stories are part of our calling.

THE VISION

Once upon a time there was a sculptor. Not a very gifted sculptor. In
fact she was a terrible sculptor. She made plaster statues for convents
and classrooms and rectories, and sometimes, unfortunately, even
churches. Blue and white BVMs with eyes rolling heavenwards, a bit
like junkies'. There was never a body beneath the drapery that
swirled and was static at once, and this was always obvious. No
troubling outline of humanity to pull the mind down into the
gutter.

After all, who could imagine a statue with a shape? Apart from the
suckling madonnas, which rather made the sculptor shudder. She
had made of her religion and of her profession a suit of armour, which
she kept highly polished, cold and inimical to people. That was what

she wanted. She liked the shine of the gold and silver instruments at Mass, like a surgeon's tools.

She took on many commissions at once, for she knocked out her statues fast, on an assembly-line principle. She made a row of heads, then hands, feet, draperies, etc; then assembled them all. It was most efficient.

One evening she was in her workroom, having assembled a row of statues, when a strange thing happened. One of them grew and grew until it stood full-grown in front of her. And the rest lined up behind it, but kept their size, like an army of gnomes.

The full-grown statue looked very unhappy.

'What's wrong, Milady?' she asked it, not very certain of the form of address. After all, it must be – ? Who else could it be? And yet she doubted it, somehow. The statue had an animated quality to it. It was a cartoon vision.

The lady nodded. 'Caricature,' she said sadly.

'Whatever do you mean, and how do you know what I'm thinking?'

'I always do,' the lady answered. 'It isn't much fun, believe me.'

'I believe you. But what's bothering you?' the sculptor remembered to ask.

'Just look at me.' The lady flapped her draped arms, sneered at the plastic rosary threaded through her fingers. She began to pull at her clothing, frantically, but of course it wouldn't come off. And if it had come off, there would have been nothing underneath.

'Exactly,' she said angrily, advancing on the sculptor. 'Nothing underneath. A plaster cast. And it's all your fault.'

The sculptor stared.

'Tell them to come to me about their real problems,' the statue added unexpectedly. 'You know. Too many kids. Frigidity. All that. I know all about it. And get to work,' she said sternly, and disappeared.

The sculptor turned back disconsolately to her work and her life and her religion. What was she to do? Give her statues bodies? How could she?

But she picked up a piece of clay and began, breathlessly, shaping it. Breasts first, with sweaty hands. By the time she'd draped it, the thing looked like a sex goddess. She went to bed and dreamt of angry armies of statues on the march across the ceiling. When she woke up, she was able to persuade herself the whole thing was a dream.

But not for long. The statue, the cartoon character, came back. This time she came back as a stripped cartoon: naked. The sculptor hid her eyes, but she still saw her. The lady was bossy and insistent. She was, in fact, not at all ladylike. She knew what she wanted. The sculptor took a long trip. She needed to get away. She travelled and looked at hundreds of statues. She studied them. The lady would appear, and pose in front of them, nude, lewd, rude. She made faces. She was never satisfied with the sculptor's rare efforts. The breasts were too saggy or too pert. The belly was too big, the legs too short. Or the whole thing was too 'perfect', too anonymous.

The sculptor dragged herself home, discouraged. She stepped into her workroom, and who was there, waiting for her? The blood rushed to her head. She exploded.

'Get out of here,' she shouted. 'Just get the hell out of here, I don't care whose mother you are. Or how many angels you've laid, either.'

The woman looked back at her gravely. Then she threw back her head and laughed.

When she woke up the next morning, she made her last statue. It was simple. It was not draped. It wore a dress, of all things; an ordinary sort of dress, such as someone might have worn. It had an ordinary face and a somewhat amused expression.

A priest bought it for his church garden. He was perhaps somewhat nearsighted. She was installed, and the sculptor got a job as a waitress.

The statue's fame spread, in whispers. She was known to have laughed on several occasions. She was also good if you were pregnant. She didn't give spontaneous abortions for the asking, though; she made you consider, whether you wanted the child or not. Sometimes you found you didn't when you thought you did, or vice versa. She was good for pre-orgasmic women, too. Her advice was to let it well up from inside you, like a spring. Not to look for it outside yourself.

Eventually the whispers grew too loud, and the priest removed her. She was wrapped in an old blanket and put in a basement. Lo and behold, when the new priest went to look for her years later, she had become just an ordinary, draped BVM with a sickly smile and doped-up eyeballs. They said it was a miracle. The sculptor, when she read about it in the paper, threw back her head and laughed so that her breasts shook, making some of her customers in the restaurant distinctly uncomfortable.

WHEN THEY BURNED US

When they burned us it was not their hell we went to. When we
burned we felt nothing. It was someone else's screaming we heard.
The angels had come for us and we were shy to meet them. Some of
us turned back to see our bodies writhe while our ears filled with
something like music. Some of us cried and in this fleshless
weeping we smelled the birth dreams. We shuddered and we stopped
our weeping.

The angels gathered us – yes we were like flowers – and took us to
this place we call end of desire. It did not look the same or
different to each of us. There were rooms to explore. They were
changing. We came to know the living through this changing.

We were happy not living. Our lives were gardens we could visit.
We could do the weeding and then other gardens would be changing.
A spark might run up the place we used to call our spine.

This continued endless. New ones coming from accident or sea
drowning. There were no signs to mark us, to show our difference
and maybe we were the same. Our shapes were changing. We knew
each other and timelessness passed.

They say no sounds of war reach heaven. Where we lived our deadness
we could hear war. We drew deeper into end of desire.
Til the sainted ones came. The ones who stayed only briefly so
to know them we would visit their time again and again.

We began knowing the need for returning. We were still without
marking and we knew each other. We heard angels gathering and
we were angels gathering ourselves. We had forgotten hunger and
now we hungered for time. We hungered for blood and muscle and bone.
End of desire changed. An old rhythm drew us out.

Lauren Liebling

WATER WOMEN

We do not want
to rock the boat,
you say, mistaking
our new poise
for something safe.

We smile secretly
at each other,
sharing the reality
that for some time
we have not been
in the boat.

We jumped
or were pushed
or fell
and some leaped
overboard.

Our bodies form
a freedom fleet
our dolphin grace
is power.

We learn and teach
and as we go
each woman sings;
each woman's hands
are water wings.

Some of us have become
mermaids or Amazon whales
and are swimming for our lives.

Some of us do not know how to swim.
We walk on water.

Alla Bozarth-Campbell

II

FIRST PERSON PLURAL

BAD WEATHER

When in bad weather
Everything I try to hang onto breaks off
To wither in my hand as if I had poisoned it
I have stumbled out to meet
This gang of peace women
So diverse, live and kind
I bike back in the rain of relief.

In my street in a bad gale
The polythene on the rehab bangs like the sails on a
rapt whaler
That is my stuttering generation beached
On Greenham Common with ninety-six Cruise missiles.

We sit there with pink hair
Blankets in the sleet
Cadenzas in the benders
We, the road, the trees
Branded with the searchlit shadow of a fence.
What I hear tonight
Is that violated by nuclear missile warheads
Stealthily we are
As witches in the ditches
Pregnant with new babies, great sea-faring girls.

Bryony Dahl

FRIENDS IN DEED

Mary E. Hunt

Women friends are the best antidote to patriarchy. The way in which we provide for one another, make space in our lives to invite others in, and act in unlikely coalitions of justice seeking friends gives me hope and energy for the task of social transformation.

As a theologian I am concerned that women's friendships be seen in the light of ultimate meaning and value. I hold them up to the light of theological investigation. They reveal dimensions of spirituality and the divine which help to explain why women friends are so central in our lives. Of course this has not been done in the mainstream theological conversation. Women are not assumed to be moral agents whose experiences reveal anything significant. Further, it is feared that if women's friendships are subjected to too much analysis they will reveal that women love women.

My perspective is that of a white middle-class, North American, Catholic woman. I do not make claims for other women, nor do I claim to be fully inclusive in my analysis. But I invite all women to name their experiences of friendship and to evaluate them critically as data of revelation.

My starting point, by contrast to that which has passed as *the* theological position, is that women are moral agents. We are capable of revealing and constructing the deepest meaning and value in human experience.[1] I also presume that women's love for women, including sexual expression if mutually chosen, is healthy, good and natural. My starting point alone distinguishes my reflections on women's friendships from any which have emerged from the mainstream theological/ethical sources.

Most models of living in 'right relation' or making friends are based on male experience.[2] For example, in the bibliography used for one of the few courses on friendship, the readings chosen, i.e., the work which has been done and is considered important, ranges from Plato to St Exupéry.[3] Of the materials listed, only a fraction are by women. Few if any even mention women's experience as different from the presumed male norm. This situation is being corrected by women, especially the work of Lillian Faderman, Lillian B. Rubin and Janice Raymond.[4] But much work remains to be done if the record is to be corrected, and women's experience is to make a contribution to ethical reflection.

This essay is an effort to reinforce the importance, especially for women ourselves, of being active and intentional in the development of our friendships. Such is a strategy for overcoming patriarchal oppression in these times of backlash against the limited gains which we have made. I spell this out more fully in *Fierce Tenderness: Toward a Feminist Theology of Friendship*.[5] In this essay I look at a very limited but central part of that analysis.

I will look at women's friendships in three aspects. First, I will explore how women's friendships manifest themselves in actions for justice. Second, I will suggest how such experiences suggest new norms for human sexuality. Finally, I will point toward several aspects of the divine which are revealed through women's friendships. I conclude that a society which does not value and nurture women's love for one another cannot expect to achieve a healthy, life-giving future. That this is true for most societies is measured by the bellicose attitudes which result in nuclear madness and global economic chaos.

Women make friends with women despite strong messages and taboos to the contrary. There is little or no literature on female bonding patterns. Certainly nothing like the 'classic' texts on male bonding that explain away the savagery and gang behavior of males exists in the history of females of the same species. Women friends develop our relationships in the tasks of survival and in the delight of womanspace which is a respite from an otherwise patriarchal world.

Nowhere do we read of female sowers/gatherers being friends. They simply carried out their womanly tasks to nourish their families, while the hunters forged bonds over against their beasts. Women's bonds emerge as part of a need to build networks to make the survival tasks a little easier, to secure a toehold for more women, in short, to do justice. This pattern has not changed drastically over the course of western history. Indeed, as feminist inroads have been made, it is clear how dramatically women's survival can be coopted. Our bonding as women is not simply gratuitous, but focused on our need for justice.

Gains achieved by feminists for all women in the last twenty years would not have been possible without strong friendships among women. In fact, friendship was a by-product of many consciousness-raising groups. Women discovered that the patriarchal conditioning that they had received, which taught them not to value other women, to see other women a competition for men's attention, and later men's protection, was destructive of their deepest selves. Women found in one another the essence of humanity which they had been taught to encounter only in the otherness of a male. Many discovered that the otherness of males was, like the total otherness of a patriarchal God, a source of alienation and death.

In women, on the other hand, the nurture and challenge of common humanity, without the alienation of male privilege and male conditioning in patriarchy, was a relief, a revelation, a delight. Women's friendships, in our time of feminist consciousness, take on the centrality that they have always had for women. But now we are willing to call them by their names. No longer are we simply going out with the girls for a change, going to hen parties, just chatting over the back fence with the neighbour lady, drinking coffee with the mothers of our children's friends. We now call our women friends by their names. We acknowledge their centrality on their own terms, in our lives.

Women have always been friends. Patriarchy eclipsed the meaning of such friendship by insisting, with the help of the Christian churches, that marriage and not friendship was the ideal for human interaction. Gradually women's friendships receded into the background until only lesbians were said to love women. Anyone else who would proclaim love for another woman would be counselled that she liked her, but that love was an experience and an attitude which one 'saved' for marriage. This served to isolate lesbians from other women, to the point of distinguishing 'real' women from lesbian women over whom they love. Obviously 'real' women love men, while lesbian women love women. Thus 'real' women cannot love women, that is, have women friends. What an efficient way to limit women's friendships and so coopt women's work for justice. Until this mistaken notion is corrected women's friendships will be only in thought and not in deed.

Women's friendships today are a patchwork of activity. The old notions are broken down in communities of women who work to transform the social and political structures which kept us from one another in the first place. We encounter one another in the organizations and actions which are our work places and our woman-constructed oases from patriarchy. These places include political parties and feminist bookstores where change takes place; universities and factories where women make their living since they no longer depend on (or cannot live on) men's money; clubs and sports facilities, child-care centers and women's base communities, where we find our needs met and our values reinforced.

What we look for are friends who share our perspectives, women who will 'Accompany us then on this vigil and . . . will know what it is to dream.'[6] Most such persons are our colleagues and our confidants, our sister construction workers on the project of building a just and inclusive society. That most of our friends are women should come as no surprise to those who realize what it will take to overcome patriarchal domination. That some few are men is not a contradiction. They too can commit to the life-changing attitudes necessary to become part of the feminist revolution for survival on a friendly planet.

Friendship is the mortar that holds the bricks of a new social construction together. This is something that many pass over, at their peril, in a desperate effort to employ private solutions to what are obviously structural problems. But women who love women understand this dynamic as an excuse not to allow its logical conclusions to disrupt the narrowly cast social order. Better, even liberals reason, to call friendship a bourgeois luxury which cannot in itself lead to change, than to admit that women's friendships are evidence of the very changes they abhor. Women's friendships deny the need for men to be central to every human exchange. This is where the presence of open lesbians becomes something that a patriarchal society must erase.

When women, all women, probe our life experiences, more often than not we find that we love women. We know that the distinction between lesbian women and so-called 'real' women is false, that it is a successful effort to keep women apart. There is only one common element in women's very diverse experiences, namely, gender oppression. Everything else is class, race, culture, age, etc. specific, and cannot be claimed as universal.

There is a common lie in patriarchy which is recognized by women when we reflect on our lives. The lie says that we do not love one another. Once that lie is named as a constitutive part of all women's oppression, and once its converse, namely, loving women as friends, is affirmed as part of all women's liberation, then a patriarchal barrier is demolished and a feminist future is possible.

This is why loving women is a political activity. It is not the privatized activity of mysterious feelings, though of course friendship can never be reduced to a political agenda. Rather, it is the delightful experience of finding that body and spirit need not be split, that friends can be lovers, that colleagues can be friends, that the world need not be a dichotomized, alienating environment. This is the work of justice, to transform the ideology of oppression into an invitation to communal liberation. Friends make it happen, and having friends with whom to work makes it easier.

I would not want to move on to a discussion of how lesbian experience can help to create new social/ethical norms in sexuality without acknowledging that women's friendships are not tension-free and perfect simply because they are between women. To the contrary, human nature is poised in and poisoned by patriarchy. Likewise, no human relationship is uncomplicated; friendship is not a cover for differences but a forum for their expression.

Just as women's friendships provide energy, so too does the breakup of women's friendships produce pain, loss and serious cause for soul searching. But when I look at the most effective groups of women, whether feminist collectives, women's business partnerships, dynamic editorial teams, or feminist lobbying groups, inevitably I can trace the energy to a few good friends. I am told that this has been true in women's religious communities, though their canonical connections to a patriarchal church have resulted in the misogynist ban on so-called particular friendships.

Women's committed friendships are not the 'neurotic minuets' of dependent misfits, but the generative, community enhancing friendships of embodied women.[7] It is this very embodiment, especially when expressed sexually, which terrifies a patriarchal society. It must be addressed if the full potential of women's bonding is to be unleashed.

My second point is that this new acknowledgment of women's friendships has important ramifications for our common ethical framework on sexuality. Our embodiment as friends is not something that we take lightly, nor something that we pass over just because a patriarchal society would have us divide our emotions from our sexual expression. While there are many ways that friends relate in an embodied way, some of them are more problematic in patriarchy than others. I focus on these as a way to reinforce what must be transformed.

In patriarchy, sexual expression is understood to mean genital sexual activity. But our feminist insights into the connections between spirituality and sexuality lead us to affirm that 'embodied energy' takes many forms in addition to the delight of genital sex.[8] We share meals with friends; we play sports, and enjoy music and art together. We comfort and congratulate, challenge and chastise, all in embodied ways. Yet a patriarchal society focuses on genital sexual activity as the pinnacle of human sharing, and then prohibits it between women. The ravages of heterosexist patriarchy result in the sexual and economic control of women, at least in part, by prohibiting women from forming intimate relationships.

What then does women's intimacy signal? First, it is intimacy and not genital sexuality that women focus upon in friendships. The danger of this is obvious in that it can reinforce the idea that feminists are so busy liberating the whales that we have no time for sexual pleasure for its own sake. This is not what I mean. I mean to imply that who sets the agenda in ethical conversations is the key to their outcome. This is especially important for people who come from religious traditions which have had heavy doses of guilt attached to sexual expression whether within or outside of marriage. As women begin to set the agenda, the conversation is shifting away from genital concerns and toward intimacy.

Second, women's tie of sexuality with friendship is unique in the history of sexuality. Heterosexual marriage is the usual licit locus of sexual expression in most societies and certainly in the mainstream of the Christian tradition. But friendship is not the hallmark of heterosexual marriage by any means. Convenience, family ties, erotic love, financial necessity, habit, and the like are far more likely to be cited as the reason why persons get and/or remain married.

Likewise, in many gay male circles it is sexual expression and not friendship which receives central attention. Here a whole economic infrastructure of bars and baths, clubs and gyms is set up to facilitate not friendship first, but some semblance of genital sexual expression. The AIDS crisis is changing some of this, but it is changing it from this reality to something more like what women friends seek, namely, companionship, care and intimacy.

Third, women's intimacy with one another breaks down the double barrier that says that sexual pleasure is the proper domain of men (whether together or with a woman), and at the same time that women are less disposed to relate sexually. Women's desire to relate sexually with one another is the most obvious proof that men do not have sole possession of sexuality, a cultural lie which has served male ends for centuries. At the same time, women's sexual expression is part of women's larger choice to bond as friends. This is evidence of the fact that human beings can make intelligent, reasoned, thoughtful choices about sexual expression without being overly controlled and excessively rational.

It is usually said that sexual passion is so consuming that it must be controlled. But women's experiences, as articulated in conversations, novels, movies and now even in theological reflections, is that choices can be made about sexual expression as in every other domain. I do not mean to deny the power of passion to invite the serendipitous. But I do mean to put to rest the prevalent idea of sexual expression, particularly in religious literature, which would have us believe that animal instincts overtake us to the exclusion of thoughtful choices. This image, especially as it provides an excuse for male behavior and a reason for male-made laws, completely denies women's more integrated approach to sexual expression. Thus, to formulate norms and laws on the basis of male experience is seen as inadequate to reflect human experience.

We can see then how women's friendships challenge the sexual norms of our time. We insist that sexuality be replaced with intimacy as the springboard for discussion. We reveal that sexual expression is tied to friendship first and foremost. And we affirm that women are sexual beings of the first order, on our own terms. Now our experiences can be added to the cultural mix in order to discern what norms we wish to pass on to the next generation. This is what friends are for, to experience and pass on the best insights of a people.

Finally, friendships between and among women provide hints and glimpses of the divine reality in which we participate. Every culture fashions its notions of the divine on the basis of what it values most highly. Hence our current Christian usage of God as ruler, king, lord of all who is omnipotent, omniscient and omnipresent. This formulation makes 'good sense' in a culture in which persons who fulfill this job description for God rule the world. But as women's influence increases it is not naive to suggest that friendship may overtake monarchy as the prevailing image. My suggestions which follow are meant only to get our imaginations in gear. You can add your own as we theologize from women's experience.

We need to look at who our friends are to begin to imagine how new visions of ultimate reality may lead us toward justice. I begin with the Goddess of Justice. She is a friendly sort. Her open arms and ample bosom spring from my imagination as symbols of love. No longer is Justice blindfolded and impartial. Rather, like the divinities of other liberation theologies, she is biased in the direction of those she loves, particularly those who have been marginalized. This goddess points toward a way of being in our culture which nourishes and comforts.

A female figure is not accidental. She is a symbol of a believable friend who can be trusted; she emerges from the experience of women friends. She reflects that experience. She is a visual source of a culture's possibility to be just.

Another image is that of Presence, a constant companion, like Sophia or Holy Wisdom, whose energy and brilliance are necessary for the transformation of the current social order into a just world.[9] This kind of divine force is the source of our belief in the essential goodness of creation. Our optimistic posture toward the future, even in the midst of nuclear madness, is derived from this depth image. We receive, create and pass on the Holy. She is a good friend in troubled times.

A final image of the divine is that of Many Women, the image of divine community in which we participate. Here we see that no image can be individual or private, but because friendship is a relationship such images must always be communal. Many Women are found in women's spaces, at music festivals and conferences, among friends at holiday times, at international gatherings. Women from all over the globe join in sustained conversation, enjoyment, dancing and the building of friendships.

The results, however fraught with differences and difficulties, are momentary experiences of a how a just world might operate, how it will feel to be in harmony. These moments are fleeting and illusory, but they provide enough of a glimpse to sustain the vision of justice which most of us have hardly seen. Of course men and children will need to be integrated, but for now such women's events give us a sustaining taste of a preferred future for which we can work. This is the function of a religious vision, a spiritual symbol.

Friendship, especially among women, provides a compelling model for justice-seeking people. It is with friends and as friends that we can approach the future, in a nuclear age, confident that there might be a future to pass on to our children. Women friends, loving well and working for justice, are motivation and sustenance enough to keep us moving.

NOTES

1 Beverly Wildung Harrison, in *Our Right to Choose*, Boston, Mass., Beacon Press, 1983, makes a persuasive case for women's moral agency.

2 The notion of living in right relation is spelled out very forcefully in Carter Heyward's *The Redemption of God*, Washington, D.C., University Press of America, 1982.

3 This bibliography comes from a course entitled 'Friendship' by Ralph B. Potter at Harvard Divinity School, 1980.

4 The following are relatively recent works in the field: Lillian Faderman, *Surpassing The Love of Men*, New York, Morrow, 1981; Lillian B. Rubin, *Just Friends*, New York, Harper & Row, 1985; Janice Raymond, *A Passion for Friends*, Boston, Beacon Press, 1986.

5 Cf. *Fierce Tenderness: Towards a Feminist Theology of Friendship*, San Francisco, Harper & Row, 1986, forthcoming.

6 Excerpted from 'They Have Threatened Us With Resurrection,' in *Threatened with Resurrection*, Julia Esquivel, Elgin, Illinois, The Brethren Press, 1982, p. 63.

7 This expression was originally used by John Frye. While the origin is uncertain the phrase is descriptive.

8 This expression was used by Marilyn Thie in a conference on sexuality and spirituality in Washington D.C., June 1984.

9 'Sophia' is a term Elisabeth Schussler Fiorenza explores in *In Memory of Her*, New York, Crossroad, 1983, while Holy Wisdom is an expression that Rosemary Radford Ruether uses in *Sexism and God-talk*, Boston, Beacon Press, 1983.

9

A TIME TO REFRAIN FROM EMBRACING

Polly Blue

When I feel as I do at the moment, I think of this as my Jesus year. That's not original – it's an in-joke with a friend who is also thirty-three (the traditional age of you-know-who at the crucifixion) but it's a clue to my tendency to grand doom-laden sulks. I look in the mirror and the shape of jolly, sensible single schoolteachers who I despised when I was fifteen settles on me like cold rice pudding. This after twelve years in the women's movement, fourteen since 'coming out' as a lesbian, and seven of (mostly) self-chosen celibacy. I must confess at the outset that yes, yes, I blossom and grow all over the place like a briar rose, I learn new hobbies, I have energy to spread around like jam, I am the solitary magic huntress in the forest, the wise spinster, the renewed virgin that meets the last unicorn, but damn it, I still feel like a failure.

I don't feel terrible on my own – far from it, I live with friends in a noisy, open household and hoard my moments of privacy. I don't feel asexual (yes, since you asked, and *everybody* confronted with the word celibacy does ask – I do masturbate a lot). I don't feel unsupported or unloved (except sometimes, and everybody feels those things some-times). I even have an odd sort of niche in the church, which as it happens, employs me in an office job, despite the fashion for 'Family Worship' spreading like wildfire in cheerful disregard for the number of people excluded by the notion. I don't bemoan my singleness, or indeed anything. I think I know how I came to be here.

I feel muddled nostalgia for the lesbian feminism of the mid-1970s. There was something, then, about being mad, bad and dangerous to know that was exhilarating as well as terrifying, and also fun – though since I tried to hang around with radical feminists and change the church at the same time, I never quite fitted into either. Nowadays, with my feminist rage unimpaired, and my clarity, I hope, undiminished, I still sometimes feel like – well, a spinster in my thirties . . .

> 'Our heroine is the unmarried only child of a Rural Dean, slightly above average height with soft brown hair, regular features, and a becoming modesty of demeanour. Her mother's friends kindly call her a charming girl, though her girlhood is behind her. She walks each day to her small job in an institution with a history of good works to the East London poor. She helps mind the children and would like to improve her crochet.'

I'm sorry, I'll read that again.

> 'A tall, freckle-faced lesbian/feminist poet in her thirties, involved in the women's peace movement, lesbian and gay bereavement counselling, and a ragbag of local causes, she seems deceptively vague. Shuffling around from meeting to meeting in overlarge boiler suits, chaindrinking cans of Carlsberg Special Brew, Aquarian detachment in her ice-blue eyes, she first reveals both her intelligence and her passion in sudden blinding flashes of witty and accurate irony. She is unnervingly self-sufficient. . . '

There, that's better.

Enough of these distorting mirrors – what of singleness, celibacy, and the questions it seems to raise for everybody? Let alone the answers . . . 'I'm writing about celibacy,' I said to a feminist friend recently. 'Celibacy? I don't believe there's any such thing,' she replied. 'I define celibacy as a positive choice of the single life for the sake of Christ in response to the call of God', says Donald Goergan.[1]

'In general usage', says *Our Bodies, Ourselves*, 'it has come to mean abstaining from genital sex in our relationships with others, even if temporarily.'[2] We are dealing with a Loaded Word here.

God is, you will recall, supposed to approve of people, especially women, who don't 'do It' except within marriage. Almost anything any of us were taught about sex and religion starts from here, from being good girls keeping ourselves for good boys. And somewhere in this part of our collective history, the word 'celibacy' and its bedfellows (bedfellows?! cellmates, then) chastity and virginity became thickly encrusted with holiness; barely able to move. 'Celibate' just meant 'unmarried' once, before the church got hold of it (for men, mostly – but more of that later). It has never quite seemed to sit easy with its original or its newer meanings for us who see it through this veneer of sanctity. Even in our generation, and particularly our generation of the women's movement, where the word had a fashionable aura for a while, it still carried a feeling of shining-eyed commitment, intense and full of meaning. Suspicion about the definition of terms set in among many of us, especially those who saw the pattern for this chosen aloneness as churchy and joyless.

We all know, too, that we are supposed to have been living through an age where expressing our sexuality is supposed to have become, or at least have started to become, liberated and liberating; through such an age, and into a conservative backlash. Even without the more obvious rubbish attached to the 1960s 'sexual revolution', it is at least clear that questions have been flying around in the air which won't easily be made to creep back under the carpet. And what is equally clear is that society is quite unable to accept innocently, now, at face value (if it ever did), the lifestyles of those 'abstaining from genital sex' without wondering what's wrong with them – with us. To take another kind of example, most of us have known strong, creative, sexually non-committed women who often chose their lifestyles without calling themselves nuns, or feminists, or celibates, or indeed anything – the ones who were named spinsters or maiden aunts by other people. They may well have been our aunts, in fact. The more the questions about sexuality are begged, the odder seems the space inhabited by maiden aunts (or nuns, come to that). And though the questions are more usually begged in male terms (leaving 'devil-may-care bachelors' unscathed and doing nicely, thank you) even feminists, among all our own questionings and redefinings of our sexuality, still share this sense of oddness when we look at our own aunties, and start racking our brains for the hint of some woman friend that could have been their secret lover.

It must be time to start asking some different questions.

SO THE FEET WON'T STICK OUT

Captivated by the aura of this word 'celibacy' I tried to explore its churchy meanings – its ascribed relationship to God – and instantly became trapped in fog. The mystique of nuns makes the reality elusive; and I am reminded, by one of the ex-nuns writing in a recent book on lesbian nuns, that a character in Djuna Barnes's *Nightwood* claims 'the contemplative life is an effort to hide the body so the feet won't stick out'.[3] The nuns I know are eager to say that they have bodies, have feet even, and are sexual people – but something feels not quite explained. The writings, too, of modern women in all kinds of religious orders handle poverty and obedience better than chastity.

They are articulate about the need to travel light in quest of God, and be freed for their particular ways of prayer and action; and many of them emphasize their sense of community, and their sexuality as 'embodiment'. But for all that, they seem to answer the criticisms of the 1950s, i.e., what's a nice Christian girl like you doing without a home of your own – more confidently than those of an age asking hard questions about sexual lifestyles and options, in the church as well as out of it. I don't mean this to sound like harsh criticism, and there are exceptions to it – simply, I'm left with a hunger to understand better. A sense of something not quite said.

Most of us think of celibacy in the church as meaning the unmarried state of certain (male) priests. Priestly celibacy confers a shaman-like purity of intention and freedom to make decisions, including those affecting women's lives, without being cluttered and confused by their messy realities. It also seems, to many of us, to draw an improbably large number of men who actively and passionately dislike women and are happiest in a world that claims a divine right to contain and exclude them. This is not true for all celibate priests; nor for all homosexual ones; nor is it the mainspring of all the church's sexism (the evangelical end of the spectrum has its own sinister games to play). But we experience it as too widespread to be coincidence. It is partly this singleness-as-male-power aspect that has made celibacy a difficult idea for some women who are both feminist and Christian, and makes them keen to affirm their own marriages as a corrective to the works of this unholy brotherhood.

But the history of all this for religious, and especially women religious, has got to be different. Donald Goergan tries to write for religious of both genders, and breaks new ground in suggesting that their friendships are good and are, 'affectively', sexual. Having indicated that 'Roman Catholic tradition has given rise to three major ways in which we live out our call. These have traditionally been listed as celibate life, married life, and single life,'[4] he affirms that 'Celibacy should be a deep engagement in counterculture because the person sees that there is value there and not sacrifice.'[5] He is clear, however, that this is a special state because it is a Christian response to God. Although I call myself some kind of Christian, I feel detached from all this. The choices for the women I know, and the calls to them, come through much muddier water.

It is hard, I know, to struggle from outside about how modern nuns feel about themselves, but all the talking and reading I have done in

58

order to give me some ideas leaves me uneasy – it is such a very different picture to the historical roots, to start with, which Marina Warner indicates when she observes that 'the little hard-won independence of nuns was gained at other women's cost, for belief in the inferiority of their state underpinned it.'[6] Well – there are historical roots to all sorts of women's lifestyles which, to say the least, involve some dealings with 'belief in the inferiority of their state'. But this is more (based on a parade of attitudes and statements from the 'fathers' which are all too familiar, in essence if not detail, to Christian feminists, but have an extra grisly charm when angled in this direction); this is the special holiness of virginity especially for women. I know, of course, that celibacy and virginity are not the same thing, but in this historical context, the argument applies.

Between the familiar mess of Hellenistic dualism and blaming Eve for almost everything ('For as childbirth was woman's special function, and its pangs the special penalty decreed by God after the Fall . . . the evils of sex were particularly identified with the female. Woman was womb and womb was evil'),[7] emerges a picture of women able to claim an extraordinary freedom in Christianity in direct proportion to the extent that they could purge themselves of their womanliness (which also meant physicality, sexuality). Marina Warner names some of the women who made extraordinary contributions to history from within the convent, but concludes that their freedom as a solution is 'completely inadequate. For the foundation of the ethics of sexual chastity are laid in fear and loathing of the female body's functions; in identification of evil with the flesh, and flesh with woman.'[8]

This seems to have nothing to do with modern ideals of community and embodiment, but gives them a not unsurprising context. I do not want it all to argue with women who devote their lives to others with courage and dignity. I have been inspired by their intellect, their love, their creativity and their laughter. I have no quarrel, of course, with those who say they are nuns and also feminists. I just wonder – and feel as though most people wonder – whether a life commitment with its roots in such a swamp is the only or the best way. The tension, not so much with male society's fantasy of itself where 'everybody's doin' it', but rather with the genuine questing for alternatives in the world at large, the church and the women's movement, feels real and bewildering.

Many of the women writing in *Breaking Silence* have clearly, by the time of writing about their pasts, had it with the church and all its works. A depth of honest and painful feeling for these communities of women they have left behind them is very clear – as is a strength in the various ways they have discovered to claim their spirituality since, over a range of almost every possibility known to women. But a minority of them are still nuns, and one of them has this to say:

> We can be completely non-physical and yet so possessed and unfree that we are uncelibate. Or we can be physical while being free and still celibate. This has proven true for me. During the periods of my life when I was very emotionally involved with a woman, I gave up all freedom. I was completely attached, either wanting to be possessed or to possess. Because I was unfree to be myself or to love others, I would call myself, during those times, uncelibate. During my life now, when at times I express my love sexually, I feel free. I neither possess nor feel possessed. I live my vow of celibacy; my vow to love all. I am committed to my group of sisters, as well as to my special friend-and-lover.[9]

The cynical part of me reads this as a description of the enduring fantasy of almost any lesbian feminist, one of open lovingness which is genuinely possible for much of the time in the best relationships, but surely almost never for all the time. If it truly says what *celibacy* is, the definition has certainly shifted a long way.

But in the end it is in this book, too, that I find the cameo which speaks most to me, in the context, of a woman's experience of God; and it is one which cuts through the official churchiness, though it may sound whimsical out of context:

> The postulant teacher said we had infringed on the teacher's authority. After her 'hell and damnation' instructions, I'd go to chapel and say, 'God, you're not like that, are you?' The answer came back: 'No' and I'd say 'I didn't think so.'[10]

Despite the joyful, sexual, wise, funny and loving nuns I have met, and despite their 'deep engagement in counterculture', I am still aware of something which God isn't like for me either.

To one ex-nun I spoke to, celibacy was only ever possible within the sense of the presence of God as a real person, in which her sexual energy was a tremendous power, redirected – yet she spoke of the sourness that could result in some nuns when the source of the energy was unacknowledged, and the difficulty of the teaching that she 'should have' been enabled to be totally available to others. To her, although desire had always been present, and promiscuity understandable, the reality of the love of God had been so intense that it had demanded the same fidelity as any committed love relationship – the ideal of the presence of the beloved. Talking to her, I felt some of my doubts receding, and we agreed on the sense in which, after years of each in her own way being celibate, we were both used to a certain kind of freedom, and mildly preoccupied with a bewilderment as to what to do next.

SHE WHO HAS CHOSEN HER SELF[11]

It seems almost a truism to say that a choice made within a structure, supported by vows and intended to be a life commitment, is entirely different from a choice (or yet again a set of circumstances or something on the sliding scale between), that leaves one temporarily single for a year or two. It is honestly hard to say how pure a choice the latter can be (as it is for most – all? – sexual choices). It certainly arouses mixed emotions about aloneness itself. While it is easy to see how learning to be autonomous can be a growth process, whether autonomy and celibacy are synonymous is, to say the least, another question. It is exciting to feminists, of course, that various cultures celebrated virgin goddesses. A proportion of these recovered their virginity after taking lovers – whether we approach them with detailed research or romanticism, that much is common knowledge. It is their power and autonomy that draws us. So, too, with Mary Daly's reclamation of the word 'Spinster' – 'She who has chosen her Self, who defines her Self, by choice, neither in relation to children nor to men, who is Self-identified . . . a whirling dervish, spinning in a new time/space.'[12] In this context of power it seems like a simple right to choose, not only how and with whom to conduct sexual relationships, but also whether to.

And yet – assuming for a moment, that there are simple choices, and trying for simple definitions – even locating this clear simple choice involves chipping away all the things it equally clearly wouldn't be. Guilt about being sexual; refusing to be sexual; being 'between relationships' and not minding, or pretending not to mind; turning aside feelings of sexual inadequacy, sexual rage, sexual guilt or sexual just-about anything into 'good works'; any avoidance or almost any pain – to name but a few. Those of us left naming ourselves as celibates by the end of this weeding process would need to be very definite and impossibly strong.

How, actually, do we ever make sexual choices in a society which distorts virtually all of them, especially the choices that make us pitiable – a poor thing, a 'sexless' woman? There are untold numbers of people who are simply single today – whether or not they have at some time been in marriages or relationships which failed, whether or not they have children, whatever they do now about their sexual needs and desires. Society can cope with almost none of them. Of course, many of them – of us – didn't choose to be here, and there is a degree of bravado involved in saying some of us did, and more of us found it at least partly a good place to be.

As I write, the more recent 'Doonesbury' cartoons in the *Guardian* feature a woman who has sent out copperplate invitation cards reading 'Ms Marcia Feinbloom is happy to announce she is calling off the search for Mr. Right and invites you to a Celebration of her Singularity.'[13] The perverse courage of this ritual – the celebration of the autonomy to be and do and travel and dream alone – equally celebrated in such statements beloved of feminists as the Joan Armatrading song 'Me, Myself, I' (and even she wants a boyfriend *and* a girl [for fun!] about her life someplace) – still struggles along against the pressures of loneliness, and of being thought odd. Tricia Bickerton, who has run workshops of Women Alone at the Women's Therapy Centre and written on the subject in *Sex and Love*, comments:

> To be alone . . . at times . . . has even assumed an ideological status within the women's movement, indicating a strength and independence in not compromising with a man. However, despite these changes, most women still wish it were different. It may sometimes seem less painful to be alone than to be in an oppressive relationship; but it nevertheless is painful. This is not surprising given the weight of continuing patriarchal pressure . . . even women friends who are in couples sometimes wish the woman on her own was attached, especially if she seems to enjoy her freedom. She has a disquieting effect, and poses questions they prefer not to consider.[14]

Bickerton is writing particularly about heterosexual women who find that through feminism they are undergoing changes at a rate the men in their lives can't keep up with. And feminists have found the ideal of women claiming aloneness rather than relationships with *men* intoxicating for the reasons already made clear. There is a strong body of opinion that heterosexual women can decide to stop their sexual involvement with men and become, if not lesbian, at least more women-identified. 'Celibacy' has been tacitly and more readily accepted as part of this process. By contrast, I, going in for grand declarations that I was now being celibate, realised that my friends found this terribly funny – not merely because I was being theatrical (though I was, and had a justified reputation for it) – but because I was somehow ineligible to define myself thus. (I wasn't leaving men; I was a lesbian already.) So . . . somehow I am cast in the role of one challenging such deep-held unease in everyone that I am regarded as either extraordinarily hung-up, or just by being here, asking especially disquieting questions. Or both, of course.

Our Bodies, Ourselves is noticeably more cautious, now, than in its first American edition (Boston Women's Health Collective, 1971), about celibacy. But there is still an enthusiasm for the good experiences of autonomy and solitude:

> many of us have entered periods of celibacy with apprehension – we have feared the insecurity of being without a partner. Often this anxiety diminishes because being alone is a very positive experience. It has given us back our integrity, our privacy, our pride. Of course there is a difference in how we feel when we choose celibacy and how we feel when being without a sexual partner is not our choice. But either way many of us have found that periods of celibacy, a month, a year, or even longer – can be freeing and growth-producing. We are freed to explore ourselves without the problems and power struggles of a sexual relationship. We can begin to define ourselves not just in terms of another person.[15]

Integrity. Privacy. Pride. And the gifts of self-understanding to carry back into relationships. In the writing and thinking of feminists concerned with spirituality, especially those on the fringes of Christianity, the language of exile, Exodus, the journey, figures a great deal. The journey is outside the safe places; it is through hostile territory; leads to the discovery of hidden treasures; and, although in one sense the community of women travels together, in many other senses a frightening aloneness is a part of it. A need to know how to travel light, to be self-sufficient. To trust oneself to have what one needs, and to discover the way. It is especially difficult to travel into the darkest parts of oneself unless one travels alone. By that I don't mean the darkness of sin or guilt, in the Christian sense of hidden grubby bits that only the X-ray eyes of God the all-seeing can penetrate the nastiness of, but the darkness that feminists have celebrated, overturning the dualism, and naming the darkness as the womb, the place of birth, the chaos we must explore – and the abyss, too, the place of the angel of death and the mystery of life.

None of this is instead of loving, or instead of the gifts women share with one another. It is not instead of our responsibility for the whole earth. Yet I am suddenly reminded of the image offered by a male Methodist minister called John Kennedy, who is one of my work colleagues, and who spent several years in Sri Lanka, as his personal ideal of what a human being is. It is of a person kneeling in the Temple of the Tooth in Kandy offering a flower. There is no sense (in Buddhism) of a God to please and placate. There is no sense of offering to, or trying to impress, other people. The offering is entirely of the self. The flower, once offered, may wither. It is not an offering which will feed the hungry (the poor you will always have with you); it is the self, known and offered freely, in a form at once beautiful, fragile and strong.

This sense of the self is not the whole story for me – it is a valuable part of the truth. I certainly don't suggest it as an apologia for solitude. It is simply one of the gains I have had a glimpse of. In the end, I find that women spending time alone spend it neither in temples, nor, would you believe, on mountain tops, but feeling freed simply to do other things. In the peace movement, for instance, the threat to life sometimes seems too urgent for us to find the distractions of passion anything but irritating. We often find we can't carry on like that – we need the possibilities of our loving, and life is a business of being in bodies which need each other. But despite the doubt, anxiety, lack of clarity, and social oddness, there is still growth in aloneness – growth in integrity, privacy and pride. Here is part of a talk by Jackie Marshall, for the Gay Christian Movement Women's Group, on 'Living Without Relationships':

> There is a choice – to search for reassurance, comfort and distraction by getting involved with every other person who might give a 'go' signal, and some have. Or alternatively use it as a time to assimilate what has gone before, and then to rethink, reshape and rebuild. I chose the latter. When the more powerful emotions – passion, anger, jealousy, despair – receded like some storm at sea, I found myself beginning to enjoy a feeling of transcendent self-control. And so such a 'downtime' can be used to polish up good habits and tackle the bad ones . . .
> A time to make new friends, develop new contacts, explore new haunts.
> A time to improve skills and get some more qualifications.
> A time to recover lost ambitions and interests . . .
> A time to reflect that perhaps one of the problems about being gay is that you can develop such a siege mentality that life can consist of only two subjects – lamenting about the relationship you're in, or lamenting about not being in any relationships.

A time therefore to discover life beyond the blinkers, and grow . . . Not that I wouldn't change all this overnight of course when the right person comes along.[16]

ALONE AGAIN NATURALLY

Now I suppose I must tell my own muddled tale. I have been alone for about seven years. Without sexual relationships, that is; not entirely without occasional sexual happenings and confusions (with women and with one man, who was even more surprised than I was), so my claim on the label 'celibate' is not pure and incorruptible. When I first declared myself celibate it was in the wake of a bitterly-felt intense bereavement. I can think of all sorts of excellent reasons to believe that I've been kidding myself about my own clarity. Nor have I spent the last seven years on a constant spiritual high of incessant growth and learning in the extra space and time. There's been some of that, certainly. How much more or less of it there's been than there is in the best stable relationships, I'm less inclined to make glib assumptions about. Nor do I have a specially-nurtured fount of love to spread round the human race because I'm not putting it into a relationship. I'm sometimes stroppily independent, sometimes sulky, and fairly often bitchy.

In fact, I led a solitary country childhood like something in an over-the-top Victorian novel, and was good (too good?) at being alone by the age of eight. (Seriously – I was the only child in a huge vicarage, a mile and a half outside its village, and surrounded by fields of cows. I played weird let's-pretend games in the attic all the time. I also thought I would be a great poet and die tragically at the age of seventeen, lacking, you might say, normal perspectives.)

By 1978, I had already been tossed and torn most of the possible, and quite a few impossible, ways between Christianity and feminism, and had just left the church for the second or third time. Between a high Anglican upbringing, which I'd started trying to reject at the age of eight (that's not an especially grand boast – vicars' kids are usually 'difficult') and a few years of bloody struggle in Metropolitan Community Church as it became more evangelical (in London) and worried at whether I was 'right with God' I'd acquired an intriguing and exasperating overview of how churches worked. I'd also read

65

voraciously in the books coming over from America about women's spirituality. And had some of the very private experiences that are impossible to write about without sounding sensational. The sudden flashes of intense knowing that all living things are united, not in some Nirvana-like blob of sacrificed identity, but in a way that includes all of their own selves, be they whales or willow trees, or come to that, women. The sense that what unites them is called love. The sense of actual human love and courage changing the world. And the sense, whatever else God is, of dotty, comfortable conversations with some-one whose sense of humour is as ironic as mine without the bitchiness, and whose seriousness more passionate without the bitterness. I was intermittently hanging on to Christianity because it had some kind of potential for not being completely other-worldly, and therefore be-cause all of the major religions were so much worse. I'd drifted in and out of churches so much that the edge felt like a natural place to live. My friends in the church were mostly still concerned with introducing women into the priesthood or with changing the language of liturgy – we didn't talk much of exile yet. (My other, radical feminist friends talked about witchcraft, but in a way that felt equally incomplete for me.) Rage and isolation made me less, rather than more, articulate – I used to sit around the edges of Christian feminist groups, weeping or snarling, and being thought awkward.

All of that is who I already was, in my 'spirituality', when my lover was killed. Bereavement, again, is at least one other story from the one I'm telling here, but interlocks with it. Much of what happened to me that in spiritual terms was part of grief – a sense of being lost in the middle of a huge grey cloud where light was irrelevant to me, for days at a time, and a frantic search, of some sense to make of death. This took in long earnest conversations about reincarnation and dreams about dead Irish nuns; and days spent in the British Museum gazing at mummy cases. I'm told, and I believe, that some form of this batty urgency is natural. What I remember is suddenly realizing that I'd always had a superstitious fear that if I let go of Christianity I would fly off into a black hole. Now I was in a black hole, it didn't matter. I poked hopelessly around in the rubble, in an unchosen aloneness, which many people experience, but a desperate one for all that.

What happened to me in sexual terms was part of grief as well. The relationships of the women around us were mostly fluid, so that the fact that I needed not to be in a relationship at all was seen as part of my insanity. I therefore alternated between disastrous minor sexual skirmishes, telling everyone that I didn't know what I wanted of my sexuality and was being celibate. When that household broke up, I rushed off into the wilds of Wales to live with my aunty – yes, a 'maiden' aunty – and be celibate 'properly'.

In Wales I both let my life fall completely apart and started to pull it back together. And I came to another hard-to-describe sense of God – or anyway, Love – not having let me go, and of the black hole being a healing process. I don't mean this in a narrowly Christain sense – narrowly Christian senses, whether I was in the church or out of it this month, weren't so important. There aren't exact words for everything I do mean by it – some of the closest are both well known and biblical:

> If I went up to heaven you would be there;
> If I lay down in the world of the dead you would be there.
> If I flew away beyond the east
> or lived in the furthest place in the west,
> you would be there to lead me,
> you would be there to help me.[17]

And for much of that important year, I was desperate, too. I was pulled more and more to London by aching loneliness for the friends I loved there. I can't pronounce, simply, on which parts of all this happened in my 'sexuality'. They did all happen because I was spending time alone. I began to sort out my practicalities; and on the face of it, all my projects for the next few years were entirely down to earth – I headed back to London, took a typing course to make myself employable, got various jobs and lived with various friends. And, despite the odd burst of romantic love, stayed alone. I should try to explain this, I suppose – though I also know, from being a lesbian if from nowhere else, the tiresomeness of being expected to justify oneself. I should at least find something more convincing to say about it than that I feel strong now, and that though I don't remember deciding to live this way, I must on some level have meant to, and mean to still.

As it happens, I never fell in love again with anybody who had the slightest intention of falling in love with me; and of course, bereavement itself casts longer shadows than I once imagined; and I haven't hung around so much with other lesbians anyway, of late; and of course the line 'I'm being celibate' is an easy defence. I know all this is not simple.

There are two other parts to this story. One is that a weird combination of coincidences has brought me back around to the church, to work for it. What started as a local office job in a relaxed, trendy-community-work-ish setting has entangled my enthusiasm. This time, it is being around people who know a lot and care a lot about the inner city area where we all live that has drawn me – I find I learn more every day, and feel more for, the pain and oppression, the courage, hope and fun of people in the East End of London. Whatever my 'spirituality' is now, owes a vast debt to them.

And there is the women's peace movement. Being involved in Tower Hamlets Women's Peace Group has meant, among other things, working closely with an extraordinary group of women, feeling vulnerable in a lot of ways, some of which are like rubbing ground glass into old wounds. It keeps dragging me out of cosy solitude, all right. And it is our passion, the political possibilities of our loving, that we are inspired by and fight with. Too many other stories here, especially about Greenham, which is hard to write about without seeming to exaggerate; but the intensity of fear, rage, courage, laughter, pain, love, empowerment and possibility is personal, political, sexual and most definitely spiritual.

You will be wondering, Gentle Reader, what it means that I still define myself as a lesbian. So am I, rather. To start from the over-obvious, it is neither what I do in bed nor yet what I used to do in bed but haven't much lately. Part of me is still drawn to the radical feminist dream of modelling my whole life in a way that enables me to be for women, making my own rules outside society's limitations, free and politically clear and creative and good. The truth (surprise surprise) is both more and less complicated. Even in the mid-1970s, trying to hang around radical feminism and Christianity simultaneously, the *last* thing I felt was a wonderful unity of personal and political possibility (lacking a male lover, and therefore merely having the most repressive of the major world religions to lick into shape). These days, even my utopia is less clearly defined. Something holds me back from defining my lesbianism in terms like:

> I mean the term 'lesbian continuum' to include a range – through each woman's life and throughout history – of woman-identified experience . . .

including the sharing of a rich inner life, the bonding against male tyranny, the giving and receiving of practical and political support.[18]

And the 'something' is not that those things are not important, but perhaps, as Elizabeth Wilson points out, 'This definition is reductionist, since it collapses lesbianism and feminism (and indeed femaleness) together.'[19] It matters, naturally, that I was involved in the gay movement what seems like a thousand years ago, before I called myself a feminist. I first 'came out' in a difficult place (Aberystwyth, Wales, in 1972, as contact address to a student 'Gaysoc' with four members). In the end we cling to the parts of our identities we sweat blood to claim. And in the end (so help my politically incorrect soul) all I can say is that I have loved women. Nor does it mean nothing that I never happened to have – and also never chose to have – and am unlikely ever to choose – a sexual relationship with a man. Whatever happens in the future from here, it will still be with women.

I am partly scared, now, of how comfortable I feel. It seems a massive undertaking to change – and has nothing to do with Ms Right galloping round the corner on a white charger to rescue me. Every way I know of 'being' a lesbian – socially, I mean – is somebody I once was, in some other space and time and the way I should take out of here is certainly not backwards. When I know what *I* need to do next, perhaps I'll do it. In the meantime, it's been interesting . . . *Our Bodies, Ourselves* says: 'When celibacy no longer feels good we want to change it – but that's easier said than done. And it feels harder the longer we have been celibate.' Hmm. I knew this would be hard to write about honestly. 'The big problem', said my ex-nun friend, 'is where to go now.' Quite.

And yet I do (usually) feel good, sharing my life with friends, spending a lot of time alone, and generally being sexual with nobody but me. A part of the story is that I have moods where I know I am stiff to friendly sensuality – hugs – because they release old pain – but only a part. I was afraid for a while that I was trapped forever in grief, but trust myself now not to be.

I have begun to write this story many times, always thinking that I would hit on some clear definition of celibacy that would prove I knew exactly what I was, and am, doing. God laughs up her sleeve, but gently. I have learnt some scraps of truth by being alone, which I might have learnt anyway. And as for the women who stay alone for years, for lifetimes? 'All shall be well' said one of them whose name we don't even know (Julian was the dedication of the church she lived alongside). All is not always well – nobody who has ever crossed the doorway of an old people's home, whose residents are always mostly single or widowed women, would want to romanticize their kind of silently-screaming loneliness, or doubt that society doesn't have the shred of an idea what to do with them. But there are a lot of survivors around; women who manage, and hope, and struggle and laugh alone, and know there is a future. I've at least learnt to listen to them.

NOTES

1   Donald Goergan, *The Sexual Celibate*, New York, Seabury Press, 1974, p.108.
2   Angela Phillips and Jill Rakusen, *Our Bodies, Ourselves* (UK edition), London, Penguin and Allen Lane, 1978, p.84.
3   Djuna Barnes, *Nightwood*, first published 1936, quoted in Rosemary Curb and Nancy Manahan (eds), *Breaking Silence: Lesbian Nuns on Convent Sexuality* (UK edition), London, Columbus Press, 1985, p.71.
4   Goergan, *op. cit.*, p.105.
5   *Ibid.*, p.121.
6   Marina Warner, *Alone of All Her Sex*, London, Weidenfeld & Nicolson, 1976, p.78.
7   *Ibid.*, p.57.
8   *Ibid.*, p.77.
9   Sister Hana Zarina in Curb and Manahan, *op. cit*, p.143.
10 Marie, *ibid.*, p.105.
11 Mary Daly, *Gyn/Ecology: The Metaethics of Radical Feminism*, Boston, Beacon Press, 1978, p.3 of Introduction.
12 *Ibid.*
13 Garry Trudeau, 'Doonesbury' cartoon in the *Guardian*, 23 July 1985.
14 Tricia Bickerton, 'Women Alone' in Sue Cartledge and Joanna Ryan (eds), *Sex and Love: New Thoughts on Old Contradictions*, London, Women's Press, 1983, p.159.
15 *Our Bodies, Ourselves, op. cit.*, p.84.
16 Jackie Marshall, Gay Christian Movement Women's Newsletter, Spring 1983.

17 Excerpt from Psalm 139, Revised Standard Version of the Bible.
18 Adrienne Rich, 'Compulsory Heterosexuality and Lesbian Existence',
    quoted by Elizabeth Wilson in 'I'll Climb the Stairway to Heaven:
    Lesbianism in the Seventies' from *Sex and Love: New Thoughts on Old
    Contradictions, op. cit.*, p.187.
19 *Ibid.*

10

THE LION IN THE MARBLE
Choosing Celibacy as a Nun

Hannah Ward CSF

One of my franciscan sisters, fully habited, was travelling by coach. In front of her were a mother with her young daughter, the latter fascinated by this rather odd-looking figure sitting behind her. After much peering between the seats, puzzled looks and loud whisperings, the embarrassed mother explained that 'it' was a 'nun'. The little girl, with curiosity still unsatisfied, peered once again between the seats and politely asked my sister, 'Excuse me, do you have breasts?'

The title of this book, *Sex and God*, may sound to the world of traditional religious celibates like having your cake and eating it. That phrase itself is worth thinking about briefly, for it assumes a very negative quality. There's a sense of outrage if, whatever the situation, someone manages to 'have their cake and eat it'. Why? I suppose it has to do with the guilt so many of us feel ourselves when things go really well for us. We feel we don't deserve so much . . . and neither, therefore, does anyone else.

Now, the last people who should have 'so much' are nuns. For centuries we have prided ourselves on how humble and self-sacrificial we are: therein lies our identity. How often do you hear nuns say that they are nuns because that's what they really *enjoy* being? Well, that's *my* starting point and in what follows I want to share some thoughts and feelings from within my experience of celibacy as a choice of sexual lifestyle.

Before I start I need to clarify the way in which I'm going to use one or two words. First celibacy itself. The name of the actual vow I have taken is 'chastity', but I shall use the words 'chastity' and 'celibacy' as in my case synonymous. I shall refer to all women in similar vows as 'nuns', even though strictly speaking I am not a nun but a 'sister' (the difference lies mainly in the type of order and the degree of 'enclosure' within a convent). It is hard to talk meaningfully about the collective experience of contemporary nuns as orders vary so much from country to country and between Roman Catholic and Anglican/ Episcopalian churches. In particular many of the radical questions that have been asked by Roman Catholic nuns in the United States have barely appeared on the horizon of Anglican convents in England which tend to be very much more conservative.

Finally, by way of introduction I want to outline three assumptions I start with. The first is that I do not think 'religious' celibacy (that of a vowed nun) is different in essence to any other kind of chosen celibacy. The experience of one may be different to another because of context and collective history, but I do not accept, for example, notions about God giving nuns, but not other celibate women, special grace to live as such. My second assumption is that I have the right to choose for myself how I express my sexuality and celibacy is a valid choice. Third, I don't regard celibacy as any kind of idealized end in itself. The phrase 'celibate lifestyle' is really more accurate as indicating something pragmatic and functional rather than a mysterious ideal. Celibacy allows me to do the things I want to do and to organize my life according to the values I hold.

I belong to an Anglican franciscan order of sisters and brothers totalling some 45 sisters and 195 brothers. The brothers have houses in various parts of the world, the sisters only in Britain and the United States. We share a common Rule but sisters and brothers each have autonomous chapters (our decision-making bodies) and their own Minister Provincial responsible for what goes on in a particular province. We wear habits as 'the norm' (which means some of us do all the time and some of us rarely do), and we take vows of poverty, chastity and obedience. We have a four-fold office (four services a day) and many houses have a daily eucharist. The Rule also prescribes an hour's private prayer a day.

One of the notable characteristics of my community is the vast difference in the style of our various houses. I began my life in community, like all our novices, at our convent in Somerset. It is a fairly large plant housing about 15 sisters, 4 elderly women whom we look after, and up to 16 guests. The work is centred on the house which is situated in a very rural part of the countryside. Each day is highly structured around the four times of prayer, a daily eucharist and two half-hour periods of silent meditation. Authority is clearly defined with a Guardian in charge of the house and a Novice Guardian responsible for the training and general well-being of the novices. Sisters have no personal money though they may ask for some on their monthly day off.

From Somerset I went to live in a mixed house in East London. The setting was a very poor part of the inner city where the population was predominantly Bangladeshi with a small remaining Jewish community. I worked with the single homeless and was involved with various local campaigns and churches. We had no one 'in charge' in our house but made corporate decisions and spent money when we needed it from a common purse. I returned to Somerset for a further two years during which time I set up an education project at the convent working with local schools. At the end of that time I asked to move to my current house in Paddington, West London.

I now live in a house with two of my brothers, and a young New Zealand woman and a young man neither of whom are members of our order. Most of us pray together in the morning and in the evening before supper. Once a week we hold an informal evening eucharist in the house to which other friends come. We each have a part-time job to earn our living and pursue our own particular interests. The house is very unstructured and we give each other a good deal of personal space and privacy. Together as a household we try to provide space, food and a comfortable place for groups and individuals who come here, most of whom tend to be living or working in some sort of 'fringe' situation. They include peace activists, Christian feminists, housing campaigners, the homeless, the unemployed . . . our friends. Many who come no longer find a comfortable, if any, place within the institutional church, and our own relationship with the institution has included painful confrontation.[1]

So that's something of the context in which I have lived as a celibate woman – a range of very different experiences, albeit within the same religious order. But my context is also saturated with the history of images of former and not-so-former days . . .

Images and stereotypes of nuns abound. There are the traditional images of the nun as Bride of Christ, consecrated virgin, obedient handmaid of Church and Lord. There are pictures of nuns meekly kneeling before a crucifix or dressed in white for their betrothal to Christ. Then there's the image of the nun as whore in pornography;

the virgin who must suffer humiliation before her spirit is finally destroyed. Susan Griffin[2] has shown well enough the relationship between the mind of the pornographer and that of patriarchal Christianity.

Perhaps closer to home there's the Julie Andrews image: the sentimental nun from the sentimental order where everyone understands and celebrates the wedding we've all been longing for. Or there's the victory we celebrate of the nun who finally turns her back on the medieval masochism of her convent in *The Nun's Story*. For those who prefer 'fact' to 'fiction', there are always documentary shots of nuns feeding the starving, comforting the poor, or standing in the congregation for 'Songs of Praise'.

If you don't have TV and don't read pornography there is an increasing variety of advertising posters. Here we have our eyes caught by nuns with fast cars or doing 'unusual' things . . . like (shock! horror!) using a computer.

I find it painful to look at the stereotypes and to think about the theology which surrounds the old images. I can find little meaning in those images that relates to my own life, and the stereotypes create a significant barrier which makes it hard to be taken seriously, especially within the feminist movement. This is a pity as I believe there are some interesting discussions to be had between, for example, feminist nuns and radical lesbians about the shape and vision of separatist communities and the way in which such groups inevitably take on a focusing role for the wider movement.

When I joined my community I had no image of myself as a Bride of Christ, no inkling of what consecrated virginity could be about, and I could barely spell 'sublimate' let alone know how to do it. Celibacy was just part of the package I was buying. I had thought about it but I didn't see it as an idealized end in itself. I found little help in the various theories presented to me either.

First, there is a 'negative ideal' type of theory[3] which continues to influence prevailing attitudes, values and atmospheres in some of our houses. This type of theory emphasizes sacrifice and self-denial. It is also founded on the splitting of spirit and matter which can be seen clearly in the following quotation from part of our source documents called the *Principles*:

> [The vows] stand for the ideal of perfect renunciation of the world, the flesh and the devil, which are three great enemies of the spiritual life . . . The brothers and sisters are bound, like all Christians, to resist and by God's

grace to conquer the temptations of the flesh, and to live lives of purity and self-control.[4]

The celibate woman gives up the joys of sex and childbirth, not for any rational reason understandable in human or worldly terms, but because she has been called to do so by God. So, for example, in one recent book on celibacy we get:

> the spiritual rational level (of celibacy as renunciation) offers the religious an opportunity for redemptive 'death'. In renouncing marriage, a spouse and children, we give to Christ our wish to be remembered in our offspring and by them.[5]

Such views tend also to emphasize that without a 'vocation' to do so, a person cannot live creatively as a celibate:

> Therefore they (members of the order) look to [God] with confidence to give them the grace needed for this life, which, if they should undertake it contrary to his will, would be to them a state of greater rather than less distraction than that of marriage.[6]

Celibacy hardly appears an attractive option!

I was never too good at sacrifice, but I am something of an idealist. The more positive idealism of celibacy is expressed in justifications like 'being free to love everyone' or 'being constantly available'. But I find problems in that position too. Who am I kidding if I pretend I can love everyone, let alone love them equally? I don't see Jesus loving like that; rather, he loved some more than others and his loving of the 'beloved disciple' and the woman traditionally thought to be Mary Magdalene, for example, caused jealousy and scandal.[7] The notion that I am a bottomless pit of love which I can spread around equally and the idea that I can be constantly available betrays the temptation to buy into the superhuman stereotype of the sentimental movie. The truth of the matter is that I need friends, I love some people more than others, and just like any one else I can burn out or dry up if I don't acknowledge my limits and my need for intimacy and nourishment.

It seems to me that the way in which we split matter from spirit, body from mind and soul, is at the heart of what is evil and destructive in our world. Christianity has been used to legitimate the splits and the tradition of celibacy has been understood as one of the primary ways to deny the body and live somewhat prematurely in the spiritual realm. However, I regard the healing of those splits as the current most important human quest and it's what I see my own spirituality as being about. In my search for ideas and models I looked to my own franciscan tradition and found an interesting mix in Francis's own life.

Whilst reading Susan Griffin's Prologue to *Woman and Nature* Francis sprang quickly to mind:

> And when we hear in the Navaho chant of the mountain that a grown man sits and smokes with bears and follows directions given to him by squirrels, we are surprised. We had thought that only little girls spoke with animals.[8]

Little girls, Navaho Indians, and a thirteenth-century religious fanatic from Assisi; stories of Francis preaching to the birds and his 'Canticle of Brother Sun' in which he refers to the natural elements as sister and brother, are fairly well known.[9] There seems to be some hope here – a religious figure taking seriously the notion that God as creator is intimately involved in creation. But the trouble with Francis is that he can't believe that God looked at *him* and said 'indeed it is very good'. The result is a real masochism in which Francis continually abuses his body, tellingly refers to it as 'Brother Ass', and finally kills himself through sheer self-neglect. Of course, that's all seen as proof of his special holiness, but it's also quite inconsistent with the way in which he relates to the rest of the created world. His only redeeming feature on that score was the apology he made to his body when his maltreatment of it was pointed out by another brother.[10]

Today in my community we are less dramatic in the way we misuse our bodies, but the sense that they are not actually 'good' is still around. It is reflected in overwork, what and how we eat, lack of physical recreation, distrust of comfort in our houses, and hard physical work as though it were a means of punishing our bodies. In our liturgical life it is reflected perhaps in one of the most important franciscan feast days – the feast of the stigmata which celebrates the wounds Francis received to his hands and feet, identical to those of the crucified Christ. In my own community, at least, it is the wounded, broken body of Francis we remember more than his intimate relationship with creation. We have focused on the split and ignored the synthesis.

Having found little inspiration in the model of celibacy provided by Francis, I turned to books on the subject.

What pertains to the vow of chastity does not require explanation, since it is evident how perfectly it should be preserved through the endeavour in this matter to imitate angelic purity.[11]

Thus spake St Ignatius. We all know what chastity is about; it's about not 'doing it' – no need to explain any more. We flap our angelic wings and bury our heads – or rather our bodies – in the sand. That's sorted that out . . . or has it? When we talk of questions raising their ugly heads we usually mean ugly bodies . . . and so with questions about the meaning of celibacy.

Most religious orders in the last 20 or 30 years have made radical changes in how they understand the vows of poverty and obedience. It is recognized that historical and cultural circumstances change and that what is an appropriate expression of poverty and/or obedience in one place at one time might not be so in another place or at another time. In the case of my own order, our understanding and expression of poverty and obedience differs greatly from one house to another. It is widely accepted that this is appropriate.

But not so of our vow of chastity. We *know* what that means and see no particular need to undertake the same radical reappraisal as for the other vows. It is not generally accepted that celibacy might mean something different in London in the 1980s from what it meant in Assisi in the thirteenth century. True, some superficial norms have changed, such as sisters visiting each other's rooms, mixed houses, etc., but nothing that really forces us to ask what celibacy *means* today. It remains non-historical, a state of life given by God for all time. What's more, to make mistakes in the interpretation of the vows of poverty and obedience, or to break those vows, is not only excusable and forgiveable, but sometimes thought to be a necessary part of learning boundaries. I have never heard the same said about celibacy: the line between success and failure is absolute (and situated somewhere around the waist) – you either succeed or you fail in your attempt to keep the vow.[12]

Most books about celibacy are obsessed with questions about 'how far can I go?' The lines themselves may have shifted a bit, but line-drawing is still the focus of much of the discussion around proper sexual expression for women and men vowed to celibacy. We are encouraged to see our bodies cut up into those bits which are reasonably safe and cuddly, and those bits which represent danger and plain unchastity. Most modern writers reckon you can do most things that don't affect the gentials. Rereading a popular book on celibacy recently, it reminded me of the worst sort of sex manuals which tell you that you only have to wriggle into the right position for an ecstatic experience every time. Except with celibacy, you *don't* have it.

It's not that I don't think boundaries are a good idea. In the intimate relationships I've had as a celibate I've found the spelling out of clear boundaries necessary for a creative and happy relationship. What bothers me about *focusing* on these issues so heavily in relation to celibacy is that it denies that I can define my sexuality in relation to myself and makes it difficult for me to affirm the goodness of all my body rather than just bits of it. It prevents us as nuns speaking really positively about our sexuality and what it means to us. It stops us healing splits within ourselves and within others.

The question for me is not whether I can live creatively as a celibate, but whether I can live creatively as a celibate within a community which seeks (as I believe it does) to reinterpret the tradition I have just described. Is it all worth it in the end? I don't know the long-term answer to that question – I'm not forced to take life vows for another four years – but I do feel it's important to claim and use the power and authority of such a strong tradition if it's possible to do so in the cause of the gospel and in the overthrow of patriarchal religion. I'll try now to explain what I value in my own celibate lifestyle and how it provides me with a structure and framework within which I can express my commitment to healing splits in myself and in the world.

The word 'celibate' comes from the Latin 'caelebs' meaning 'alone'. I regard my commitment to celibacy as a commitment to aloneness; not a life without friends and intimacy, but a life whereby I value and affirm a kind of inner aloneness. I couldn't have said that when I joined the order – celibacy was just part of the overall deal. However, I do remember a friend at college saying to me that, 'You'll have to have lots of affairs or become a nun.' She was bemoaning my failure, as she saw it, to settle into a 'serious' relationship that had marriage on the horizon. And there is something 'natural' and 'me' about celibacy. I don't think I could sustain a life-long relationship with only one other individual, nor do I think I would cope well with the insecurity of numerous affairs and accompanying separations. Celibacy has always felt like quite a good option for me.

In defining celibacy as being about aloneness I don't mean either that I spend all my time on my own or that, so long as I don't have a *permanent* relationship, anything goes sexually. I find I cannot divorce the celibate part of my lifestyle from the rest of my life and talk about it in a vacuum. It seems to me that all the bits of our lives are interconnected and what we do or don't do in one area affects another and so on. My way of telling whether this or that relationship is OK is not with reference to some hard and fast rule about which bits of the other person I do or don't touch with bits of me, but about whether *as a whole* it 'fits' with the rest of my life. That includes how other people I live with seem to feel about my relationship(s).

The sorts of practical questions I would ask would be something like:

- Am I spending so much time with B that I'm hardly ever at home with the people I live with?
- Am I pouring so much emotional energy into my relationship with B that other friendships start falling apart as a result?
- Am I failing to get on with work or other interests I want to pursue?
- Am I spending sufficient time on my own for my own sanity?

These are not different questions, I suspect, to those that anybody asks, whether in a sexual partnership or not, about what sort of relationship they want with another person. The only differences might be in who the other person/people are who have demands on my time and loyalty, and how much time I need to spend on my own.

One other difference for me as a vowed celibate within a particular community is that I am in some sense accountable to the rest of my order. I find that a very difficult issue and one that has caused, and continues to cause, pain for both me and some of my sisters. I know, for example, that there are some who might be upset by what I have written here. I find the only honest thing to do is to follow my own path, sharing my thoughts and visions with close friends (including some in the community), and being as honest as I can with myself and with my order. I can't pretend to make a very good job of it, but for feminist nuns as for so many women today, role models are scarce.

I am a nun because I enjoy being a nun. I don't think my six and a half years in a religious community have ever been without some struggle, but it has also been the place where I have learnt most about God and most about myself. It's been the place where I have had to live the relationship between my sexuality and my spirituality. Anne Dickson, in her book *The Mirror Within*, writes that when a woman 'finds her body she finds her sexuality – and her own way of expressing it'.[13] It's been as a nun that I've found my body and thereby my sexuality. Perhaps 'found' is the wrong word – it would be truer to say I'm finding them.

I'm hopeless at practising what I preach. Ironically for someone who has never bought the traditional view of self-denial, let alone self-castigation, I began discovering my body when it almost collapsed from exhaustion. Two years ago, whilst living at my convent in Somerset, I became ill; I was treated for exhaustion and anxiety but the experience was one of breakdown, of giving myself permission to stop and fall apart. It was both frightening, as I didn't know how far I would fall, and a tremendous relief because I had known for some time of its inevitability. I had driven myself hard, worked furiously, and been constantly anxious about much. In the time that followed I let go of many things and waited for the world to collapse. It didn't.

I was forced during that time to listen to what my body was saying. I was shocked by my illness because it had not been the result of some airborne disease which had happened to come my way. Rather, I was largely responsible for the state I now found myself in. That recognition, far from paralysing me with guilt, gave me a considerable sense of power – power to co-operate if I so chose with my own inner healing processes. I had talked about all that before – to *other* people – but now it was time to put my money where my mouth was and, among other things, I began regular exercise sessions in my evening prayer slot. The daily scenes of me hot and sweaty in a sports shirt were to some of my sisters a confirmation of my sickness: others joined me. I felt as if I was using my prayer time more honestly than I had ever done and I enjoyed it enormously. It was one of the few moments when heaven and earth seemed to touch.

Through the experience of illness and gradual recovery I discovered that my attitude to my body changed radically. It became a part of me it hadn't been before – it could nourish and it needed nourishment. I felt a greater sense of warmth towards myself and I felt affirmed in my choice of a celibate lifestyle. I think it was to do with the word 'choice'.

I said at the beginning that I didn't see religious celibacy as being any different to other kinds of chosen celibacy. But the experience of deliberately *chosen* celibacy is probably very different to an enforced celibacy for whatever reason. I think that's true, not just because of the desirability of options, but has also to do with whether or not *I* define my own sexuality.

A woman's sexuality in our culture is commonly defined only in terms of her sexual partner who is usually assumed to be male. She is only sexual if she's 'doing it'. That's why society does not commonly distinguish between sex and sexuality – it sees both only in terms of coupledom. But my sexuality, with all its power and energy, is for me too. We discover our sexuality when we discover our bodies because our sexuality is about the nature of ourselves as embodied beings – about how we relate to the world and to one another *as bodies*. The choice is ours to decide how we relate as embodied beings and celibacy, as I see it, is just one of the options.

To regard myself as the Bride of Christ would be once again to allow my sexual identity to be defined only in relation to some other, albeit a divine other. Women have always had to have some man around to give them a sexual identity – forbid earthly creatures and it has to be God. I think that's one reason why the book *Lesbian Nuns*[14] caused such a stir: nuns saying they weren't interested in *any* kind of husband.

Spirituality. It's not a word that I find easy to use. It conjures up images of kneeling in bleak churches, whispers, guilt, specialness . . . husband holiness. The problem is I can't think of another word: I shall use it to mean an attempt to get in touch with what I experience as in some sense 'beyond'. Spirituality for me is about quality rather than transcendence. There's a story I like which explains what I mean. A little girl was taken by her mother to see a sculptor. What she saw was a big shapeless block of marble being chiselled away at by the artist. Some weeks later they returned to the studio and there in the place of the shapeless lump was a beautiful marble lion. The little girl gasped and asked the sculptor in amazement, 'But how did you know the lion was in the marble?'

Seeing is believing, but easier said than done. Sometimes to see means sitting or standing still for hours, days, years . . . like the artist, the lover, the hermit, the woman at Greenham Common. We all have different things we want to see, our own places to sit, and a variety of symbols to help us focus and prevent us from giving up. We have our own dreams and behold our own visions. Sometimes we sit with those who have already seen, other times we simply block each other's view.

One of the things which strikes me more and more is how important it is where we place ourselves to look. Our bodies matter, and it matters what we do with them. There's a strong tradition, common in monastic houses, that we must pray unceasingly however and wherever we are: we feel prayer *ought* to be the same in whatever circumstance, and we are suspicious of special 'atmospheres' (unless, of course, it's a church) as if they are the antithesis of 'discipline'. But that's just not true. Words like sin, oppression, exile, obedience, crucifixion, even 'Lord', feel quite different facing the fence at Greenham Common than they do in Westminster Abbey.[15] Where I place my body will affect what I see and what I hear. It will also affect what other people hear me saying.

So what's all this got to do with being a nun? I suppose it has to do with where I find I can see the clearest . . . the margins, the outskirts, the fringe. My lifestyle provides me with one way of living marginally to a society I feel is fundamentally sick. The vows I take express some basic human values which are not very popular ones, at least not with those who hold the power in our society. Materialism thrives with advertisements which encourage us to buy all we need for a happy and carefree life; a rather private nuclear family is regarded as the all-important 'normal' social unit; we need never be alone with 24-hour radio and TV; women who leave home to wage peace rather than war are regarded as insane; and the law must be upheld at whatever cost to civil liberty. Those of us who refuse personal possessions, turn our backs on the nuclear family, and proclaim that our obedience is to God can't help but find ourselves in some sense 'counter-cultural' if we take our vows seriously.

The celibate part of our lifestyle challenges not only the notion that the nuclear family is the only viable social unit, but also the assumption that women are always sexually available for men whether as wife or lover. A friend asked me the other day where the pain was for me in celibacy. I found her question very hard to answer because I wanted to say there wasn't any. That's true in so far as I don't go through agonies of frustration or of wanting children, but there is the inevitable pain of choice. Whatever sexual lifestyle we've chosen we all suffer or celebrate the limitations of choice. What's usually assumed, though, is that it is only celibacy which is about 'not having' rather than having something different. As a celibate I believe I have something different, but equally worth celebrating and enjoying . . .

The 'not having' image is very strong. Sexual partners, particularly marriage partners, are often referred to as 'your other half' or worse still 'your better half'. It implies that those of us on our own are *only* a half, that we are not whole people. My experience of celibacy is the opposite of that. It struck me very forcefully at a workshop once how closely related was my understanding of my sexuality and my spirituality. We were invited to draw images of both. The image I had of my spirituality was a spherical object, like a globe, resting in the palm of my outstretched hand. I was still as I held it and it was infinitely lovely. The image I drew to represent my sexuality was a similar object with rays going out from it indicating that it was about relationship, although the rays didn't actually touch anything else. Both images were complete in themselves, both had a quality of wholeness, and both 'belonged' to me and in a way *were* me.

Moments when I am most consciously in touch with either tend to be when I am on my own, when I experience myself as essentially separate and alone. Paradoxically they are also moments when I tend to feel connected with the natural world, just another piece woven into the fabric of creation. They are fleeting experiences of wholeness and synthesis, times when the various 'bits' which are me seem to connect. In all that, the truth which I proclaim as a celibate has to do with ultimate aloneness. At the end of the day, we are all on our own; in the language of traditional Christianity, we stand alone before God. Our society wants to kid us otherwise and we fall often into the trap of thinking we can merge with another person or with a group. We can't.

It sounds from what I've just written that I'm constantly fleeing to mountain tops or lake sides (if only . . .) but that's not the case. The other truth for me in discovering where I need to sit or stand to see is that I must do it where I am – in the kitchen or bathroom, at work or in the local pub. It matters how I cook, what I eat, how much sleep I get. I'm quite convinced those things contribute more to the state of my soul than how many times a week I fail to get to morning prayer or whether or not I go to church on Sunday morning. Occasional retreats to the mountain are only necessary to regain a sense of priority and balance. I find it almost impossible to withdraw regularly within the city, even though I think it's a good idea!

Finally, I want to return to what I said about not being able to carve my life up into bits and talk about particular aspects of it, in this case celibacy. When I was asked to identify the pain in celibacy by my friend, I could only think of pain which goes with my overall lifestyle. Being counter-cultural in the 1960s was fun, but in the present age it's suddenly got serious. Whether we feel the power of church authorities or secular authorities, cross the fence and we know all about it. It pains me that we split so much within the feminist movement arguing over ideological purity. We have so much strength together and so many stories to share. One of the most important questions for me right now is whether the monastic tradition can be reclaimed and in what form. Convents down the ages have been powerful separatist communities which have often provided women with the only alternative to a servile marriage. Perhaps the future lies in separation from the institutional church. I don't know, but I know I want to share the vision and ask the questions with all my sisters whatever their sexual lifestyle and whatever name they give their search for the beyond.

NOTES

1   Most recently we found ourselves at loggerheads with the Church Commissioners (who manage the Church of England's wealth) and diocesan authorities over the proposed sale of a redundant church site for luxury housing.

2   Susan Griffin, *Pornography and Silence*, London, The Women's Press, 1981.

3   See Roger Ruston OP, 'Religious Celibacy and Sexual Justice', a paper given at the Provincial Chapter of the English Dominicans, April 1982, and reproduced in *New Blackfriars*, June, 1982, pp.260–74.

4   *The Principles*, The Society of St Francis, 1984.

5   Joyce Ridick, *Treasures in Earthen Vessels: The Vows*, St Paul Publications, 1984, p.45.

6   *Ibid.*

7   Mark 14:3–9; Luke 7:36–50; Matthew 26:1–13; John 19:26; 20:2; 21:20–23.

8   Susan Griffin, *Women and Nature – The Roaring Inside Her*, London, The Women's Press, 1984, Prologue.

9   See Celano, *First Life*, Chapter XXI, in *St Francis of Assisi, Omnibus of Sources*, ed. Marion A. Habig, Franciscan Herald Press, 1973, pp.277ff. This very early biography of Francis gives an account of various stories of Francis preaching to the birds, talking to rabbits, etc.

10 *Ibid.*, pp.530f. from Celano, *Second Life*.

11 St Ignatius, *Constitutions*, Part VI, Ch.1, no.1; in Francis J. Moloney SDB, *Disciples and Prophets – A Biblical Model for the Religious Life*, London, Darton, Longman & Todd, 1980, p.100.

12 Ruston, *op.cit.*

13 Anne Dickson, *The Mirror Within*, London, Quartet, 1985, p.119.

14 Rosemary Curb and Nancy Manahan (eds), *Lesbian Nuns: Breaking Silence*, USA, Naiad Press, 1985.

15 Angela West writes: 'On August 31st 1984, ten women arrived at Blue Gate, Greenham Common to do the night watch for the peace camp there – and simultaneously to keep the vigil of the Passion based on the gospel of St Mark . . . The women of the camp welcomed the night watchers and extended the hospitality of their fire, before going off to sleep under their sheet of polythene. The vigil women remained around the fire to keep the watch, gathering each hour on the hour to face the guarded gates of Greenham, and to sing a psalm, read from the Bible and pray.' From 'Greenham Vigil – a Christian women's theological initiative for peace' (unpublished paper).

The Greenham vigil is held on the last Friday night of the month and if you are interested in taking part contact Angela West, 91 Bridge Street, Osney, Oxford OX2 0BD.

III

BODY THEOLOGY

PERFORMANCE

Choosing her moment with care, she steps into the light at
    the centre
And dances for the audience an outrageous ragtime gavotte
With the startled Hound of Heaven.
We frown at her unrespectful clown face; her hands
Place more stars in the air.

He, the rogue magician,
Already at the shimmering table
Surrounded by sweet perfumes and holy vessels,
Almost affects not to notice the up-staging.
She is his daughter who chooses this moment called church
    to be undutiful.

He is said to image Christ
He does not dance.
Somewhere in all the achings of women to claim their
    holiness
To be seen standing in the light at the centre
To celebrate the earth and the flame, the spells of love
and healing, the ring dances
Is the justice of her cheekiness

At her age I, another priest's daughter
Also knew which things were true
And which are theatre that I might as well perform in.

They catch one another's eye
But his movements start to echo hers
Tom and Caitlin, MAGIC ACT EXTRAORDINARY
Roll up and catch a glimpse of the world shifting.

Handing him the props, the wine and water
Not humbly but like a rebel co-conspirator
She bows, but her eyes gleam
Distant applause.

                                        Polly Blue

A WOMB-CENTRED LIFE

Una Kroll

When I was a child I lived for some time with a family of Russian Orthodox Christians. This meant that we spent several hours each Sunday in church. From my point of view it felt like heaven to be there. The richness of the music and ritual, together with the fact that I could not understand any of the words that were being spoken or chanted, meant that I had time to absorb the atmosphere surrounding me during the time we were there. It was, I now realize, my first experience of living in the dark, nourishing womb of God. At the time, of course, I did not know this. I simply felt safe, warm, and loved; but at the same time I was conscious of movement as if I were swimming easily towards a light which drew me to swim out towards the horizon to see what lay beyond it. I am surprised that I should use a visual image to describe what was happening because I could not see anything in that church. For one thing, in Russian Orthodox churches the worshippers stand during the whole of the service and I was standing there surrounded by the black-coated figures of my mother and her friends. On the rare occasions when I opened my eyes I was too small to see anything other than their clothes. For another, all the exciting bits of the service took place behind a highly decorated wooden wall-to-floor screeen and were invisible to the lay congregation crowded into the space in front of it. True, from time to time, the priests came out through doors set in the screen to chant blessings or read the gospels but, as far as I was concerned, that was something that mattered to grown-ups not to children, and in any case it was in a foreign language. So it was the music and the smell of incense that delighted me. Why then did I translate that experience into images that were felt and seen? I am not entirely sure of the answer but it has to do with experience and with the way I identify experience with God and God's womb in terms of a journey which involves birth and coming into the light. Maybe it involves a dim memory of my own birth into life. What I do know is that this very early experience of worship created a memory that was real to me and that was to be repeated at other times of my life in different circumstances. It was an experience that I learnt to trust, have identified with God, and have called 'living in the dark womb of God' only since I learnt to accept the goodness of my own and other people's wombs and to understand how God can dwell in, and work through, my womanhood as well as allowing me to dwell in God's creative womb.

At the time of my first experience, however, which must have been when I was about four or five years old, I simply connected the experience with God. After all I had been told that God lived in a church and that I could meet God there, so accepted our meeting joyfully. We did not meet again for quite a time and our next meeting did not occur in a church at all but quite unexpectedly in the middle of the night when I was alone, frightened, living away from my mother, and tormented by an older child who was a bully. After our meeting the bullying did not stop but I had acquired the strength to survive pain and fear and my own impotent rage. By this time God was real. It matters not to me now whether my experience was real or a figment of my imagination for I believe that God can work through our dreams and self-delusions and I do not look to prove God's existence through my subjective experiences of reality, merely to share something of that reality by describing it. My direct experiences of what I call God are quite rare, unexpected and surprising to me, but their effects last for long periods of time and can sometimes lead to radical alterations of direction and lifestyle. That is what confirms their reality for me.

When I was growing up I understood none of this, never spoke of it to any adult, but accepted the meeting as important. My next meeting happened when I was eighteen years old. I was an undergraduate medical student at Cambridge at the time. I had told a lie to a friend who asked me if I was a Christian. 'Yes,' I had answered, knowing it to be untrue. That lie made me more ashamed than any other lie had ever done so I went into a church to think about why I had said such a thing. And met God again. It so happened that a priest was in that church hearing confessions, so, knowing absolutely nothing about ecclesiastical custom or sacramental practice, but dimly aware of a need to seek help, I went and said sorry to God and another human being for my lie. The church and the priest happened to be Anglican, which also happened to be the church of my baptism in infancy, and, to his credit, the priest coped with this uninstructed penitent without surprise and so I became a practising Christian.

I found myself belonging to a community dominated by rational thought and an insistence that God was a 'perfect gentleman' whom I, as a woman, should be honoured to serve all the days of my life, preferably without asking any awkward questions about the purpose of my life as a woman with a womb. Women's wombs were their *raison d'être*, I gathered, and I could fulfil my purpose in life either through childbearing or consecrated service as a nun. 'Be good, sweet maid, and let who will be clever,' was a good motto for a Christian woman I was told, but if I also wanted to use my mind in God's service I could do so provided I was willing to become an 'honorary' man, adopting his traditions of prayer and ways of doing things. Having been endowed with a good brain, a first-class education, and a desire to become a Christian doctor of medicine, I learnt to treat my womb as an organ of convenience which I could forget or at least ignore for long periods of time.

So I set out to become a 'mind-centred' person who would be able to ignore the insistent claims of her womb by offering herself to God as a nun. Mercifully, at this point in my experience of life I re-discovered the womb of God through prayer, recognized the God I had met as a child, and allowed myself to be nourished by that wonderfully enclosing dark love that lay beyond the reaches of reason and correct behaviour, but which also had everything to do with the way I could live as a Christian woman if I dared to let God work through my womb. This time it was more difficult for God to arrange our meeting, for I had become an instructed Christian rather than the uninstructed young child or adolescent whose life had been touched by God so swiftly and surely so long ago. I had been a Christian for ten years. I knew about doctrine. I knew about the Fatherhood of God. I knew all about the sub-ordination of women as a theological proposition. I knew that most priests distrusted women's intuitions and ways of doing things, and I had certainly learnt to distrust my own woman-hood over the period of those ten years. I had also learnt to distrust my own way of praying and was busy trying to learn to do what I was told to do by priests and nuns who were older and wiser than I. So I did not make it easy for God, or for myself. In fact, when God and I did finally meet I thought I was deluded and was convinced that the experience was the product of my own sickness. Yet, the darkness, the warmth, the sense of movement towards light, the sense of being born were all there if only I would dare to let go and enter the experience of being in God's womb ready to be born again and become what God wanted me to be. Here in a way the images I am using cannot express what I am trying to say. I was drawn into that darkness time and again, but I could leave it when I wanted to and so for a long time I did not stay in God's womb long enough to go through the experience of birth. Yet my longing for God was so great that I returned to that dark nourishing experience time and again with the easy familiarity of a child who recognizes her mother in a crowd of people. In time I accepted the goodness of the prayer. I knew I was being invited to stay. The effect of the prayer was that I was learning to love myself as God loved me, as a child, as a woman with a womb, as a woman 'created in the image of God' who was 'like' God and bore God's image in the whole of her being, including the whole of her sexuality. My experiences of femaleness began to assert themselves in my prayer life and now I no longer treated them as distractions but as God-given feelings that could teach me more about God. Many of those feelings had affinities with my knowledge of God through direct contact and that was how I gradually began to ignore the patriarchial messages I was receiving from books, priests and teachers and to trust God to teach me through this prayer of 'indwelling' in God's womb. In time, and it took years rather than months, I was taught by God to be thankful for and to trust my own womanhood, and to love and trust other women too. In time, too, I came to understand that my own experiences as a woman could teach me more about God and so my ideas about God began to expand as my understanding of what it meant to be a woman grew.

The story of how that happened is part of this essay. I want to share with others the experience of learning to live and pray with the mind and heart centred in the womb. When I speak about having a womb I am using the word to describe more than an organ which is capable of nurturing an implanted embryo and of bringing a child to birth. I am using it to describe an amalgam of elements in a woman's life which give her the ability to describe herself as a woman even if she is either born without a uterus or loses it during her lifetime, even if she has no ovaries or loses them during her lifetime, even if she was born a transsexual. Genetic sex, gender and the inevitable conditioning that all human beings are subject to from the moment they are named as female all combine to create a person who is womb-centred, a woman having a womb even if she disowns it, that is to say she is a person with a particular perspective on life because of her nature. Moreoever it is my belief that her perspective which is womb-centred is also God-centred because she is created in God's image.

Unlike men, women bear God's image in a dynamic way which is marked by periodicity, indeed marked throughout her life by changes in rhythm, large and small, which enable her to be in tune with other rhythms in creation which are also in tune with that aspect of God's creativity. In saying this I am not denying periodicity to men. They too are subject to rhythmic changes in their lives, but in a more explosive and less regular way when they are young and in a less obvious, more gradual way when they grow older. Their rhythms are as important as womens' but no more important or valuable. There are occasions when the joint rhythms of women and men can lead to their participation in God's birthing creativity, not necessarily through physical parenthood but also by becoming parents to ideas, books, businesses, religious communities and other enterprises. However, I have not touched on men's periodic rhythms, simply because I want to concentrate on the importance of rhythms in women's lives.

I want to look at this marvellous dynamic periodicity which is so characteristic of all women's lives to see how it affects our understanding of our womb-centred lives as members of God's family. I am writing as someone who has lived through adolescence when I discovered the meaning of sexual joy in my life, by falling in love, as young people do, passionately, for all time, which turns out to be a shorter time than expected. In adult life I was able to celebrate my fertility. I have now come to the post-menopausal phase of my life when I am no longer able to bear children but remain a complete woman. In describing my own experience as a woman I do not seek to make generalizations. I simply feel that an open celebration of the importance of the womb in one person's life offers an experience against which other equally important and varied experiences can be measured. In finding and claiming my own womb as good I also discovered the womb of God. I came to that discovery in stages.

FINDING THE WOMB OF GOD THROUGH REJECTION

Life as a womb-centred person began for me with rejection by my father. Having been previously married to a woman who had part-nered him in the birth of two girls, he had ardently desired to see a son born out of his union with my mother. I was a disappointment. He left our lives before I was two years old; I had already begun to experience the rejection of my womanhood.

That rejection was to be reinforced by other rejections so that when I grew into an adult I attempted to ignore my own womb and to behave as though it were a nuisance rather than an asset. I soon learnt to enjoy the status of being an 'honorary man' and felt flattered when men 'accepted' me provided I behaved as one of them.

My mother, herself rejected by her father, found herself left with a child she had not wanted in the first place. I remember her as a large person with a fiery temperament which fuelled her tendency to erupt into volcanically destructive rages. Between these periodic and ter-rifying displays of anger she was woman of sparkling personality, with a generous nature and an infectious capacity for laughter. She was also a woman of great courage and determination who fought tena-ciously against loneliness and poverty. She gave me life, taught me how to survive in a hostile environment and protected me from the consequences of being a woman by forcing me to learn to use my mind in such a way that I might escape the kind of material hardships that befall millions of women who do not receive a good education. For the first eighteen years of my life I lived in her shadow. I both feared and adored her. She sought unconsciously to turn me into a boy, chose my profession of medicine for me, encouraged me to live single-mindedly and propelled me into adult life as a de-sexed person who could pass myself off as a woman or an honorary male according to the company I found myself keeping. Yet, by the grace of God, neither my mother nor my father, a legendary figure whom I saw but three times during those eighteen years, destroyed my womb. True, I did not love my womb: I felt its effects in my body each month, but ignored their significance. Memory tells me that I resisted nature's rhythms, denied the goodness of my own thrust towards life-bearing, and attempted to beat my body into subjection by a fierce discipline, which began at the age of eighteen when I became a Christian, and continued for the best part of the next ten years.

None of this do I now regret. The way of negation was for me a way towards the discovery of my own womb and of God's womb. When eventually I did claim my womb I did so with a full understanding of the symptoms and signs of the disease of sexism which had afflicted me and trapped me for a time into denying my 'self', that precious 'talent' which is God-given and meant to be used productively and to the glory of God.

In describing what happened to me as a child and a young woman I am offering others an experience which I hope will help some of my sisters and brothers who have undergone similar experiences of rejection to take heart even if they now do feel imprisoned by their early conditioning. Liberation is possible. For me, it came through Christianity, and that, perhaps, to some people will seem very strange. It is, however, true.

My first ten years as a Christian were bewildering, self-negating, womb-denying. Five of them were spent as an ascetic, five as a nun. All of them were passionate and, as I now realize, helpful to my development as a woman, for, as so many other people have done, I discovered that by rejecting my own womb in an attempt to search for a God 'beyond parts or passions', I could not destroy either it or my 'self'. When I sought God in a dedicated life of prayer and community life as a nun I found my womb again enclosed in God's womb, kept safe there until I could reclaim that part of myself which was precious to God and remains so until today. This I now know to be true not only for myself but for all women, even though I know that some women have been unable to integrate God's womb and theirs into their lives as Christian women because of the inability of many Christian communities to acknowledge the presence of God's image in women.

It is a matter of regret to me that some of my friends have only been able to discover the goodness of their womanhood by leaving the Christian church altogether because they have mistakenly equated some of the patriarchial attitudes they have found in some Christians with Christianity. Mercifully, God cannot be imprisoned in any institution and waits for us both inside and outside the communities we call churches.

Anyone who takes prayer seriously and is willing to go on this journey of pilgrimage hand in hand with Christ will find themselves in the end, will discover themselves as God sees them, and will eventually begin to look at the world through God's eyes rather than their own.

It takes some people longer to learn how to do this than others. Everyone's journey, my own included, is unique, yet there are, I believe, similarities in our lives which enable us to sympathize, and even sometimes empathize, with others whom we meet along the way. This hidden glorious community within a community, this company of friends, helps us to keep going onwards. Christian friendships are given to us by the love of God at points along the journey when we most need help. Such friendships have been rich in my life, offsetting the negative experiences of my early life. Paradoxically, I do not think I would have had such treasured relationships had I not also had knowledge of the impoverished relationships that can come through rejection.

FINDING THE WOMB OF GOD THROUGH EXPERIENCE

I found my own womb again through prayer which I thought was taking my life in the opposite direction but which led me directly towards God's womb. In a convent nuns spend several hours a day attempting to meet God in prayer. Prayer in this context is not talking to God, or asking God for favours, but is an attempt to be still. Stillness of this kind means leaving thoughts and feelings behind so that the person who is praying is really empty. God comes into that emptiness in silence so profound that the host person is unaware of God's presence at the time, but may know that God has been with her or him by the fruits of the encounter which are apparent later on. What happened to me was that I 'knew' nothing during my prayer times but found that in my times of routine work, study and recreation I was increasingly aware of and happy about my womanhood and began to be able to reclaim my sexuality. I claimed my womb again through the experience of rhythmic helplessness which comes most obviously to every woman who gives birth to children but which is also available in less obvious ways to women who remain childless. Most young women are reminded of their inability to control their own lives every time they see menstrual blood. That mysterious rhythm takes place independently of them, yet demands their attention and participation. This recurrent sign of womanliness tells a girl she is a woman, tells a woman she is a potential mother, tells her when she is pregnant and finally tells her when she is past childbearing age.

On the other hand, when men bleed their loss of blood is a sign of warning, a sign that if the flow of blood is not staunched they could die. When, however, women bleed from the womb their loss of blood is a sign of life, of hope, of fulfilment, of completion. Menstruation brings with it the mysterious joy of being able to share in God's work of birthing.

The inability to control this God-given menstrual rhythm symbolizes the helplessness of women to control their lives. When women accept their natural rhythms and allow themselves to work with them instead of against them they also learn to be flexible as well as practical. Living so close to nature helps most women to accept their own temporality and mortality. Men are just as dependent on God, just as helpless to control their own lives, just as vulnerable and mortal as women but they are not subject to regular reminders as women are and so they sometimes delude themselves into behaving as if they were in control of their destinies and immortal. In order to do this they have to reject the helplessness which symbolizes the limitation of mortality and unfortunately often do this by a display of powerfulness, arrogantly assuming that they have the right to dominate those who are so obviously 'out of control' of their own lives. This kind of behaviour may help some men to stave off the knowledge of the inevitability of death but paradoxically leads them to flirt with death every day of their lives in an effort to prove that they are in control rather than God. Such behaviour is most obviously apparent in the 'war games' men play with both conventional and nuclear weapons.

Menstruation is a hidden sign of human vulnerability. Pregnancy, on the other hand, is an outward and visible sign of human dependency on God. Women and men alike are able to exercise some control over their destinies. They are, for instance, able to prevent pregnancy by one means or another, but once a woman becomes pregnant she becomes part of a process of nature over which she has no control. A pregnancy once started will have its end in birth even if a miscarriage occurs, even if the birth is premature, even if the child is stillborn, deformed or handicapped.

Pregnancy gives an individual woman a personal experience of helplessness which is more sustained and powerful than any experience in a man's life other than the experience of death. It is, of course, true that men submit to temporary helplessness during orgasm and during illness. Many of them may feel it when they go to war as front-line soldiers. Everyone will also experience such helplessness during the transition from life before death to life after death, but then they cannot tell us what that experience is like. Many women, however, live with this kind of helplessness for comparatively long periods of time. Most of them will live through their pregnancies and can therefore describe their experiences of powerlessness during the labour of birth.

That experience has happened five times to me. Happily, we have four children alive. Our first child has no name, for she or he died during an early stage of pregnancy. Nevertheless, I had already recognized the symptoms of pregnancy. My mind was already attuned to expectancy. My body had undergone subtle changes in its rhythms and in its biochemical make-up. I was already aware of the inevitability of birth. That is a fact which confronts all pregnant women, even those who seek and are granted therapeutic abortions.

This kind of physical helplessness had a profound effect on me and on my understanding of God. I realized, as so many others have done, that resistance to the inevitable accomplishes nothing but increased pain, anxiety, even terror, whereas co-operation with nature makes birth easier, quicker and safer even if the child does not survive the act of birth.

Giving birth is a frightening yet exhilarating participation in God's work. In recent years the multiplication of monitoring devices, surgical techniques to induce labour, and other interventionalist tactics have given many women the illusion that human beings control birth rather than God. It is important to remember that no woman would need obstetric care and intervention had she not conceived. It is her sense of moving towards the critical point where labour of one kind or another is going to happen that is so important throughout the time of her pregnancy.

It is my belief that all women are endowed with the ability to respond to the demands of pregnancy, labour and motherhood whether or not they have children. This mysterious ability to give birth is so familiar to most women that they take it for granted rather than reflecting on its effect on the way they live their lives. It is so strange and unintelligible to many men that they distance themselves from it instead of recognizing that they share in birthing just as much as women if they can allow themselves to experience powerlessness, vulnerability and dependence on God instead of pretending to be able to control everything all the time.

Physical birth has profound spiritual effects, giving most women an ability to flow with events rather than trying to stand out against them. This quality stands them in good stead in other aspects of their lives. It may be easier to acquire the qualities needed for mothering if you have experienced the birthing of children but the ability to be a 'good' mother is innate in most women and can be learned by women and men who are willing to allow themselves to explore other areas of their lives where they experience helplessness or a sense of being carried along by forces which are greater than themselves.

Attentiveness to my own experience of birthing has enabled me to be more aware of the way in which God is creative in and through Creation, helped me to pray more in accord with God's will and to accept the intimate link between birth and death that forms part of my daily life, by finding and dwelling in the womb of God and seeing life from that perspective.

FINDING THE WOMB OF GOD THROUGH LOSS

Birthing and dying are very similar events. Those men and women who do not have the joy of physical parenthood can often understand what birth is like if they look at their own experience of death in going through the 'mini-deaths' of life which are a preparation for final physical death. The experience of 'mini-death' often comes to men through the loss and grief that accompanies an unsuccessful courtship, a marriage breakdown, sudden unemployment or retirement from work. It may also come through temporary impotency, loss of face, surrender to an enemy, or imprisonment of various kinds, including illness. Women share these experiences but add to them the experience of menopause after which it is impossible for them to give birth to children.

All women who live long enough go through the experience of natural menopause, a time of profound hormonal changes in their bodies when one phase of their lives comes to an end. Many women fear this time of change, feeling that it will have a profound effect on their sexual lives and status as women. Instead, they can, I believe, welcome the menopause as a liberation from some of the responsibilities of womanhood in order to find pleasure and fulfilment in others.

Although I have not yet known the joy of becoming a grandmother I have experienced the freedom that comes to post-menopausal women who remain sexual persons. I welcome the certainty of not having to think about pregnancy. I know that I do not now have the necessary years ahead of me when I would be strong enough to nurture children on a full-time basis. Yet, I have found that my ability to be a 'mother' has increased now that I no longer have to cope with the demands of a family of growing children. Life as a post-menopausal woman has led to the discovery of aspects of my sexuality that I did not have the time to explore when I was younger. This new-found freedom to explore has also led to my becoming willing to accept new interests and adventures which are certainly just as fulfilling as the experience of parenthood. In my own case, for instance, I have begun to enjoy creative recreations like gardening, which I did not fully appreciate when I was younger. I have savoured friendships in a different way. I have become a 'spiritual' granny to several young women and men. I have developed a tenderness for and understanding of old people that I did not have as a younger woman. I have a delight in the 'present moment' that is heightened by my acceptance of the inevitability of my own death. I have a new eagerness to share experience through writing. Yet I feel that I remain womb-centred though I find it hard to express this reality in words.

Menopause comes early enough in a woman's life to give her the time to learn to grow old gracefully without giving up her enjoyment of being a woman. That experience of 'loss' comes to most men only at retirement and is then often accompanied by a loss of income and status that are painful and sometimes lethal. Moreover, the changes in a woman's body are so definite and obvious to her that she is encouraged to accept her advancing years and adapt herself to a different way of living long before she grows old and set in her ways. She therefore has an advantage over most men in facing the great changes which come through retirement, bereavement, and one's own impending death.

People who try to defeat death by remaining perpetually young in appearance and behaviour never have the joy that comes to women who can adapt to post-menopausal life. The menopause is a profound change involving the surrender of power and ambition into younger hands, involving pride in past experience and a willingness to share one's acquired knowledge without trying to impose on other people, involving ultimately the acceptance of help from other people who are younger and stronger than oneself.

It is easier for a woman to accept change as she grow older than it is for a man simply because the changes in her body are definite and obvious. It is, however, no less important for men to learn these lessons of change and ageing. Men can learn from women even though they do not share exactly the same experiences at the same point in their lives. It is, therefore, a great joy when men can acknowledge their differences from women and yet feel able to admit to their similarities so that they are willing to listen to women's experiences and enjoy their mutality as human beings made in God's image.

FINDING THE WOMB OF GOD THROUGH ECSTASY

Moments of ecstasy have recurred like grace notes throughout my life. Without ecstasy my life would have been sadly impoverished. The ecstasy of sexual union is akin to that of ecstatic prayer. Both involve a loss of self-consciousness, a sense of merging with the beloved object of desire, a sense of nothing being more important than one's lover's happiness. I have lost myself in ecstasy again and again, more easily, perhaps, with a man than with God, but certainly with God who has sought me out as a lover on occasions when I have been waiting in prayer. Now that I am older I think that God is as present in the ecstasy of sexual union as in that of unitive prayer but when I was younger I could not face that truth so easily. Ecstasy has given zest to my life. I could not have known what it was like if I had not been taught by God to love myself and so to begin to love others as myself.

I have reached an age when I can look back on the experiences of my younger years to celebrate and rejoice in various events that have happened to me because I have lived a womb-centred life. Yet I am still young enough to remember the struggle I had to accept the goodness of my self, my sexuality, my rhythmic periodicity.

I do not now regret those years of rejection because the acceptance of my womb when it happened was archetypally complete. Yet they were sterile years and I hope that fewer women of our time and after will have to go through the kind of oppression and suppression that was usual for women of my generation.

Just as it is important for individual women to move on from childhood to womanhood, passing through the gate of the menarche, and from their birthing years to fruitful maturity, through the gate of the menopause, so it is important that generations of women do the same in their corporate struggles to free themselves from the shackles their societies have imposed on them in an effort to keep them perpetually chained to their domestic roles as children, wives and mothers.

As women we are beginning to celebrate our heritage. We have accumulated a wealth of knowledge about our past. We are beginning to be able to claim and rejoice in our womb-centred lives without finding them imprisoning. We need now to be able to move on to give birth to all kinds of ideas and changes and people who will start from points which women of my generation took decades to reach.

It is, I believe, important that older women like myself should rejoice in the fact that our children do not have to struggle in the same way that we did. Their struggles are real enough but fewer of them should need to start from the perspective of self-denigration, secret shame about bodily functions and sheer ignorance about female sexuality that many women of my generation did. At the same time younger women need to have compassion and understanding for those older women who cannot move out of the dependency roles in which they were raised and which confined many of them to the status of children in societies where 'daddy always knew best'.

The many determined attempts made by church leaders, politicians, and cult heroes to reduce women to the status of household slaves will be impossible if the generation of younger women now alive are confident enough about their womb-centred lives to claim and use their gifts as women rather than as honorary men.

It is, in my opinion, high time that women begin to insist that men should live more natural rhythm-centred lives than they presently do. It is also high time that men begin to listen to the wisdom of women so that together they may contribute to the welfare of each other and God's world in ways that acknowledge the sovereignty of God who is incarnate in women as well as men, yet who remains beyond the reach of all sexual images.

13

NOTHING IS SACRED, ALL IS PROFANE
Lesbian Identity and Religious Purpose

Elaine Willis

I want to outline an autobiographical process, that is, parts of my life that have contributed to patterns and movement within it. My journey into female friendship and loving, into questioning the values, purpose and commitment with which I was being asked to live and carry my life, pre-dated all my interest in organized religion. However, both were easily colonized by the patriarchal structures of the Anglican church, not least because it purported to take my awakening adolescent guilt and creative energy to make something good of them. Perhaps I recognized the threat at an early age, for I recall refusing to get confirmed at the anglo-catholic church up the road when I was ten or eleven. Instead I got my mother to agree to send me to a strongly evangelical church a much longer walk away, and what I remember valuing most about it was the people-centredness of its life.

During this time I had my first boyfriends (we met at the church youth club) and discovered the great wealth of feeling and affection I had for some of my girlfriends at my single-sex school. Happily, one of these also attended my church; thus religious intent became inextricably linked to female friendship. At school, the first of my women communities, I felt myself academically inferior and from the wrong background; my school reports described me as boisterous; and I placed great hopes in my teacher of religious education, whose laughter and sensitivity held me spellbound.

In the study of my life it appears that sexuality and religion have always been entwined in my search for harmony with myself and my loving of women.

At college, after my first love affair with a woman, in which I felt I had at last gained clues to the mystery of life, I began to wean myself away from the increasingly suffocating dicta of evangelical Christianity. Others, had they known what I was doing or feeling, would have cast me out as sinful, dirty, rebellious, in need of redemption and forgiveness. I did not feel this need; I felt arrogant knowing this. So it was that the writings of T.S. Eliot, Bonhoeffer, Wittgenstein and Marx moved into the vacated spaces along with reams of my own poetry and the study of human feeling wherever it could be found – in music and film, letters and conversations. All of this I can now only interpret as my attempt to reconcile my passion for a woman lost in love with spirituality as I had accumulated it in adolescence and early adult life. Looking back, I realize I always justified my mainly nonsexual involvement with boyfriends on religious grounds, citing relevant pieces from the Holy Book to guard my space and fend off the invasion. At least I suppose I had the good sense to use the sword against the sword-maker; and its effect held out long enough for me to find softer and more rounded ways of expressing my woman-loving which gave some affirmation to being alive.

One other relationship with a woman, again furtive and unacknowledged as to what 'this' was, saw me pass from college to teaching, but distance and guilt soon made this fail, and for the four years in which I taught I had no further sexual relationships with women. Instead, I attempted two abortive and unsatisfactory relationships with men, neither of whom seemed to understand how friendship and sensuality could be forged between us on the way to the bedroom. Until this day I do not know if I ever had intercourse with a man, though I do recall one painful time of fumbling and disconnection when I found blood, presumably mine, on the sheet after all the huffing and puffing had ceased.

By now it was my turn to know both the visible and less obvious admiration of some girls in my classes. With one I developed an intellectual and spiritual rapport which was quite beyond my understanding and disturbing to me in view of my past and our age differences. We discussed books and authors, poetry and human endeavour; she talked to me about art. We laughed a lot and kept in touch for a while after we had both left the school. We never spoke of the meanings of what passed between us but we undeniably gave each other support at a vital time in our lives. During all of this I was struggling to come to terms with the final loss of my first lover, who married at this time. I survived that pain in isolation, and used my Christian religious language as a tool for survival. No doubt the signs of struggle were there for all to see but I did not let on and for the most part journeyed alone, refusing to accept my loving as sordid; I knew that on it my world was built.

Eventually, ill-health pulled me spiralling downwards. The struggle between private self and public persona had taken its toll and its internalization had wrecked my stamina and wellbeing. After lengthy sick leave I made my decision; somehow I had to get out of the institutionalized structure of schools into more open space. Ironically and naïvely perhaps, I chose to attend a theological college and train as an Anglican deaconess. At that time I was still unable to connect the personal to the political because my own identity was as yet unnamed. There is no doubt, however, that the motivation to make this move was one towards personal liberation.

Parents and friends were simultaneously aghast and curious at my decision. I started going to church regularly again – a passport to my new career – and began moving back towards the institutional centre. It is as if my life was about to become the screen on which all iconic assumptions about womanhood converged. In 1981 I wrote:

> My two years in theological college formed the context within which I came to own my relationships with and loving of women that for years I had disowned by living both a public and a hidden away life . . . I soon discovered that to do this within the ethos of the theological college and in relation to the structures of the Church of England was a dangerous albeit challenging adventure. Whilst the theological college was busy defining the Godhead, articulating in abstract forms the various christologies, eschatologies and epistemologies and ignoring the significance of human experience to theological content, I continued a different journey.[1]

I considered myself alienated in three major senses: the first, because I was a woman seeking to discover a meaning for Christian ministry whilst the theological college was geared to producing a male priestly caste; the second, because I was a lesbian woman seeking to affirm lesbian/gay existence whilst the Fathers were keen to enhance married, heterosexual life and the nuclear family; the third, because I was interested in decentralizing authority from the clergy to a shared concern amongst the laity whilst the church authorities were preoccupied with the economic factors influencing ministry, incorporating women in order to keep up the 'clerical' numbers and maintain the ecclesiastical machinery. It became clear to me that ordination provides an insurance policy for men in same-sex relationships that is unavailable to women who find themselves in a similar situation.

During my second and final years in theological college my time was taken up by various ecclesiastical power games as I looked for a job. But I refused to disown or secrete away my personal life in order to find employment. Even the women to whom I could go for advice would not stand by my side for fear of threatening the interests of women's position in the church and the ordination of women in particular. 'We must not get distracted from the main fight,' I was told.

It seemed that 'my sort' – academically able, pastorally competent and liked by others, the church wanted; but 'my sort' as a self-defining lesbian woman, it could not afford to take on. Three bishops in turn refused to give me a licence which prevented my doing any job in the Church of England; the third bishop did so even though I had obtained a chaplaincy post through routine application and inter-view. I left theological college in July 1980 without a job and not knowing where I would live. I continued to be unemployed for several months before obtaining part-time work. These were the external events surrounding a time of intense pain and anger during which I felt dispossessed, discriminated against and powerless to counteract the church's influence on my life. The same hands that put bread and wine into mine at the altar rail betrayed trust and exercised power in voyeuristic and under-hand ways, all to protect 'the faith', the position of the clergy, and the status quo. All in the name of Jesus, for the love of God and the liberation of the world.

It could almost have been one of those classic stories of martyrdom, at least then I would have played a legitimate woman's role in the eyes of the Fathers, sacrificing myself for the faith. (Even the Fathers allow for the possibility that an individual's conscience has a right to contradict the dicta of church authorities.) Instead, I became the iconoclast itself as religious and sexual identity fused to range against the forces of internalized and repressive icons. The process was intolerably painful, only just survivable; it was also exhilarating, illuminating and elemental. Through it I became woman (strange as it sounds, I had never known I was before), lover of a woman with whom I was to live; most important, my inside began to connect with my outside. I had found the source of my liberation and in touching this had become feminist, political and other-women-conscious, almost without knowing that this had transpired.

Life since then in the 1980s has been a new kind of living, my sexual identity and energy charging the atmosphere of my relationship style,

107

political efforts and consciousness of how oppression operates in our society today. For me there is a discontinuity between life since theological college and life before it. If life before theological college was the precursor to the iconoclasm, life since has constituted digging around in the debris, studying the texture and colour of the pieces where they are identifiable, and deciding, whether intuitively or by rational deliberation, what baggage is both necessary and desirable for carrying on. There have been some new discoveries once time has allowed some of the shattered pieces to be cleared away. More basic has been the need to recover the will to live, to say 'yes' to going forward.

From amongst the debris I quickly discarded organized religion. Rage, a physical feeling of sickness, prevent me from comfortably entering churches or participating in forms of traditional Christian worship. Much of it feels irrelevant and ludicrous. Its power, however, cannot be underestimated; lesbian women's lives are rendered invisible always by it; it is a tamer of the wild and the great leveller of human life, an obscene caricature of what ritual and symbolic actions can accomplish for human life. I do not speak to or of God any more. The very term encapsulates to me all that is anti-life: otherness, keeping women in our place, requiring affirmation of white male supremacy over others' lives at all costs. I have tried discussing other concepts of God with women friends since and although intellectually I can concede to some of their perspectives, at a gut level for me this does not work. The iconoclastic experience shattered the Godhead into a thousand pieces; I feel that it will never be reclaimed. I have not thought lately of Jesus as icon, as an example to follow or a life to emulate. The 'perfect man' image is dead to me and all crucifixes appear stiff, inert and impotent. I am relieved at no longer having to do mental acrobatics to imagine what life was like as a first-century male Jew in order to understand how I should live my life today as a twentieth-century white lesbian woman living in England. The motivation for moving towards others and out into the world is no longer fuelled by theological models or Christian inspiration: my many books about both remain on my bookshelves as historical reminders. I no longer open them. I have not kept in touch with many of my friends who continue to hold a traditional Christian religious commitment. I find that I want to break their images and cannot tolerate the ways in which they hold me to account when using them. They remain on the inside protected by their icons; I am on the outside, belittled and excluded. It is difficult, on the whole, to find ways of crossing the divide, particularly when those images have forged our friendships in the past.

Yet amongst these shards have been other more useful pieces. I have been known in recent years to remember some of the Gospel stories and to use some of the images that were footholds for me towards the iconoclastic experience: exodus, visions and prophecies, broken jars of ointment, siding with the poor and oppressed, liberation theologies, all have served to help me relate my individual woman-meanings to cosmic connections and to work towards building a sense of community and support with other women.

Temperamentally it is difficult for me to be politically active because of the private and individualized religious patterns of my past. I know too that the idealist/visionary within me who once related so intricately to Christianity now weaves her way through other ideologies and symbols in the hope of finding new clues and signposts. It would be good to believe that I shall never fall into the trap again, but all institutions have the characteristics of churches, and what I decry and reject in the latter I do not always do with other structures. Often I become aware of the similarity between Christians and politically correct feminists and I baulk at both. Such ideologues do not help us to claim and live our lives. The need is much more for knowing ways of self-acceptance and making intimate and social connection with others.

I want to focus on five aspects of this autobiographical process because I believe that in them lie clues to what might underlie the formation of a reconstructed spirituality. These aspects I shall describe under the following headings: naming and owning; pain and passion; love and sexual intimacy; vision and transformation; reflection and revelation.

NAMING AND OWNING – A LIBERATING PROCESS

For many gay people, the experience of 'coming out' has been a delectable and traumatic combination of relief and revelation. Making a statement about ourselves in this way can mean that we cease to be victims of our cultural inheritance and conditioning and start to become survivors of it. For women, however, such survival is often against all the odds as we are bestowed with secondary status, and experience multiple forms of discrimination on the basis of race, class and sexual orientation. By 'coming out' as gay or lesbian, we participate in a continuing and converting experience, a transforming act. We find that the closet door once prised open can never be closed as tightly again and that moderation is no longer an affordable life pattern. Once the unspeakable is spoken, confrontation – with friends, colleagues, relations – is created in ways which, for our survival, is only accomplished at a cost too great for the going back. I recall a period of eighteen months in which those who knew me found that they had to take on themselves the responsibility of choice in their relationships to me as they questioned and faced up to their assumptions about my identity and consequently their own identity too. No longer were they able to avoid naming that which many of them felt to be unnameable – that someone whom they knew and cared about was normatively different, that is, *homo-* rather than *hetero*sexual.

In our heterosexually dominant culture it is assumed that the everyday cues of body language attracting us to people and arranging our social relations are normative to all people. These fundamental modes of relationship, initiation, creation and sustenance are vital if people are to interrelate; with only heterosexual forms available to them, gay people can find it particularly hard to work towards the formation of relationships. To own the sense of 'difference' that we feel as gay people has been one way towards empowerment. Negatively, this sense of difference can make us feel so isolated and alienated that it reinforces fear about ourselves, perpetrating a hidden or 'closeted' life which may lead to exaggerated forms of social, emotional or mental ill-being. Positively, a sense of difference can be a way of enhancing self-image so that, alone or together, gay people begin to live a more integrated, less self-destructive lifestyle. Together, these experiences of 'difference' can help to develop chameleon-like instincts for survival in threatening environments as well as colourful displays in enriching ones. Chameleon modes are also subversive because I take from them what I need to recreate a culturally alternative world in which I learn to take on the experience of loving 'against the odds'.

PAIN AND PASSION

The passion and pain of woman-to-woman loving is the matrix within which every lesbian woman's life is held. It is our baptism and fire of inspiration. Lesbian lives are ones of excess – of too much or too little, too bold or too afraid, too alone or with too many lovers. Lesbian passions enliven, heighten, separate; they enslave, run havoc and evoke fear. Our pain camouflages, paralyses and distracts; it also sharpens, accuses, enrages. The passion and pain involved in lesbian relationships are intense and acute with every woman having her story to tell of longing and betrayal, of ecstasy and comfort. Such stories told and retold help to bring joy and healing out of what may have been difficult and first-time experiences whether in relation to a first lover, the ending of a marriage, discrimination at work, or harassment on the street:

> I always knew from quite young that I was attracted to my own sex and at the age of eighteen had a serious relationship with another woman which was doomed from the start because of the stigma attached to being a homosexual. I ran away and after several years married a farmer. I knew I could never love him as he loved me but I thought I could cope with it. After more than twenty years of married life the bombshell burst. Another woman ten years my junior fell in love with me. When I found out, that was it! We were both prominent people in our community and with all the pressures involved, we eventually fled. Three times we ran away together, each time going back to try and settle into our respective marriages, but the last time we left again after three weeks and made a new life for ourselves at the other end of the country . . . We would still be together if we had not husbands and families; she and I will come together I'm sure. There could be no one else for me.[2]

Another tells of the importance of the woman who becomes a first lover:

> Without her support and friendship I doubt whether I would have been able to name my feelings and involvement with women as 'lesbian'. It surprises me sometimes how little things have changed: I remember close friendships with women at school and college and that it was these women who gave and helped me to keep my sense of self. But naming my feelings and choosing to make them central does make life different.[3]

> She said if she had not met me she wouldn't have told her employers that she was gay and then she wouldn't have got the sack. I felt so guilty and thought that I should have fought against the feelings and left her when I realized it was deeper than mere friendship.[4]

Yet the times of healing and of joyful meeting are never totally absent:

> I was left with a hell of a lot more than just pain after our relationship. It still feels like one of the most powerful and important things that has ever happened to me and pain actually feels like part of my strength now.[5]

To arrive at a shared and affirming love of a woman is nothing short of miraculous if one considers the extent of homophobic[6] attitudes, the internalization of guilt and the many other forms of alienation that lesbian women have to overcome. Such alienation, much of which is the product of religious practice and belief, internalized into lesbian existence, constantly impinges on any interaction between women. As Judy Grahn says: 'The subject of lesbianism is very ordinary; it's the question of male domination that makes everybody angry.'[7] Women have been growing more aware that 'negative attitudes towards homosexuality have been correlated with attitudes condoning the inequality of women. This finding is not surprising because both same-sex behaviour and the equality of women disturb the traditional notion of what it means to be male and female.'[8] Nevertheless, there are always times of self-doubt when the dancing demons within demand 'are you sick?' or taunt that as lesbians we are not normal. Then, there is the need to tame again the voices which mimic and to transform fears and confusion into sources of insight and empowerment.[9] Lesbian women with whom I have talked say that their deepest fears and greatest strengths have emerged from the passion and pain of their woman loving.

The writings of Adrienne Rich and of Audre Lorde have been particularly helpful in enabling me to move nearer an intuitive grasp of movements within me in relation to the pain (fear of loss) and passion (longing for the other) of my loving of other women. I am persuaded that there can be some clarity and that there are words to break the silences of our lives even when we are afraid and confused, if only we will take courage by speaking our words or crying our tears or shouting our rage or holding one another in our arms. All these actions speak to tell us that we are alive, groping our way towards growth and freedom for which we have to take some responsibility:

> In the cause of silence, each one of us draws the face of her own fear – fear of contempt, or censure or some judgment, or recognition of challenge,

of annihilation. But most of all I think we fear the very visibility without which we cannot truly live ... that visibility which makes us most vulnerable is that which also is the source of our greatest strength.[10]

Nothing is as visible as the loving, intimate relationships of our lives which lesbian women so often deny ourselves the right to claim:

> each of us knows in her heart that being lesbian is more than a bedroom matter. It is the hinge upon which our identity moves, the vital integrating centre of our personality, the well of our religious imagination, the deep source of our power as we work, play, suffer and struggle. In fact it is all of our lives.[11]

By speaking out and naming such knowledge, by sharing perspectives borne out of the struggle with our own selves, women begin to build community, support, and networks. In short, we create the social and political structures that we need in order to find a way to exist in this homophobic world. It was Susan Sontag who wrote, 'I want to save my soul, that timid wind';[12] for me the phrase intimates the fragility of the steel-strong efforts of many of my lesbian friends to survive the almost non-survivable. By entrusting part of our 'timid wind' to other women we can know that we are touched and alive and by so doing we say 'yes' both to ourselves and to life itself. Yet the big question for us all 'is how to hope and what to hope for',[13] when the limitations imposed upon our lives appear to be immovable and insuperable.

LOVE AND SEXUAL INTIMACY

It is a fact of life that lesbian women are again and again forced back into the arms of women friends and lovers to seek comfort and salvation. Personal intimacy and sexual encounter provide the material of our passion and pain, involving a plaiting of desiring and being desired, of loving and being loved, of longing and melting, of attending to and being nurtured by, all of which create experience that can model for the life of the world beyond our individual selves. We may come to echo Mary Daly's words even though we are not always able to practise the art: 'The reign of healing is within the self, within the selves seen by the self and seeing the self. The remedy is not to turn back but to become the healing environment.'[14]

In order to create this healing environment we must first create a map for our own journey:

> suppose the old covenant were now rent asunder? She feared the consequences which this reading must have. Soon she would get up, wake Mara, go with her into the bedroom. They would take off their clothes; it would be troublesome, but it was part of it, things had to start like that. It would be a new beginning. But how is one to make oneself naked for the very first time? How is that to happen if one cannot rely on skin and smell, on a curiosity fed by many curiosities? How produce a curiosity for the first time, when nothing has yet preceded it?[15]

Our map creation commences the first time we approach another woman:

> It has taken me eleven years to realise that I am gay and I find it a struggle as I am totally inexperienced and probably need some guidance. I have no friend [meaning *lover*] and am not involved in any relationship.[16]

I well recall the ways in which my first lover broke through my lifetime of isolation to show me to myself. That she later denied the reality of this did not affect the consequences of such a revelation, nor did it prove, as I assumed, to be as complete a revelation as I supposed. This connection between sexual intimacy and maturing self-identity is of key importance and seems to defy ideological packaging, whether religious or political:

> The crisis of self vs. society explodes in sexual experience. Sexual arrangements provide an important set of terms by which we negotiate as we mature, the relation between who we are told and allowed to be. The negotiation is complex, and long, and indeed unending, because sexuality is multi-faceted and changes with age. Notions of political correctness therefore constitute psychological foot-binding.[17]

Often we adopt heterosexual customs which do not belong to us, and use them against our own best interests, so it is not surprising to me that healing is slow in coming and that many of us do not make it en route. In our sexual lives many of us still perceive ourselves as victims, making a battleground of our most intimate encounters, continuously raging and warring so that we might remain survivors. In this context

I fear the extent to which my lover becomes my deliverer, my goddess. How can any of us survive or fulfil that role? How can we not fail to be enraged or disappointed, adulatory or over-dependent on the other? It is in this area of womanly intimacy that we can least afford to be *laissez faire*, grabbing what we can from each other, renewing energy for the 'real' struggle which is often perceived to go on outside the 'closet' and not within it. Personally, my private world is often the most closeted, most disclosed; yet disclosure here seems to hold one of the keys to resistance and transformation in the social world. Experience demonstrates that others' homophobic fears are located precisely in this area of intimacy; this understanding should provide us with one of the major reasons for developing our own at-homeness in an area provoking real hostility in others.

Sexual activity is a natural and necessary part of lesbian relationships. The sharing of bodies, their warmth and texture, movement and shape, can be one of the most healing, affirming and beautifying experiences that two women can share. Equally it can be one of the most alienating, endangering the journey of all future relationships. Lesbian women hold no premium on 'getting it right' where sex is concerned and certainly many (mostly men) are curious about what women do in bed together. 'People always bring it down to "how far have you got?" physically. They ask as if it is my duty to tell them and as if I should have no doubt about letting them know. One friend reacted as if I were ill and suggested a "cure", that of grabbing the first man and heading for the bedroom to "see what I was missing"!'[18] Sexual intimacy between women can never be procreative and this *positively* allows a freedom for different emphases to emerge. Such emphases do raise questions for all women about the goal and value of intimacy.[19] Suffice it to say that these are located more in the question 'Who are and can we be to each other now?' than in 'Where can this get us?' It is not possible to select out *the* lesbian sexual act and make it into something else. There is no ideal lesbian sexuality or sexual mono-culture to define. All we know is that such intimacy creates unspoken forms of enriching knowledge:

> I was not going to say
> how you lay with me
>
> nor where your hands went
> and left their light impressions

115

nor whose face was white
as a splash of moonlight

nor who spilled the wine
nor whose blood stained the sheet

nor which one of us wept
to set the dark bed rocking

nor what you took me for
nor what I took you for

nor how your fingertips
in me were roots

light roots torn leaves put down –
nor what you tore from me

nor what confusion came
of our twin names

nor will I say whose body
opened, sucked, whispered

like the ocean, unbalancing
what had seemed a safe position.[20]

There is no doubt that we can encompass destructive experiences in our desire for intimacy; our passion can overwhelm and divert us into places we would rather eschew, leaving us at best vulnerable and at worst disempowered by our own emotional life and involvements. Any hope of deliverance by my lover is dashed in a moment of realization:

I enclose and imprison the images
of those women I have loved,
their warm, rounded bodies
that have held me tight
releasing the life-blood within me.
We shared dreams, and our knowledge of one another
led us to trust, hope, believe
that our loving might change the world,
all the time not noticing
that what it did was to change us, ourselves.
Far too late we discover
that the world is us
and we have such limited capacity for change.
Our loving travelled before us
to where we have not been able to follow.[21]

What has become clear to me is that lesbian women must seek to know the goal of our desire if we are to transform our love 'from a bewildering passion for one person to a deep rooted lust for life'.[22] How we shape and hold that desire is a spiritual process for us all, the main motivation for our desire often being that of falling in love. Or it may be that love is the predominant way in which we attempt to construct our desire and our pursuit of intimacy. Whatever the case, love is revolutionary because what we are taught is dirty and disgusting becomes beautiful and affirming; what we are taught is unnatural and perverted activity can be a more natural homecoming than ever imagined, releasing flowing streams of tenderness and shared vulnerability. Such revolutionary loving:

> moves us . . . toward both intimacy and collectivity, and back to self, and again toward society. Since sexuality is the sculptor of desire, since gender organises sexuality and shapes part of desire into the self, since gender, as we know it, is born of sexual oppression, then feminism, for me, must be a struggle for sexual emancipation. For we must make sure that we desire all we can so that we will be able to create, and therefore get, all we desire.'[23]

'Really being in love means wanting to live in a different world.'[24] Nothing is sacred; all is profane. Love itself, presumed to be a natural goal of human existence, is subject to scrutiny and redefinition. As with our sexuality, love is also birthed by means of the historical events shaping our experience. We are trained to subvert, to juxtapose, to flaunt, to confront all that denies us our desire to live. We seek to warm processes of transformation into life by our very being.

VISION AND TRANSFORMATION

I have outlined the ways in which lesbian intimacy challenges the assumptions of the dominant culture. In view of this it is not surprising that the external constraints constructed to deny such intimacy are both extensive and deeply rooted. It should not surprise us that religious belief and practice greatly contribute to the implementation and reinforcement of this oppression. I have already indicated that lesbian culture resists such oppression by naming as 'other' the forces that are 'ranged against us' and 'within us', and in so doing begins to consolidate power structures from which to act. Challenging heterosexual and patriarchal attitudes is a way of re-visioning the world in which we live. However, the central question for me as a lesbian woman must be this: how possible is it to strive towards claiming difference, which has distinct characteristics contributed to by our social and political relations, whilst affirming the sorority of all women and the humanity of all people? Can I move towards a critique of my daily oppression and forge action against this whilst acknowledging and celebrating my connection to and my dependence upon particular other women?

The answer in part must be that the possibilities change with the interplay between our personal, social and political lives, that various dances emerge historically and actually at any given time. At present it is more possible to come out as lesbian, not least because we ourselves own that need and possibility. However, it is less possible than a few years ago, to get feminists to give vast attention to lesbian womens' lives, even less possible to force great social changes in favour of lesbian women. It would seem that, at a basic level, most of my lesbian friends are digging in and holding on to what has been gained; the advance, at least in the public arena, has been halted even though much activity is in evidence. The political and economic climate of the 1980s is challenging us, extending our resources, exhausting our energies and sowing seeds of division and rivalry. Possibly our generation have lived our adolescent meanderings and pulled ourselves to full height ready for solid exploration just as the winds of political fortune have changed. My grandmother used to say when I pulled grotesque and funny faces as a child, 'You want to be careful, the wind might change and you'll stay like that!' We both used to laugh, but her words hinted at a truth: when the winds of fortune change is it better to be privately insular than to be publicly left out in the cold? Better to become invisible again than to be left adrift on a sea of visibility with no obvious signs of support? In the changing winds, lesbian women are deciding which 'face' we want to be caught wearing when the time to account for our lives arrives. For many of us, survival has to be prioritized over and above sexual politics or notions of sisterhood.

The process of envisioning and transforming lesbian life and culture is a daily task involving sensitivity and imagination. Networks have been evolving in order to provide tools of relevance to our lives, and connections have been made between our own oppression and that of others. The cost of such engagement is hard to quantify: energy that might have gone on personal intimacy and relationships has been sacrificed to the public arena; frenetic campaigning activity has usurped reflection; the goals of liberation have seduced us away from noticing the routes by which we do or do not choose to travel; ideological concerns have distracted from spiritual needs. At times I find it hard to see a way forward and only feel that there can be no going back; my own life and that of those around me can at times feel so circumvented that my 'chameleon mode' is switched permanently to that of the outside world. At such times, I struggle to believe in a process of transformation. Against all these things I have to carry the belief that lesbian intimacy, constructed by desire and shaped by ideology, does help to shape and reconstruct human life.

REFLECTION AND REVELATION

Why do we seem to reserve our most painful and destructive words for those who are most like us? Is it characteristic of human beings that, in feeling powerless and in order to rise above oppression, we bait and bruise one another instead of those who impose such conditions upon us? At least in this way we may feel that our words have the possibility of resonating in the echo chamber of our shared lives and so fire our passion, assuage our pain, purge our guilt and clarify our vision. We may move towards breaking our cycles of self-abuse by revealing the truths of our loving if only we do not turn our backs on each other in anger, being too hurt or vulnerable or naked to remain in each other's presence.

Adrienne Rich's 'The Dream of a Common Language' contained from the first words that invited images with which to celebrate my love of women. Above all else Rich knows that engagement and disengagement are part of the same action: reflection births insights for action, and revelation gives way to a place beyond words.

Most lesbian women live within others' constructs for our lives. Forced to use the words, culture and forms of others we become the invisible lovers, resistance-fighters, grief-carriers, freedom-makers and truth-seekers. To take power over our lives we must move into the most dangerous places within ourselves for such power comes from moving into whatever I fear most that cannot be avoided. But will I ever be strong enough again to open my mouth and not have a cry of raw pain leap out? There are no universal lesbian cultural norms or survival tactics, no ideology or common understanding that pre-exists our lives. We create ways of living and loving as best we can in ways not always competent or effective, fumbling our way towards one another and hence to ourselves. The times of reflection are as necessary as maintaining our economic independnce; they may also be as difficult to obtain.

SURVIVING FOR A FUTURE

'If you bring forth what is within you, what is within you will save you. If you do not bring forth what is within you, what is within you will destroy you.'[25] For many women, the role and purpose of religion is experienced as opposite to that which gives purpose, meaning and shape to being alive. Rather, it obstructs, defines as irrelevant and renders invisible lesbian existence. Generally, traditional religion ignores the reality that sex and gender identity fundamentally informs and helps to create religious experience. In denying spirituality as a vehicle by which women come to discover and own their lesbianism, religion excludes them from this form of liberation. So it is that 'since most traditional religions view homosexuality as a sin, their self-definition as lesbians also precludes participation in organized religion.'[26]

Any woman defining herself as lesbian may have religious and spiritual aspirations to which she seeks to give expression, some of which may be the products of traditional religious definitions and values. As adults we tend to hold on to our adolescent views of primary religious concepts, and for some of us brought up in a western Christian tradition such concepts include the male identity of the godhead, our submission to that figure and behaviour that is deemed appropriate both individually and corporately to express that relationship. All of this well suits the dominant culture which shapes our daily life: patriarchal views of the western godhead, a commitment to the dominance of heterosexuality over all other forms of sexual expression, to the power of men over women and children, to the assertion of a white racial identity over all other forms. All contribute to the distortion and eventual destruction of lesbian identity. A lesbian woman may continue to hold adolescent and patriarchal views of religion, orienting herself towards her community whilst simultaneously struggling towards self-identity and spiritual liberation. Such a woman may well find that the way in which she centrally identifies herself oscillates between religious and sexual identity both of which are fundamental orientations towards the world. So it comes about that lesbian women may be both oppressor and oppressed by the internalization of their alien religious and sexual identities. Martin and Lyon articulate this:

> Many women have said that the awareness that they were lesbians caused them greatest suffering in the sphere of religion because they expected to be denied salvation. Some still attend traditional church services, but in a closeted condition, where they hear, as a part of the church liturgy, periodic denunciations of homosexuality.[27]

Traditionally religion has set out to control and define the kind and purpose of sexual identity and relationship between people, if only to prevent us all sinking into some individualistic/narcissistic pool of self-indulgence. However, religion has contributed as much to the privatized and alienating consumerism of individual by individual as has sexual activity itself. In reality sex is not only about bodies or religion but about abstract aspirations and ideals. Both are inextricably bound to our human existence which is both gender- and culture-bound, emotionally propelled and circumstantially constrained.

For many lesbian women, traditional spiritual life is doomed from the start. In my life, ribbons of Christian religious thought and forms pass through my life but for the most part I find them redundant and irrelevant, preferring to seek out new words and forms for my journey. Some of these, as indicated previously, have their roots in my religious past and have as their goal some form of transformation of our lives:

> We do battle, not only with the ghosts of patriarchy within us, but with reality again: we see men are still in power, and to survive we transform, re-tell old stories, listen, hear again. This is a kind of bravery and I am in love with this quality and this affirmation. Do you see what I see? And there is joy in these shared perceptions and a kind of healing.[28]

Today, even with my women-friends, words, education and economic independence, I feel that mostly my energy goes into trying to survive. The striving to self-define, to connect with other women, to value this earth and strive for justice, to learn to trust intimacy – all these I

121

struggle towards. Often I am seized by despair, overcome by the alienating structures that permeate my daily living, only to be pulled up by those women who are able to see a way forward when I cannot. It does not feel a grandiose spirituality, nor worthy of the term; it is without a god yet struggling from a place of self-denial towards affirmation of self and the other. I tend to support a model of women's friendship rather than women's sexuality as an envisioning guide. Mary Hunt suggests that such friendships 'are mutual, community-seeking, honest about sexuality, non-exclusive, flexible, and other-directed.' This model feels 'more adequate because it acknowledges that it is not sexuality *per se* but friendship which determines what the quality of life can be.'[29]

Lesbian women are seeking the creation of a quality of life which is inclusive of ourselves, in which we might celebrate our intimacy and friendship, and make the contribution of our lives wholly visible, without fear of harassment or discrimination. Reweaving our past and envisioning our future whilst endeavouring to survive and live the present is a process involving faith – faith in the possibility of a different world when we cannot know that such change will occur. It is a case of dipping hands into our own and each other's womanly wounds and attempting a process of reintegration via a 'meaningful frame of reference of life in a hostile society'. My own religious autobiographical process has helped me to see that I am 'not power-less but conscious'[30] as a lesbian woman. Such consciousness pushes me onwards in the reclamation of my life.

NOTES

1   An autobiographical story (unpublished) written for Feminist Theology Project, 1981.
2   Personal correspondence.
3   Personal correspondence.
4   Personal correspondence.
5   Personal correspondence.
6   George Weinberg, 'Homophobia', in *Society and the Healthy Homosexual*, Gerrards Cross, Colin Smythe, 1975. Also consult Jonathan Dollimore's 'Homophobia and Masculinity', a paper presented at the 1985 Theory and Text Conference on sexual difference held at Southampton University. Also Adrienne Rich, *Compulsory Heterosexuality and Lesbian Existence*, London, Onlywomen Press, 1981.

7 Judy Grahn, 'A History of Lesbianism', in *Lesbian Poetry: An Anthology*, Elly Bulkin and Joan Larkin (eds), Watertown, Mass., Persephone Press, 1981, p.70.

8 Jeannine Grammick, 'Homophobia: A New Challenge', in *Social Work: Journal of the National Association of Social Workers*, vol.28, no.2, March-April, 1983, pp.137–41.

9 *Ibid.*

10 Audre Lorde, *The Cancer Journals*, Spinsters Ink, 1980, p.21.

11 Barbara Zanotti, 'The Vision that Claims Us', a talk given at the 1984 Conference for Catholic Lesbians in USA. Excerpted in *Images*, vol.2, no.4, Highspire, Pa., December, 1984.

12 Susan Sontag, 'The Pornographic Imagination', *A Susan Sontag Reader*, London, Penguin, 1983, p.300.

13 May Sarton, *Journal of a Solitude*, New York, Norton, 1977, p.62.

14 Mary Daly, *Gyn/Ecology: The Metaethics of Radical Feminism*, London, Women's Press, 1979, p.339.

15 Ingeborg Bachmann, 'A Step Towards Gomorrah', in *The Other Persuasion*, Seymour Kleinberg (ed.), London, Pan, 1978, p.250.

16 Personal correspondence.

17 Muriel Dimen, 'Politically Correct? Politically Incorrect?', in *Pleasure and Danger: Exploring Female Sexuality*, Carole S. Vance (ed.), London, Routledge & Kegan Paul, 1985, p.144.

18 Personal correspondence.

19 Gayle Rubin, 'Thinking Sex: Notes for a Radical Theory of the Politics of Sexuality', *Pleasure and Danger*, op. cit., p.26.

20 Joan Larkin, 'Some Unsaid Things', *Lesbian Poetry: an Anthology*, op. cit., p.46.

21 Elaine Willis, unpublished poem.

22 Lucy Goodison, 'Really Being in Love means Wanting to Live in a Different World', in *Sex and Love: New Thoughts on Old Contradictions*, Sue Cartledge and Joanna Ryan (eds), London, Women's Press, 1983, p.66.

23 Dorothy Allison, 'Public Silence and Private Terror', *Pleasure and Danger*, op. cit., p.148.

24 Goodison, op. cit.

25 Susan Griffin, quoting Alice Walker in *Made from this Earth*, London, Women's Press, 1982.

26 Deborah Coleman Wolf, *The Lesbian Community*, Berkeley and Los Angeles, University of California Press, 1980, p.82.

27 Del Martin and Phyllis Lyon, 'Lesbian/Woman', in *Images*, vol.2, no.4, San Francisco, Glide Publications, 1972, p.34.

28 Susan Griffin, *Made from this Earth*, London, Women's Press, 1982, p.123.

29 Mary Hunt, 'Lovingly Lesbian', in *A Challenge to Love: Gay and Lesbian Catholics in the Church*, Robert Nugent (ed.), New York, Crossroad Publishing Co., 1983, p.152.

30 Betsy Ettorre, 'Compulsory Heterosexuality and Psych/atrophy: Thoughts on Lesbian Feminist Theory', in *Women's Studies International Forum*, vol. 8, no.5, 1985, pp.421–8. For a more thorough analysis of lesbianism as a social movement with political ambitions, refer to Ettorre's *Lesbians, Women and Society*, London, Routledge & Kegan Paul, 1980.

14

PASSIONATE PRAYER
Masochistic Images in Women's Experience

Sara Maitland

Last year I published a novel called *Virgin Territory*. It was about sex, religion and violence against women – and the three things seemed, imaginatively, to entwine and wind themselves together into a single tight ball. One of the central questions of the novel was whether it would be possible for a woman to remain within the institutional framework of the Christian church if she tried to break away out of that tight ball, to escape from the repression of sexuality controlled by the violence of a male God towards His Women, His 'Brides', the consecrated virgins of the religious orders. The image that countered the image of 'The Fathers' – the internalized expression of that violence and repression – was the image of Lesbianism – the woman who 'walks on her own', is genuinely un-owned by the combination of culture and spirituality which we call Christianity.

In this novel there is a lesbian feminist character called Karen, who when we first encounter her is researching the life of St Rose of Lima as part of a paper she is trying to write about women's masochism and guilt. Now originally this was simply a narrative device to make it possible for Karen to become acquainted with the protagonist of the novel, a nun, whom she would not have met socially. However, as I wrestled with the novel and since I have finished it, I have become more and more curious to know and understand what Karen would have come up with had I wanted her to pursue her researches. This is not 'her' paper – I am not the sort of writer who believes in her own fictional characters in that way, and Karen (unlike me) was not a Christian. But this paper arises out of that imaginative engagement with my own fiction; and therefore with the personal imagery and experience of my own life and my own spiritual experience. This paper therefore is not only about historical ways of representing the relationship to the divine, which were formed in a predominantly – no, viciously – sexist and heterosexist culture; it is also about what affects me, and I sense other women too, now, in the present tense. My response to the material I am using is passionate, confused, pained and important. It is that sort of paper.

> It was no less astonishing that she should find room on her emaciated body to engrave in it, by her discipline the wounds of the Son of God . . . she gave herself such blows that her blood sprinkled the walls . . . and as she practised this penance daily every night she reopened her bleeding wounds by making new ones . . . Her confessor having ordered her to use an *ordinary discipline* and leave off her iron chain, she made it into three rows and wore it around her body . . . This chain soon took the skin off and entered so deeply into her flesh that it was no longer visible . . . she bound her arms from the shoulder to the elbow with thick cords . . . she rubbed herself with nettles . . . [in her full-length hair shirt] she appeared *more glorious in the eyes of God* from her having armed it underneath with a great quantity of points of needles to increase her suffering by this ingenious cruelty . . . She exposed the soles of her feet at the mouth of the oven . . . she drank gall and rubbed her eyes therewith . . . In her *ardent desire* for suffering she made herself a silver circlet in which she fixed three rows of sharp points in honour of the thirty-three years that the Son of God lived upon earth . . . She wore it underneath her veil to make it the more painful as these points being unequally long did not all pierce at the same time . . . so that with the least agitation these iron thorns tore her flesh in ninety-nine places . . . to keep herself from sleep she suspended herself ingeniously upon the large cross which hung in her room . . . and should this fail she attached her hair [the one strand at the front which she had not shaved off] to the nail in the feet of her Christ so that the least relaxation would inflict terrible suffering upon her . . . [She constructed herself a bed so excruciatingly painful that] although she was very generous still she never placed herself upon it without trembling and shuddering . . . so violent was the emotion which the inferior [i.e., her body] manifested at the sight of the pain it was to endure . . . Rose represented forcibly the necessity she felt of suffering this continual martyrdom *in order to be conformable to her divine spouse*.[1]

Rose of Lima was born in Peru in 1586 to a middle-class though not very rich colonialist family. She refused to marry, and became a Dominican Tertiary (that is a member of the Dominican order who did not live in community, but in an ordinary home) following the example of St Catherine of Siena. Although she did various works of charity, especially among the enslaved Indians – interestingly there has been speculation that she was part Indian herself – her principal claim to fame is the extraordinary life of violent and self-inflicted penance which she maintained from her youth until her death in 1617. She was canonized in 1671, the first American-born saint in the Roman Catholic calendar, and is the patron of South America and the Philippines. What is fascinating is the enthusiasm with which she has been adopted by hagiographers, and how often she appears in collections of holy biographies specifically directed at children.

Rose of Lima is an extreme example of self-inflicted penitential excess but she is by no means an isolated one. Donald Attwater in his *Penguin Dictionary of Saints* suggests a certain unease: 'such saints pose delicate questions of religion and psychology,'[2] but he immediately goes on to describe another South American woman, St Mariana Paredes y Flores, who died in 1645 but (and this is vitally important) was not canonized until 1950, whose 'penitential practices were even more startling than Rose's, so extravagant in fact as to savour of morbid fanaticism.' (Which implies he sees nothing morbid or fanatical in the extract above.)

Throughout the history of Christian women's holiness such activities are rife:

> Sr. Margaret Mary was so determined to make a complete gift of herself to the Sacred Heart that she carved 'Jesus' on her breast with a knife. Still not satisfied she burned the letters in with a lighted candle.[3]

Women flagellate themselves, starve themselves, lacerate themselves, kiss lepers' sores (poor lepers!), deform their faces with glass, with acid, with their own fingers; they bind their limbs, carve up their bodies, pierce, bruise, cut, torture themselves. The most highly praised mystical writings use metaphorically imagery from these acts: women speak of Christ's rape of them, they abase themselves, abuse themselves. Catherine of Siena gave her heart – the imaginative location then not just of the emotions, but of the reason, the personality – away, denied her own personal existence and started a spiritual fashion for 'mystical marriages' which affected the aspirations of Christian women for centuries. They did it for love of Jesus and the church applauds them.

What the hell is going on here? What can possibly lead women to believe that they are more 'conformable', more lovable to the God of creation, love and mercy, bleeding, battered and self-mutilated, than they would be joyful, lovely and delighted?

What is going on is an open expression of something that exists less consciously and concretely in a great many Christian women: a sado-masochistic relationship with God. Such a relationship with an invisible omnipresent and all-male God is an unbearable thing to see. It also gives a subliminal justification to every wife-batterer, every rapist, every pornographer and every man who wishes to claim 'rights', the rights to abuse, over women. And it is a relationship still condoned by the church. In 1950 the Roman Catholic authorities did not only canonize Mariana de Flores, they also conferred the same distinction on a twelve-year-old because she preferred death to the loss of her 'honour' – read technical virginity – at the hands of a rapist. Maria Goretti (1890–1902) had taken a private vow of virginity before she even reached the age of moral consent, and believed that her Beloved would rather have her stabbed repeatedly than 'deflowered' (I use the word advisedly, the connection between female purity and flowers in religious iconography is not casual – Thérèse of Lisieux, The Little Flower; Mariana de Flores; Rose of Lima (not her baptismal name); The Lily of the Mohawks; Our Lady Rose of Sharon, the Mystic Rose). David Farmer, editor of the *Oxford Dictionary of Saints*, concludes his entry on Maria Goretti: 'In canonising Maria Goretti the Roman Catholic Church also *honours* innumerable others who in similar circumstances preferred death to *dishonour*.'[4] This is real sexism; on this reading the church also dishonours every woman who makes a somewhat more holistic valuation of her worth. Moreover those 'innumerable others' in similar circumstances have to be *women*; but Farmer dissolves them into the universal lest the perpetrators be too easily identified (always be on your toes when women are 'allowed' to be universal human beings) and he does not ask *why*. Why should the church honour anything so idiotic? Why should we be asked to rate a silly bit of skin which may be dislodged accidentally, above the life of a 'devout but cheerful girl'? (That 'but' very nearly gives the game away, incidentally.) Why should we be expected to 'love' a God, a husband, who would rather see us dead than uphold our innocence? Why is 'virginity' the only 'grace' that can be stolen from us without our consent? (And none of this should stand against the courage of a young woman who – her bloody-mindedness hidden in masculist retellings of her story – chose her own way over male definitions of her worth.)

Before I try and answer some of those 'whys' it is important to acknowledge something quite painful and difficult that lies at the very heart of Christianity itself: Christianity is inextricably, horribly, tiresomely embedded in the flesh, in the body, in history and matter. The Roman Empire in which Christianity first formulated its theology was intellectually and emotionally committed to dualism – which does at least make the corruption and sadness of life infinitely more bearable. Sometimes this commitment was cynical, and equally often it was ecstatically mystical. Cults, like the various forms of Gnosticism, waxed fat on the attractive and comforting conviction that the body, the material world, did not really, finally, essentially, matter; that the pure soul entrapped in fleshliness would eventually burst free of its dust-inclining shackles and ascend triumphant to the realm of pure spirit. To that society it was inexpressible, and also inane ('folly to the Greeks') that 'the Word took flesh', that 'God became human' – never mind the 'and died of it'. The material and the spiritual were locked in bitter opposition and there could be neither compromise nor unity between them. Even as they admired 'how these Christians love one another' their earliest contemporaries were seriously concerned that Christians were cannibalistic, that they ate human flesh and drank human blood after making human sacrifices. They believed it because, in their context, that is exactly what the Christians were saying. Christians proclaimed the resurrection of the body (yuk!); that how you acted in history was who you essentially were (depressing!); and that salvation flowed from a God who had become so fully bodily that a gruesome and humiliating death was an integral part of divinity (weird!); Christ's resurrection did not transcend but incorporated that bodiliness (hence the stress in the Gospels on Thomas being invited to poke about in the wounds, and, more touchingly, the story about the resurrected Jesus cooking fish dinner for his gang beside a lake and eating it with them too (John 21:1–14)). This was a faith not 'for the oppressed' but for anyone who *wanted oppression to be ended*; a faith for the joyful, the life-loving, for any bleary-eyed shepherd who saw a newborn baby in a back shed and could not be persuaded that it was not a sight of glory.

But time passed and Christianity was lured further from its Jewish roots and deeper into the heart of Graeco-Roman culture; dualism became harder to resist: it underpinned all the language of knowledge. And after the first fine careless rapture it became clear that sin continued and death continued and the contemporary world could not love itself as much as God loved it, it could not accept such a simple forgiveness, such a cheap escape from guilt. Gradually

Christianity turned its flesh love inwards and against itself, focussing more and more on the suffering of its crucified leader and less and less on its wine-loving, women-loving, life-loving resurrected saviour. The source of salvation gradually shifted from faith in the power of the resurrection to copying the death of Jesus. And through this identification and the struggle to find imagery for it, Christianity developed a nexus of metaphors which were shot through with dangerous tendencies: cannibalism ('when we eat his flesh and drink his blood we proclaim your *death* Lord Jesus until you come again'); necrophilia ('the blood of the martyrs fertilizes the Church' – not their lives); incest (Christ crowns his mother as his bride; the brothers and sisters are also the lovers and spouses); rape ('Take me to you, emprison me, for I/Except you enthrall me never shall be free/Nor ever chaste except you ravish me'[5]).

This ever more enthusiastic approach to pain and death as the best way of identifying with God is best exemplified in the passion for martyrdom. The early Christians had not suffered from this disease; just as Jesus had prayed that the cup might pass from him, so Peter and his friends prayed like mad to get him out of prison; Paul pulled a quick one, declaring his citizenship of the imperialist 'power of this world' in order to prolong his life; Polycarp (*c.* AD 69–155), a great favourite with the early church, first ran away and hid, and later played verbal riddle games with his captors in an attempt to escape death. But gradually martyrdom came to seem not just a quick route to heaven but a glorious one. To suffer for Christ, to suffer and die – the worse the preceding tortures the better – became the highest desire of aspiring Christians. Hagiography is littered with individuals of both sexes who seem to have organized their whole lives around a greed for violence and death, as the way of providing their commitment – and the church rewarded them. Hagiography is also littered, it should be said, by individuals who pursued bold and joyous courses through life and met death merrily on their way to do something else; and with high-principled people, whose understanding of the destruction of selfhood that comes about through not telling the truth caused them to look death straight in its mean eyes and find it preferable to capitulation; but there remains a strain of ecstatic lust for martyrdom which can formally be described as masochistic.

This belief in martyrdom as the highest vocation weighed particularly heavily on women. One of the reasons for this is laid deep in the stereotyping of women; once dualistic thought gained ascendency within Christianity women were increasingly associated with nature and with the body while men identified themselves happily with mind and spirit: if Christianity was to flagellate and dominate its bodiliness, then women were the obvious and 'natural' matter for the church to go to work on – and what's more they need more punishment, since, being more bodily they are also more sinful.

This laid down a complex 'no win' situation for many women, best summed up in a quotation from Augustine's sermons on the martyrdom of SS. Perpetua and Felicity, who had been martyred in AD 203:

> Truly towards these women a manly courage worked marvellously when despite all the pressure their womanly weakness failed not . . . And how proper that women should cause the fall of that enemy who through a woman originally caused men to fall . . . On the same day courageous men also suffered and conquered, but their names do not commend this feast to us. And this was so not because women are to be preferred before men for their courage and deserts, but because the weakness of women made the vanquishing of the ancient enemy even more marvellous.[6]

The more heroic you were, the more it 'proved' the superiority of men.

But there is another and much more practical reason why the idealization of martyrdom put additional pressure on women: they were less and less permitted to go and seek it. Once Christianity had become acceptable to the Roman world no one was likely to be martyred just staying at home and being a Christian. You had to go out into the world, become a missionary, a writer, a politician. Increasingly enclosed within the home or the convent, women were obliged in a specific way to inflict the desired martyrdom on themselves. As early as the beginning of the fifth century Jerome was showing them a way to do it, with his women's community modelled on virginity and 'mortification of the flesh' – a rigorous asceticism. (Jerome's fasting and dietary suggestions would be one of the most efficient ways to induce amenorrhoea in an average woman – there is a clue in this.) From a lack of practical alternatives as much as anything else, women who desired perfection were obliged to internalize their desire and martyr themselves. They had to make their lover, or whatever name they chose to personify their inner passion (bearing in mind that it had to be a male personification) if it was to be 'of God' both the instrument and the object of that martyrdom. However dangerous it is psychologically to seek torture and death at the hands of someone who can be named as 'bad' – pagan, primitive, unconverted – it is infinitely worse to torture oneself at the instigation

131

of the 'good' – the lover, the saviour, the divine.

And what makes possible this dangerous inversion, this destructive and self-annihilating relationship with a God whom we proclaim to be loving, healing and liberating? Christianity here has caught women in a classic double bind; it has placed a negative value on women themselves, but a highly charged positive value both on heterosexuality and on personal love, personal passion, for Jesus. Christianity has done this valuing, moreover, within the context of a society which assumes male dominance to be both 'natural' and 'god-given'; which defines women according to their relationship with a man; and does both these things under the sheltering wing of a god who, although officially without gender, is of course always male.

A great deal of work has now been done on the ways in which women and women's sexuality have been given a deeply negative value within the Christian tradition. From Tertullian's 'gateway to hell' through Luther's brood cow and Kramer's witch, right down to Maria Goretti's honour, female sexuality is always dangerous and usually wicked. It is not just self-destructive; it is dangerous to men. In this context it is worth noticing that Rose of Lima's conscious self-mortifications began after an incident when she was five: her younger brother threw some mud in her hair; she was about to protest when he said, 'My dear sister, do not be angry at this accident, for the curled ringlets of girls are hellish cords which bind the hearts of men and miserably draw them into the eternal flames.'[7] (For which he did not get the spanking he deserved, but she went into the house and cut off all her hair and was applauded throughout catholic history. Though not, fascinatingly, by her mother, who seems to have been the only person who made any attempt whatever to moderate her daughter's zeal for suffering and is consequently condemned as a 'worldly and ambitious woman' by all Rose's principal biographers.) I will not develop here the history of the negative valuation of women, except to remind ourselves that the underlying gynophobia if often at its most virulent when appearing to praise individual women. This is evident in much Marian writing and in the eulogy of St Augustine quoted above, as it is in the quote from Farmer about the church 'honouring' rape victims.

But while the devaluation of women has received a proper attention from feminist historians and theologians, the other side of the double bind has been less noticed. Christianity places a very high value both on individual passionate intimacy with God in Christ and on its expression within the imagery of heterosexuality. This dense web of intimacy has, inevitably and sadly, usually been expressed in the language of the socially constructed family: the first person of the Trinity as Father; the second person of the Trinity as lover/husband as well as brother; the Church as Mother (taking care of things while Dad's away); and the individual soul – as well as the community – as Bride, as spouse, as household. And because of the bodiliness of Christianity the physicality of those relationships is not fully suppressed. So even Paul at his most puritanical cannot resist the sexual metaphor. In Ephesians chapter 5, for instance, we encounter a very strange cluster of images. Paul denounces physical desire roundly:

> Among you there must not be even a mention of fornication or impurity in any of its forms . . . There must be no coarseness or salacious talk or jokes . . . for you can be quite certain that no one who indulges in fornication or promiscuity . . . can inherit anything of the kingdom. (Ephesians 5:3–5)

But only a few verses later, and interestingly in an attempt to keep women under men's control, he uses directly sexual language to describe Christ's relationship to the church, naturally personified as female:

> Husbands should love their wives as Christ loved the church and sacrificed himself for her to make her holy. He made her clean by washing her in water with a form of words so that when he took her to himself she would be glorious with no speck or wrinkle. (Ephesians 5:25–27)

Indeed by the time the Gospels were recorded this image of Jesus was sufficiently satisfactory for all three of the synoptic Gospels to mention an incident where Jesus directly compares himself to a bridegroom (Matthew 9:15, Mark 2:19, Luke 5:34), while John more allegorically takes the miracle at the Wedding Feast in Cana as the opening of Jesus' public ministry (John 2:1–12). And by the end of the first century AD the Apocalypse Writer is presenting the church as Christ's Bride in the ecstatic and often erotic language drawn from the later prophecies of the Old Testament, the Psalms and the highly sensual Song of Songs.

So long as Christianity kept its primary focus on the Bride as the whole Christian community – as Paul very conscientiously does in his Ephesians passage, stressing that individuals are only living parts of the bridal body – this imagery was potentially affirmative of women; but as soon as salvation and holiness became located in the individual

133

'soul', in mystical experience and personal sanctity, this sort of language brings with it a major problem. The church, now rigidly personified as female, must be made manifest in every woman individually. Each woman, in a way that does not apply to men, must represent the Bride of Christ in her own person. Women religious until the Second Vatican Council – and sometimes still – took their solemn vows under the external form of a wedding ceremony, wearing white dresses, given away by their fathers, carrying a bouquet and receiving a wedding ring from their new husband. Even in the newer rites the sexual imagery often remains: the collect at Benedictine professions asks that Jesus 'who by the bridal bond binds the hearts of consecrated virgins to him, may make your mind fruitful through the divine word.' The new nun is exhorted to 'Keep perfect fidelity to your bridegroom,' and she replies, 'I am espoused to him whom the angels serve, whose beauty the sun and moon behold with wonder.'[8]

But the historical/cultural 'event' that finalized women's doom in this field was the rise of Romantic Love in the late middle ages, which came to overwhelm completely any sense of marriage as a communal interest, a social contract. Feminism has correctly diagnosed romantic love as the terrible disease that it is – 'You start by sinking into his arms and you end up with your arms in his sink.' While women are socially required and socially constructed to be the bearers of humanity's 'emotional life', they are the inevitable victims of a love which consciously stands over against reason ('I'm madly in love, I'm crazy about him') against community, and against individuality. Denis de Rougement in his important and excellent exposé of the origins and meanings of Romantic Love *Passion and Society*[9] goes further and claims that romantic love is of its nature morbid – it inclines towards death, self-annihilation and suffering; it idolizes emotion above the object of the emotion; it rejects fulfillment and satisfaction necessarily. Using courtly rhetoric, the language of romance (because it had become the language of Ultimate value), mystics were sucked into the romantic emotion in an attempt to express their desire: 'In flames I burn and languish crying "in living I die and in dying I live." I die of not being able to die.'[10] Teresa of Avila, a sturdy, humorous woman in her daily dealings, changes completely when speaking of her mystical experience and describes her relationship with God in terms of 'Love's dart that wounds but never kills', of the passion that sets the lover apart from the world and from all other beings; of the 'struggle of

134

love' in which it is necessary to be defeated; of the 'stolen heart', 'the ravished understanding' and the 'rape of love'.[11]

If it was bad enough to be the Bride of Christ, it is worse to be his romantic lover and still worse when the two become bound inextricably together, bride-and-lover in one. If romantic love was morbid for male lovers seeking earthly mistresses it is death itself for women seeking a heavenly master. The men were choosing their own humility before a woman over whom they had actual real power, while Christ can claim male social power over his lover's voluntary self-humiliation. The romantic lovers of literature could criticize their lady's coldness, her infidelity, her locked chastity – but an aspirant lover of Christ cannot criticize her beloved for anything because he is God and therefore perfect. If he is cold, unfaithful, withdrawn, it must be her fault.

And women are trapped here. As women they are believed (and being socially constructed to believe themselves) to all that is dark and horrible, seductive and dangerous. They are the lure, the devil's bait; they are witches and whores. They are capable of redemption only under the charge of a good man, who of his generosity will punish them, whip them into shape, make them good, if they deserve it. They are undeserving of love.

They must also, for the salvation of the world and for their own good, love and accept the love of Christ; be the perfect Bride, desired by Jesus, wedded to Jesus. To Jesus who suffered for them, who suffers still because they are not good enough, who restrains his loving hands from the punishment they deserve and he desires. This unresolvable paradox is a recipe for guilt, for that deep-laid unshiftable guilt that can be soothed only in the suffering, the physical suffering that is desired and deserved. Accepting pain from the beloved is the final eroticism, because the beloved is seeing the object of his passion as she really is, and is attending to her needs. The seductive language of mediaeval spirituality; the sentimental writing of nineteenth-century exhortation; the clear strong bell of puritan zeal; the obscene discourse of twentieth-century pornography; the mystical experience of unity – 'the wordless understanding between two lovers' – which is so often and inevitably sexual and so often and inevitably expressed by those who have no experience of the real limitations, and mockeries and silliness and compromise of physical sexual pleasure. All these say the same thing. They say Repent, repent, repent. Punish your stinking self and become worthy. If you don't enjoy the suffering that proves you are proud and need it; if you do enjoy the suffering that proves how much I love you.

Jesus demands our love, but we are not worthy to respond to his demand even though we may not disobey it. When Rose of Lima first thought of desiring a 'mystical marriage' she was thrown into paroxysms of guilt at her own presumption: 'And this humility, which made her judge herself unworthy of it, was the precious portion which captivated the heart of the Son of God.'[12] (He likes you grovelling. It turns him on???) At one point in her life the extremity of her activities led the Inquisition – in its mildest form – to investigate her. Apart from finding all her practices holy:

> They also remarked with astonishment a sort of combat between God and her without being able to determine whether God was more occupied in seeking in the secrets of his wisdom the means of exercising her by suffering than she was disposed to suffer for his love; for she showed an incredible avidity for crosses and an invincible patience over her trials and over every affliction which Almighty God sent to exercise her love and fidelity.[13]

Which sounds to me not only like a pretty traditional sado-masochistic relationship, but horribly more like too many human marriages than it does like a reasonable and willed co-operation with a God who danced with delight in the act of creation.

And do not fool yourself that this is but the extravagance of a past era. Women Christian mystics are writing the same things today.

> In the novitiate the discipline became one of my major troubles. Not because of the pain, but for some people such pain can give trouble in the sexual line. It upset me in that way. It was arousing me in that direction as nothing else had done. It even got into my dreams. *It was sheer fervour that made me continue.*[14]

> The purpose of flagellation was to dominate (to master) our sexuality. But sometimes when I hit myself I awakened my carnal desires . . . I knew that as a woman there were moments when my sexuality was there. This flagellant device did arouse my feelings and it was hard for me to control them. By obedience to the Rule I had to use that device on myself every Monday, Wednesday and Friday. There was no escape. Many times masturbation happened . . . I felt guilty and remorseful and I requested heavy penance, which was granted. Heavy penance was self-inflicted flagellation, which sometimes aroused me again . . . Some days doing this penance was quite helpful and rewarding for me in trying to achieve perfection.[15]

And no penance is ever enough, not even death, not even self-inflicted

death, because women are doing penance for the unforgiveable sin –
the sin of having been born female, having caused the Fall, having
made the death of God necessary. This sin can never be forgiven
because it can never be properly repented. For repentance to work the
penitent must (*inter alia*) sincerely desire 'amendment of life'. And you
can bash the body into submission, you can beat it and punish it; you
can try cloistered virginity or devoted motherhood; you can take
Christ as your spouse or one of his vice-roys who has biblical rights of
dominance over you as Adam had over the beasts; you can repent and
repent and repent, but you cannot amend, change, improve unless
you die (and probably not then) – so you must be punished, you even
want to be punished. It's exciting. Jesus loves you.

I have called this spiritual disease sado-masochism precisely because the woman so afflicted acts out both roles herself. She has
internalized the sadist who is her beloved other, her own projection
and her one hope of salvation. He is the lover who loves her pain and
she offers it to him humbly and ecstatically.

> On these occasions (when she was literally collapsed with physical fear of
> what she was planning to do *to herself* next) Jesus Christ several times
> appeared to her *with a sweet and gracious countenance*, saying to her to rouse her
> courage, 'Remember my love, that the bed of the cross on which I died
> for love of you was harder, narrower and more painful than that on which
> you are now lying.'[16]

Where do we go from here? I no longer want to deny the joy-
destroying masochism that I recognize in myself. I want to cure it. I
no longer want to find my spiritual or sexual thrills in fantasies of pain
and humiliation. I do not want to be afraid of or erotic with the God
with whom I want to share the work of creation and transformation.
There is quite enough actual real pain and horror in the world not to
have to inflict a new load on myself.

I believe of course that feminism has a cure, indeed is a cure.
Philosophically it does not just deny male superiority, male-
dominance-as-of-right; it also challenges the central idea of male
power, that there are any images of the divine which are not socially
constructed within history – and feminism states that anything which
can be constructed within history can also be deconstructed within
history. (Feminism is a revolutionary movement.) This means first of
all having an absolute respect for and awareness of how everything is
bound into history – and that includes ourselves, our society and
feminism itself. We are seeking neither a return to a sentimental

pre-lapsarian 'natural order', nor a projection into the future Utopia 'when the Kingdom comes', 'after the Revolution'.

And for this reason we must hold out for a more correct, more traditional Incarnational theology than we presently use. God became flesh and dwelt among us because God *likes* humanity; likes the material solidity of it. God made the world and 'behold it was very good'. God did not enter into history and bodiliness in order to suffer but in order to redeem – the suffering is quite incidental (even if inevitable). If we want to 'identify' ourselves with Christ's primary act it must be through a passionate involvement in the process of history and its transformation. The consequence of God's suffering, like its purpose, is not that we should suffer more, but that we should suffer less. Paul was absolutely clear about this:

> Jesus has brought you to life with him, he has forgiven all our sins. He has overridden the law and cancelled every record of the debt that we had to pay; he has done away with it by nailing it to the cross; and so he has got rid of all the Sovereignties and the Powers and paraded them in public . . . It may be argued that true wisdom is to be found in (rules, penances and disciplines) with their self-imposed devotions, their self-abasement and their severe treatment of the body; but once the flesh starts to protest they are no use at all. (Colossians 2:13–15, 23)

In the light of this incarnational theology we can also hold onto the Pauline vision of a corporate relationship with God – in which mystical experience, like all things, is the possession of the whole community; in which that community itself is the presence and being of love and justice is the primary image of the divine, rather than a wildly promiscuous and polygamous eternally judgmental, unamused old wife-batterer in the sky.

And once we have entered into that liberated space, even if only in our imaginations, we must hold out for a better metaphysical theology too. We need a metaphysics which denies neither history nor free will; one that does not remove responsibility for our own well-being from the community of women, but enters into that community and moves within it and within its movement. And since we now know that definitionally no man can enter into the community of women we must again crash the blasphemous barrier which has been constructed to keep our women's bodies separate from the woman-body of God. We must in our own defence and to our own glory continue the struggle to name God as not-male, and also to name her as female.

Oddly enough, against all the odds, there is considerable historical precedent to show that this works. Marina Warner in *Monuments and Maidens* gives a lovely example from the twelfth century when there was a renewed interest in the Wisdom literature:

> While Sophia/Hokmah, the beautiful bride, excited intense responses in both men and women, males show a greater need to give her an historical character and to purge the erotic force of the scriptural metaphors. The incarnational tendency of Christian imagination led the greatest thinkers to identify the bride-mother with . . . Mary . . . It is perhaps surprising that the cult of Mary is less marked in the texts of women writers . . . The asymmetry springs from the erotic character of the imagery: votaries' relationship to Holy Wisdom was changed by the question of sex. In general, while a mystic like Bernard [of Clairvaux, d.1135] imagined the Bride as the object of his love, contemporary Hildegard [of Bingen, 1098–1178] *identified herself with the symbol of transcendence itself*, not with its worshippers.[17]

In the light of this identification she not only went her own blithe and abundantly creative way through life, she was also able to write: 'The form of woman flashed and radiated in the primordial root . . . How wondrous a being you are, woman, who laid your foundations in the sun and who have overcome the earth.'[18] In her convent, and despite considerable opposition and criticism, the nuns were known for the beauty of their clothes and for the elaborate enamelled crowns they wore; they sang and feasted and laughed. She justified this because God 'had clothed the first human creature in radiant brightness.' The nuns did 'not need sackcloth and ashes to expiate worldly transgressions. She could surround herself in the abbey with women who in their very dress signalled their identity with the holy and the divine.'[19]

Now that does seem a better and a more radical thing than beating my spiritual or physical back until the walls are sprinkled with blood. And more fun. And not altogether impossible. Wow.

NOTES

All biblical quotes from the Jerusalem Bible.
1   F.W. Faber, *The Saints and Servants of God*, London, 1847, pp.27–45 (oh, yes, there's *lots* more). Faber's biography of Rose of Lima is in fact a translation and abridgement of J.B. Feuillet's French translation of an

original Italian text – though the 'evidence' must have first been in Spanish. Such a worked-over text is bound to have been affected by its series of male translators, but this in itself is interesting. All emphases here, and in subsequent quotations, are mine.

2 D. Attwater, *The Penguin Dictionary of Saints*, London, Penguin, 1965, p.300.

3 M. Bernstein, *Nuns*, London, Collins, 1976, p.298 (a seventeenth-century example).

4 D.H. Farmer, *The Oxford Dictionary of Saints*, Oxford, OUP, 1982, p.176.

5 J. Donne, *Holy Sonnets*, No.XIV, London, 1633.

6 Augustine, 'Sermons on the Feast of SS Perpetua and Felicity', from *The Passion of Saints Perpetua and Felicity* (trans W.H. Shewring), London, Sheed & Ward, 1931, pp.24–38. Augustine preached four sermons which are published with the third-century passion narrative, a first-person account by Perpetua, in a series called *Spiritual Masters*, which makes the point more quickly than I have managed to do. There is a new and superior translation of the Passion itself – an amazing and important women's history document – in P. Dronke, *Women Writiers of the Middle Ages*, Cambridge, CUP, 1984.

7 Faber, op. cit., p.7.

8 Bernstein, op.cit., p.122.

9 Denis de Rougement, *Passion and Society* (trans M. Belgion), London, Faber & Faber, 1962 edition.

10 From *Ciascum Amante*, a Franciscan Laud, quoted de Rougement, op. cit., p.160.

11 Teresa of Avila, quoted de Rougement, op. cit., p.161.

12 F.W. Faber, op. cit., p.53.

13 *Ibid.*, p.71.

14 Bernstein, op. cit., p.296 (a quote from a contemporary Sister of the Sacred Heart).

15 Maria Christina, 'South American Lawyer in a Cloister', from R. Curb and N. Manahan (eds), *Breaking Silence*, U.S.A., Naiad Press, 1985, p.205.

16 F.W. Faber, op. cit., p.45.

17 M. Warner, *Monuments and Maidens*, London, Weidenfeld & Nicolson, 1985, pp.179 ff.

18 Hildegard of Bingen, trans P. Dronke, op. cit., pp.165–6, quoted and slightly adapted by Warner, op. cit., p.184.

19 Warner, op. cit., p.191.

15

PARAGORY*

Linda Hurcombe

Once upon a nowish time there was a young woman who ran away. She had been married and had always been a loving wife and mother by society's standards. Let us call her Sarah. She had loved her husband fiercely, and doted on her children. But over the years her husband had lied to her and betrayed her, and the most recent episode was once too many. So, in spite of the fact that he had otherwise been a kind and caring companion, Sarah found that she could not, no matter how desperately she tried, reclaim her lost trust.

Since most of the possessions in her marital home were not her own anyway, Sarah travelled light, her backpack bulging with warm socks, extra layers of clothing to fend off the biting winter, and photographs of the children. Had we seen her walking purposefully along, we would have been sure that this was a woman who knew where she was travelling, but such was not the case. Sarah moved in the direction of the huge yellow-lit and rather sinister-looking city because it was *there*, and for no other reason. By the time she arrived at the outskirts she was already aching with exhaustion. Sarah trudged along the narrow congested streets, mindlessly directing herself toward the heart of the city. Her desperation grew with her hunger and aching feet. So close was she to turning back, to spending her last coin on a phone call home

(O yes, he would most surely have her back!)
that she was opening the telephone kiosk door, when, from the darkness of a nearby doorway she heard a voice, a very old-sounding voice.

'Daughter,' croaked the voice, 'help me; I need to return to a warm

---

* My portmanteau word for a story form combining the characteristics of both parable and allegory (ed.).

place, or I will die. You have been so long in coming, and I've been waiting for you.'

Sarah squinched her eyes to adjust to the darkness. Initial revulsion at the ancient gnarled vision of female ugliness soon gave way to an overpowering desire to giggle at their mutual predicament.

'Old woman, I am the last person in the wide world to help you. I am penniless, my flask is empty, I have no food or warm blankets to share, and I myself am so weak that if I attempt to carry you, both of us will most likely – snuff it!'

'Take me where I bid you,' gruffly ordered the old one – then, more gently, 'and you will be rewarded beyond your wildest dreams.'

Now, Sarah may have given up everything she understood, but her sense of humour was intact. 'Whose fairy tale am I in anyway?'

A mischievous gleam lit the old woman's eyes – did she wink?

Revived by her own irony and intrigued by the mystery of all this, Sarah gathered the old woman in her arms – ah! sparrow-boned, frail, *light* she was – the very act of carrying seemed to ease Sarah's steps. And in less time than it takes to say 'the personal is political is spiritual', they had arrived. 'Bloody predictable destination,' muttered Sarah as she eyed the weatherbeaten women's hotel. 'A stopover for the homeless battered and anonymous in the nameless city. Come to think, I suppose I fit the bill.'

'In there, number 3. Take the key from my pocket.' The cluttered yet sparse room contained a narrow bed, endless numbers of laden plastic bags, a table on which lay writing materials, a penny whistle and an undoubtedly dangerous table lamp.

'Some treasure,' grumbled Sarah; hunger, thirst and fatigue were working their effect.

The old one pointed to the bed: 'Carry me over there and put me down.'

Not so gently Sarah placed her human burden on the narrow cot. The old woman fell silent and began to remove her clothing, layer upon layer of filthy, tattered garments. As she moved, crumpled bits of dingy paper fell from her pockets. Then off with the shoes. 'At least the feet are young,' Sarah remarked to herself. When the old woman was clad only in her shapeless shift, she spoke: 'Remove this.'

Sarah's reply commingled humour and panic: 'Look, I'm no princess and you're no frog!'

Again the wink. Then, 'Don't be afraid. Your fear can destroy me.'

'OK. But no tricks . . . honest?'

'No tricks.'

Eyes shut, teeth clenched, breath held, Sarah caught hold of the shift and rather clumsily tugged it up, feeling her way, pulling each tired stiff fragile arm free. Eyes still shut, she clasped the shift to her breast.

'Open your eyes, my lamb.'

Is this how Pandora paused at the moment before opening the box – did she shut her eyes too? The moment of opening the box, tasting the consequences of this moment, the fruit of ignorance. Open your eyes, Sarah.

No metamorphosis; only the simple incredibly fragile and mutilated body of a very very old woman. Had she been tortured? Old scars, raw livid scars, open wounds, pustulent sores. Only the feet untouched. A wail escaped Sarah's lips. 'I cannot bear to look at wounds I cannot heal!'

The old one chuckled. 'Ah but already *I* feel stronger. I can help *you*. Tell me your name.'

'I am Sarah.'

'Name your pain.'

'I have been betrayed.'

'Name your deepest desire.'

'Everything.'

'Name your fear.'

'I fear you and hate myself for it.'

'Name the reason for your journey.'

'Was it to find you?'

'Name your hope.'

'I cannot.'

At this point the old one took Sarah tenderly in her arms. And it is here that our story begins.

IV

THE LANGUAGE OF FEELING

16

INNER ANATOMY OF A BIRTH

Léonie Caldecott

Then God's temple in heaven was opened, and the ark of his covenant was seen within his temple; and there were flashes of lightning, loud noises, peals of thunder, an earthquake, and heavy hail.

And a great portent appeared in heaven, a woman clothed with the sun, with the moon under her feet, and on her head a crown of twelve stars; she was with child and she cried out in her pangs of birth, in anguish for delivery.

Revelation 11:19, 12:1—2

Midnight

Laundry. Brightly coloured items going round and round in a whirl of foaming water. Is it a dream, or merely the obsessional image of a troubled sleep? I am too sleepy to figure it out. I am too wakeful to suppress it. A nameless anticipation nibbles at my bones. Which is to say that I hardly dare name it. Could this afternoon's frenzied session in the laundromat signify more than just another false alarm?

2.00 a.m.

I wake from a light sleep to feel Strat getting out of bed. He disappears into the living-room. He suffers from insomnia these days. We joke about how he is going to take the night feeds when the baby is born. But actually this sleeplessness worries me. We are going to need all our strength when the moment comes, and right now we are neither of us managing to get the rest we should. Worry, worry.

Better try and pray. After all, it is not me that's calling the shots around here. The Lord is my strength and my salvation . . . Can't quite connect the words with my feelings. I start to say the rosary, using my fingers, as I am too lazy to get up and find the beads.

Glorious Mysteries: the Resurrection, the Ascension of Christ, Pentecost, the Assumption of the Blessed Virgin into Heaven, her Coronation as Queen of Heaven and Earth. Human and perfect, virgin and mother, the paradoxes whirl round and round like the laundry, my mind spins with the stars on her head, my concentration slips.

2.30 a.m.

It isn't the laundry at all, it's the ocean, wide and deep and teeming with life. It's the whales we went to watch this summer off Cape Cod, their broad backs smooth and glistening as they surfaced near the boat. I have a love-hate relationship with the ocean, a seesaw of awe and terror pictured in terms of whales and sharks.

I roll over to avoid the dead eyes and gaping jaws; my enormous belly makes a beached whale of me. I am out of my element. My body withdraws before the advancing tide of the unknown, too slow, too slow, and the waves surge out from between my legs. I am awake and my waters have broken.

3.00 a.m.

Thank heaven we have some clean towels. It would be hard to believe that anything is happening, if it weren't for the steady seep of pink-tinged fluid down below. I haven't had any contractions yet. We have been told to go to hospital, anyway, to avoid the risk of infection (humph!) but to take our time. I am rather relishing the situation, now that I'm up and dressed and Strat is heating up some chicken soup whilst I pack the last few things. Not that I like chicken soup very much, but the Lamaze childbirth instructor said it was a good thing to eat at the start of labour, as the digestive system slows down. So I consume it in good ritual manner, whilst Strat looks for the digital watch he never wears, in order to time the contractions when they start.

3.30 a.m.

Still no contractions. I go into the baby's room and wonder how long it will be before I meet its new occupant. I finger her tiny clothes (we are sure, without benefit of science, that it's a she), and try to picture her lying in the crib. The silence of the small hours confounds the mind's eye, and my daughter remains an enigma. To me, at least.

> *Already you knew my soul,*
> *My body held no secret from you,*
> *When I was being fashioned in secret,*
> *And moulded in the depths of the earth.*

We have pinned the words of Psalm 138 onto the notice-board. This room was, until recently, my study. Now it is the locus for a new kind of activity (the old kind has been shifted to a corner of the living-room). The child's discovery of the world, and our discovery of her. To launch her on her way, we have decked the notice-board with a patchwork of data worthy of the Voyager spacecraft: snapshots of the family on the other side of the Atlantic, favourite quotes, postcards of landscapes and paintings, a photo of the earth taken from space.

> *If I take the wings of the dawn,*
> *And dwell at the sea's furthest end,*
> *Even there your hand would lead me,*
> *Your right hand would hold me fast . . .*

6.00 a.m.

We are dancing, hand in hand toward the sunrise.

Having completed the chicken soup ritual, the taxi ritual ('follow that stork!'), the stretcher ritual (some rule that said I couldn't walk to the hospital elevator), the strapping-on-of-the-monitors ritual (the baby's heart sounds like a small horse galloping into the distance), the contractions finally begin.

So far, however, they are completely painless, and pretty slow-moving. Strat and I are taking a walk to the window at the end of the labour and delivery floor, to greet the new day spreading its delicate fingers over the Boston skyline. I am still finding it hard to take this whole thing seriously. I have an urge to run around the hospital corridors like a small child, talking and singing and leaping about.

> *For behold, when the voice of your greeting came to my ears, the babe in my womb leaped for joy. And blessed is she who believed that there would be a fulfillment of what was spoken to her from the Lord.*

9.00 a.m.

What I'd really like at this point is a hearty breakfast. I wouldn't mind getting some sleep, too, now the initial excitement is giving way to this waiting game. But it's too late for that. Whether I like it or not, I am going to wait out the arrival of this child with fasting and vigil.

Strat and I say our morning prayers in between visits from the nurse and the obstetrician. I am lucky: it happens to be my own doctor from the health-centre, a gentle and courteous middle-aged man, who is on duty today. I hang on to that small sign of providence, practise my early first-stage breathing (which makes me think of an American football game – HUT-HUT-HUT AND GET THAT BABY TO THE TOUCHDOWN!!!) and try not to think about the fact that the contractions are starting to hurt.

12.30 p.m.

Let's face it, the novelty is beginning to wear off. They've banished me to the recovery floor, ostensibly so I can have something to drink, but actually because I am progressing so slowly and they need the birthing room upstairs. Apart from the unexpected appearance of Strat's father Olly, who happened to be in New York and hopped on a plane to Boston when he heard I was in labour, the morning has been pretty uneventful. Strat and Olly have gone off to grab some lunch, and even the babies in the nursery (where Martha, the brisk young nurse with a dry sense of humour, has sent me 'for encouragement') have lost their attraction. Somehow this whole thing seems to have more to do with boredom and discomfort than with having a baby.

Also, I'm trying not to focus too consciously on the fact that all the women around here look alarmingly exhausted, inching their way around in dressing gowns and slippers and sitting down gingerly on one buttock only . . .

2.00 p.m.

I am lying on the bed I will lie on after the baby is born, in a room shared with a woman who had her baby two days ago, by caesarean. Strat is sitting in a chair next to me, alternately reading theology (to keep himself awake), trying to take my mind off my growing angst with nifty metaphysical propositions, and rubbing my back when the contractions come. These are very irregular – anything from four to ten minutes apart – and when I feel one coming on, I stand up and lean on Strat's shoulder and try to remember the breathing patterns for this stage. It suddenly seems crucial to be disciplined in the face of the pain.

It is visiting time, and we are separated from my room-mate and her succession of guests by nothing more than a thin curtain. To pray under these circumstances is hard – about as hard as it would be to make love. Martha pops in every half-hour to take my temperature and to get the low-down on my contractions. It occurs to me that she'd probably be less shocked to stumble on us locked in a passionate embrace than fervently reciting Hail Holy Queen.

The worst aspect of it is that I am obliged to cross my room-mate's half of the room in order to get to the loo, which is a pretty frequent occurrence. This entails sidling by her bed like one of the hippopotamuses in *Fantasia*, grinning apologetically at the gentleman with whom she is discussing varieties of wine and food (I later discover she is a waitress, and that she worked throughout the last month of her pregnancy, a fact which confounds me with admiration). I feel as though I am in a kind of egg and spoon race, trying not to spill anything from the amniotic grail before I reach the door.

3.00 p.m.

How's it going, asks Martha. Still pretty irregular, says Strat, looking at the sheet of paper on which he's been taking note of the latest contractions. How are you feeling, she asks me. Not too great, I say, in fact here comes a contradiction right now, hoo-ha, hoo-ha, hooha, hooha, hoohahoohahoohahooha . . . You're still smiling, says Martha, it can't be all that bad. I'm British, I gasp through clenched teeth.

3.30 p.m.

You've heard of demonic possession, I say to Strat, well if these laid-back Americans don't do something for me soon, I'm going to regress into a national archetype – Basil Fawlty.

Get in here Martha, there's a good girl. Listen, I don't want to make a *fuss* or anything, but I would like to go upstairs again. What do you mean why? I want to rant and rave in private, all right? Thank you *so* much.

151

4.00 p.m.

Yes I know the cervix is posterior, just get on with it. Yes I know you have to do this during a contraction, I've read the books. WHAT DO YOU MEAN IT'S STILL ONLY THREE CENTIMETRES?

4.20 p.m.

Darkness of sorts, silence of sorts. On my own in the birthing room again, lights dimmed, sitting in one of the rocking chairs for which this labour unit is famed. A good way to be in motion without using wobbly legs. I breathe, I rock, I pray, I rock, the wood of the chair, the blue of the wall, reminds me of a Shaker house I saw a few months ago. Empty now, of course. The Shakers didn't do this, this birthing. It's another culture I've embraced, reclaimed rather, troubadours and knights of the round table and Joan of Arc taking her voices literally and riding into battle. I yearn forward into the pain, eager for a resolution. Hips into the saddle, breathless, relax, stay with the rhythm of it, don't lose the momentum. I struggle to write down the time of contractions; they're speeding up and I want to be believed. Three minutes, five, four, two.

4.30 p.m.

Don't panic. *Thy will be done, on earth as it is in heaven.* Keep your eyes fixed on a single point, the eye of the Mother. Our Lady of Czestochowa, scarred and beautiful, *pray for us.* Wish Strat would get back from his coffee-break, though he's only been gone fifteen minutes. Father and son, one pacing the corridor in the old-fashioned manner, the other with his sleeves rolled, joining in the fleshly fray.

I shift my gaze to another picture: the Annunciation from the Portiuncola in Assisi. I try to recall the warmth that swept over me this summer as I prayed in the tiny chapel where St Claire kept her tryst with St Francis. They say that any prayer sincerely offered in that spot will be answered. Whether you like the answer is another matter, of course. Up in the town, in the austere Basilica of Santa Chiara (in contrast to the jewel-box of San Francesco), they still display the blond locks that St Claire shed at the Portiuncola. When I prayed there, I asked for us to be a real family, the family I did not know as a child. As I got up from my knees, the baby was kicking.

4.40 p.m.

The problem is not the pain, so much as the thought that it might go on for a long time before I reach the magical ten centimetres. Don't project into the future, Strat always says. Where is he, anyway? And where is the nurse? Let's face it, I can't handle this situation. My body feels like one enormous bruise, being squeezed all over from the inside out. I can't seem to ride these waves, which crash upon me ever faster, ever harder, however much I try to breathe 'correctly'. Perhaps I shouldn't try. I catch the sad eyes of the Czestochowa icon. Behind the image of mother and child, another figure looms. The crucified Christ.

Am I being a coward? I ask the Mother of the Lamb. Or does this hurt as much as I think it does?

5.00 p.m.

Christ has no hands on earth now but ours, said St Teresa. She also said that if God treated His friends so badly, it was no wonder He had so few of them. I don't quite have her cheek, but I've done my share of grumbling in the last half-hour. Look here, Old Chap, is this really necessary? I mean, mightn't there be another way of going about this?

And immediately I throw up, bright green, haven't had anything except apple juice downstairs . . . There was a young lady from Ryde, who ate fifty green apples and died, the apples lamented, inside her fermented, and made cider inside her inside . . . I think I'm being made to understand something about nature and grace. Fasting means fasting. It doesn't mean the occasional apple juice on a stomach that's got more pressing things to think about.

At least I have the hands. Strat's hands, passing me the bowl and the towel, rubbing my back, my head, rocking the chair for me as my breath becomes furious, vehement, HOO-HA-HOO-HA, take that and that, take it, please, take it. I am hurtling into the unknown, rocking, harder, harder, the terror, pain, and more pain.

5.15 p.m.

Why does the doctor have to come in to examine me, when I'm in the bathroom? I mean, do they want their urine sample or don't they? I've decided I've had enough of natural childbirth, and want a shot of nysentol, if nothing else to help me relax between contractions. But they'll only give it to me if I'm over four centimetres dilated, for fear of slowing me down again. The idea that I'm feeling what I'm feeling and may not be progressing is unbearable. I think of futile suffering, torture victims. I'd be blurting secrets at the first turn of the screw, I discover. I'd have to swallow a cyanide capsule. Which is what I feel like doing now.

'I'll be back in a few minutes,' calls the obstetrician from outside the bathroom door. I try to get up and come out to beg him to stay and do the examination right now, but I can't manage it, and collapse into a heap, Strat holding me under the arms, not sure whether to run after the doctor, or stay with me. I don't know either. I weep; a fresh contraction commandeers the shaking. The bathroom is a mess. I am a mess, every biological function going at once. I've never been so humiliated in all my life.

5.30 p.m.

Impossible. Impossible to move. Impossible not to move. Sit? Stand? Walk? No dimension in which to find relief. How about kneeling? says Strat. Is this some kind of joke, I think, then I realize he is referring to a position recommended by the Lamaze instructor. Kneeling against the upright back of the bed.

I do so, and ask him to apply counterpressure against my back. He tries the tennis balls we've brought, but they are new, and their scratchy pile is irritating. Heel of your hand, I blurt (we agreed some time ago to forego please and thank you for the time being). No. Too hot, sticky. Hurts. I suddenly realize why cornflower powder is on the Lamaze list. Where is it? he asks, when I tell him to put some on his hands. Spongebag, I gasp. He rummages. I groan. In the bathroom, HURRY! More rummaging. Oh God, what was the other breathing technique? Three short breaths and out. Hurry. There's a squirting sound. Can't get the top off, says Strat, desperately. He is running round the room, banging the powder container on different bits of furniture. I don't know whether to laugh or cry. Except I'm beyond both.

5.45 p.m.

The contractions are coming every two minutes now. Still no one has come in to examine me. The nurse reappeared briefly and said she'd be right back, she had a patient about to deliver next door. It's suddenly got very busy, she said, apologetically. Trust me to give birth during a baby-boom, I thought. Still, at least I have a room to myself, and no intervention is better than too much intervention (they don't insist on shavings and enemas here; as for monitoring the baby, they only do it every now and then, leaving me free to move around the rest of the time). Right now, however, I just want someone to put me out of my misery, I don't care how.

I am describing this part from a distance, emotion recollected in tranquillity. I am not sure I could recapture its *in extremis* quality any more. Not fully, anyway. It is overlaid with the merciful amnesia that ensures I won't simply refuse outright to do this again. At one point I thought, not: I'll never do this again, but rather: I can't imagine wanting to do this again. I was struggling to hold on to some modicum of objectivity, even then. I conclude from this that objectivity remains dear to me, even when everything else has been burned away. I may not be very good at it, but it does matter.

So. I am kneeling on the bed, holding on to the upright back which has become my wailing wall as I sway back and forth in, let's face it, agony. Strat, poor fellow, is trying to comfort me as best he can. He can't take the pain away, but boy am I glad he's with me. Somewhere in the back of my mind is an inaccessible place, a serene Himalayan landscape of prayer, beyond the searing red jungle that presses in upon me now. My ears are roaring, my mouth is parched, I bang my head against the bed, shaking, out of control. I visualize my god-mother, her intense oriental face with its high cheekbones redolent of dignity and discipline. Across the ocean that divides us I cry out to her to pray for me since I can't do it for myself. You have been through this, wrapped in this heat, this blinding intensity, the unbearable mystery of bearing a child.

My God, my God, why have you forsaken me?

6.00 p.m.

We've got to call someone, says Strat, you can't go on like this. I recognize a familiar paralysis in myself: when in doubt, don't. And doubt teases me, relentlessly, right now.

I see the cord with various position controls, and the call button, draped across the back of the bed, right in front of my face. A new contraction grips me (or is it the old one, renewing its attack?), and I feel an overwhelming urge to push downwards. I punch the call button.

Yes? says the woman at the main desk, in the tone of someone taking a luncheon order.

NURSE! I scream.

Right, she responds, her voice switching to emergency mode.

6.15 p.m.

The nurse's name is Deborah, and she is wonderful. She apologizes for not having got here before, but the floor has gone crazy in the last few hours. Everyone is giving birth at once. I try to imagine all this combined labour, this universe in travail, but fail to transcend my immediate sensations.

Also, she says, as she persuades me to turn around and draws on the sterile gloves in order to examine me, no one thought I was going to progress so fast in the last two hours. For indeed, says Deborah, I am in transition. Typical. I never could time things right.

The bad news is that I'm not supposed to push just yet. The child's gateway into the world has not fully opened. This is like telling someone who is having an epileptic fit to keep their body limp. How about the nysentol, I whimper, failing to get the desired element of sarcasm into my voice. For, as I suspected, it's now too late to have it, as it would inhibit the pushing reflex. So it's to be childbirth *au naturel*, in spite of my wavering commitment to the concept. At least I'm learning to give up the illusion of control.

The torrent Kishon swept them away
The onrushing torrent, the torrent Kishon,
March on, my soul, with might!

I know it sounds impossible, says Deborah. Just try breathing instead of pushing.

6.30 p.m.

I am hanging on to Strat with the grip of a baby monkey, and panting for dear life. This can't be happening to me. Please can we go home now? But this *is* happening to me, and home is guarded by an angel with a flaming sword. My mother describes this part as 'going up the

156

wall'. I think about throwing myself out of the window, flying, exploding, a variety of cul-de-sacs. I don't deserve this. But what does deserve mean? De-serve. Who have I been serving, until now, in my life? I was, after all, free to choose. *My ways are not your ways.* Good and evil, the knowledge, the forgetting, I turn my head, complaint shudders out, I am dis-membered. This is the fruit, somehow. I don't know. I hear the obstetrician being paged in the distance.

O Mary, conceived without sin, pray for us who have recourse to thee.

Strat is whispering the prayer over and over into my ear, and putting ice-chips in my mouth. I suck at the words, mantra melting on my tongue, water of life. I am starting to see stars, my legs have pins and needles. Deborah puts her hands over my face. The breathing, too, can be abused. I am glimpsing the truth about the fallen condition. It has something to do with hyperventilation.

And ye shall be as gods.

7.00 p.m.

Try pushing now, said the obstetrician when he arrived, and let's see what happens. His name is Oswald Treisman. He was born in South Africa, like Strat's parents, trained in England, and now lives and works in the USA. There's a kind of genealogical aptness about this. He apologizes for the lack of anaesthetic. Oh well, I say between contractions, these things happen.

The room is flooded with light for the delivery. I wanted her to be born in subdued lighting, gently, tactfully. But the spotlight which is supposed to make this possible, by illuminating only the immediate area Dr Treisman needs to see, turns out not to be working. Also, the bed, which cost thousands of dollars and comes apart in the middle for a sitting delivery, has jammed and can't be cranked up to the appropriate height. Dr Treisman, who has a bad back, will have to crouch over me and the baby like a prophet reading entrails. So much for high technology.

7.15 p.m.

Good, says Deborah, you're doing good, push into the burn. And again. I remember childhood gym lessons, the girl with the skinny arms who couldn't climb the rope and burned the palms of her hands trying to slide down too quickly. Slide down and escape. But there is no escape. No way out but on.

7.30 p.m.

The sound of one woman yelling. Exhaustion banished by the beserker's roar, teeth bared, true-grit, don't let the side down, can Olly hear me out there in the corridor. Hope he can't. Hope he can.

In anguish for delivery.

Push, she says. Push and hold, he says. Anger, roaring, ripping herself apart with both lungs. Madness. Hold it, hold it, he says, does he mean hold or stop or hold to keep going? 'You're doing great, love, I can see the baby!' Strat's voice, Strat's hands, he's humouring me, I feel only destruction, death. Am I going to die?

Dust to dust.

Put your hand there and feel the head, he says, the quiet doctor-voice, seen this, heard these screams, a thousand times. See, the head is crowning. My fingers tremble, my hands aren't clean; it doesn't matter, says Deborah; they encounter an alien something, dampness, hair, O my God. I forgot to believe. Despair returns, I am too weak, I can't do it, this wrestling with the angel. I look away from the carnage, I give up, I see her, the Mother, wounded face, dark, dark, the child in her arms, both to the same crowning, the crowning of thorns. I see Him stretched out, it's the same, it's giving birth, pulling entire universes through the eye of the needle, water and blood, pierced by contempt. I push it away, I thrust it out, evict the impossible.

And: Here I am, says the angel, rising out of the sea.

The surf suspends its pounding. There's the head, says Dr Treisman. Now for these nice broad shoulders. I just heard myself agree to an episiotomy, I have no stretch left, the life-force spent, the knife releasing more blood, more water, he could cut off the entire bottom half of my body for all I care. God, how little I knew before, in that dream-world. Before the whale swallowed me.

I had heard of Thee by the hearing of the ear,
But now my eyes see Thee . . .

7.48 p.m.

Suddenly it's over, a slithering, gushing feeing, a final roar from me, then another roar, not my voice, but like my voice, the same tone, exactly. You have a daughter, says Dr Treisman. He lays her gently on my strangely deflated belly, a warm, wet porpoise thrashing in slow-motion as she becomes a land-animal between my hands.

Strat, at my side, catches his breath. We look at one another, at her, do you see what I see? Her eyes are open, fierce, blinded by the light, she has masses of hair, streaming over her head, so large, perfectly shaped, can she really have come from inside my body? Dr Treisman hands Strat the surgical scissors and he cuts the cord, without batting an eyelid. Now she is free to soar, our baby eagle; we name her after that other soaring, passionate soul, Teresa of Avila.

Deborah, full of smiles, compliments, wraps her in a receiving blanket and puts a stocking cap on her head. I offer her her first food. Tiny clenched fist, heat-seeking mouth, fastening on to my body, a survivor, greedy for life, sucking intently. Where did you learn this, Teresa? Amazing, says Strat, warm body standing at my shoulder, leaning over, protective; a Christmas-card family, complete, accomplished.

Is this real, I wonder, holding the hospital gown, a little awkwardly, out of the way of the incredible feast taking place at my breast. So. Here you are, at last.

O taste and see.

Midnight

Laughter, and tears. A baptism of fire. Lying in the sleepless hospital half-light, war hero, heroine, stitched up without a murmur, what could compare with the actual combat? Images of celebration, calling in the patriarch, wounds staunched, covered over with clean linen, laundry, ordinary thoughts return so fast, wash your hands, here she is, your granddaughter. He drops his coat, his hat, his newspapers, he tiptoes over, proffers a finger, almost shyly, holds her in his arms in gentle silence, ponders her, we are all feminized by this. Interesting headgear, he says, was she born with it on?

Images, memories, calling up the past, made strange now.

The future is even stranger. In a few hours the sky will lighten and they will bring her to me, flesh of my flesh, she who is to be my teacher, my guru in a new discipline, a new array of pleasure and pain, struggle and joy. Right now I am a little afraid, am I up to this, these years of carefulness, this new burden? My body aches, I worry about the simplest things, such as: will my nether-regions ever function normally again? I should sleep, rest. I am too confused to let go.

The night-nurse bustles in, another interruption, but she is kind, she helps me wobbling to the bathroom, she gives me a painkiller, she tucks me in and ticks me off for not sleeping – oh the contradictions of motherliness! But it works: I drift off.

Hail Mary, full of grace, take me in your arms, *blessed art thou amongst women*, I have been turned inside out, *Holy Mary, Mother of God*, tell me it's all right, all will be well and all manner of thing shall be well. *Pray for us now and at the hour of our death*.

Death. Birth. The way out is the way in. Gracefully now.

Little one I love you. You have taught me the meaning of redemption.

The way that one and one makes three.

17

ON THE EDGE (1985)

Come into my heart now
I write
whoever you are
out there
the stars are muted in the cold
there is a half moon
come into my heart
now, now
before

It is the same door
always
shut
which nevertheless
remains open

Two years old
very small
flash of light
sound of world blowing apart

Breasts gone
part of her womb
children fixed like stone
out by the water faucet.
It would take an hour
to get her back

Hole in the mountain
there past the
scrub cedar
what is it you have heard?

Substances
mixed with the water
fumes, no name
for them
smelling worse
than a sewer
you can hardly say

many barrels with a skull
emptied there
what went into the stream
radiation, mercury, tritium
so many mysteries.

Sound of world coming
apart
death of mother, father
sister ill, sickness
in the air, she
over the bridge
on the way to school

And this is not just one place
one story
but many
name them, like Arcturus, like
Sirius, full of history,
Tennessee, Hiroshima,
Desert Flats, Nevada,
Nicaragua, El Salvador
Dachau

My suitcases
in a locker
the train moving
over a line
I can't see
I am frightened
for no reason
for no visible
reason

They brought in those barrels
over the black top
and you can smell them
but it gave
the men work

Why am I not the one?
I ask, and that I have
let myself
be used
as a blind
so the others
don't see

2

Where?
Do the children even remember

have they even
been told

Sirius, Arcturus
can you ever
see them
from here?

Did they hear the story
of Mary, was it a ghost who
made love to her, tongue
in her mouth, sweet like
fruit, or Kore,
she was in the grass when

All that makes me what I am
gone, my daughter cries.

All that makes us
even the cell
brightness, the gene

a face, not as the remembered face
not weathered
by how many times the hands
the sun,

try to be calm
try to be calm
the rain on the West window
covering the bridge
I will cross over
the ones who

I burn my fingers on the
baking
bread

crying, you have it
you have it
why am I not the one

seeing my hardness in the
hardness of another

the hell darkness of winter.

3

Little child of
perfection
fingers, toes
ears, small nose
two eyes, infant breathing
mouth open
closing little cries
what if the
eyes are in
the or hands are
like lungs like gills
fingers in a circle
on the head
skin blue
what if the gene invisible
like this in the air
water smallest
and somehow inside
is this the
decision
we make
we have made
growing not
human, we look
and say.

4

Come into my heart
tired beyond speaking
I don't care
if I am not supposed
to speak

I was supposed to have this house
precipitous
almost flying
out over the water
and to wander

and witness
it is beyond speaking
really
it is a weeping
become like ice
in the bones

pieces of music
broken
then played back

poetry must be walked
comes out of the body
in measures
as if somewhere
in the body
were
an arc flashing
and we are supposed
to find this

and they would not tell him
why
the blood in his stools
right after
the flash of light

and they did not list
the retina
clouded vision
fatigue

nor the blood in the stools
of the smallest grandchild

finest dust
fine, fine dust

poetry returns to me
wild in its directions

I think of
her finger
in the fold of my labia

I think of
the salinity of cells
sweat

I think
of the one who looked for her sister
and found only a button
from an old dress
in years of rubble

don't ask me
to be calm
don't ask me to try any longer
to make sense
I am straining toward a
certain madness
it is in my body
singing with the force
of ice that
carves out canyons

5

hand knocking on the door
finds an echo
do you hear this?

it is empty
but it is also space.
It is infinitely hollow
and the wood

is burning.

6

It was not so much
the wire that held them in
as the joy on their faces
when it opened
not so much
the hard places
cancer right there
where I touched
in his body
but his question
do you believe me?

166

I believed him
I would have cupped my hands
around his ears
or held tightly onto him
earth
invisibly shaking
and say
I too
have seen

noticed
the small animals
egg shells cracked
calves unborn

7

I knew I could never
close you out, nor really
anyone for even an
instant, even if I imagined.
I have it back
now, all that I heard
some of what I know
and an aching
like a prodigal lover
barest evidence
of the greater part
the great part that is above
below around beneath
and in
us.

8

How many are moving
not in belief
only in homelessness
not in communion
only in blood and woundedness
the armed doing
what they do

for so many reasons
language
like the wings of a half dead
bird hardly
a witness
a country where only
the silent survive
even death driven
to obedience

9

what were they
and why
poetry returns
Bergen
Belsen in the barracks
many beds one on
top of the
other I have
seen them
noticed
some not able to rise
bare bone against wood
what would you say
and shit pouring from
between the boards
Birkenau
two men who are
holding an old woman
still crying
still, now,
as if to flee
now
and the trees
so straight
Dachau's ovens
in two tiers
above, below
one large
one small
long ravine for

the shooting
do you imagine
this has stopped
gravel
between the barracks
hot sun standing
torture
do you imagine
this is not happening
a precious piece of thread
here,
one bit of tenderness
and so much
nakedness made into
last glimpse, train
Auschwitz
track
one body on
another
Auschwitz, are you
still able to
say
if not me then
who?
Do you imagine it has
ended?

10

Trained rebels at the border
body counts
body bags
the increased perfection of technology
dots on a screen
so many factors
let it go out generously your love
and with no calculation
poems can be like people
aged on this earth
whose voices cut through you
whose eyes
even in memory

you cannot turn from
the pigs chosen to
burn
because their skin
looks like
human skin
and in this way
they imagine
they still
voices that cannot be
forgotten

11

I am speaking in the language of feeling
trying to tell you about
Sirius
or any of the stars
or any place
above or
beneath
or inside
the cells
the arteries
to speak of any
of the mysteries
where are they
and do the
children remember
and do we?

the plum white and green
brown branch floating
fresh again
after so many
millions of
and was there ever a day when

does it matter?
strung out like so much
icing
spelling no discernible
name
but random the testicles

ovaries
no birth a coal colored
dust over everything

something in the water
the fruit
I have said this before
a metallic taste
or no taste
I have said it

ask all you want to know
my mother tells me
and my questions
sleep with me
until I can say
you have answered and now
it is I who

one would have to love the tree in
its flowering
more than fear in its force
and hold the mouth open
against freezing

that place
inside the lips
like a rushing river
not like laser
not like radium
not like mercury
or tritium

children taking
the gleaming fish
from the water
proud
their fingers slipping
over the gills

and we did not imagine
what they put in that stream
no more than I imagined
the softness of your mouth
or
the warmth of the light
the lights around the crown
of the head

171

or in a line
in boats on the water
dotted in the hills
glowing for eight days
and more
fixed in the tree
in the eyes
in what we remember
    light
what words would you put to it
as close as my hand
what I would speak
I cannot turn from you
you cannot turn from me
and every bit of dust, every
Last breath, everything falling
under it
we have not imagined this
    light.

Susan Griffin

18

LAMMAS BABE: TEN DAYS OF HEALING
Jenjoy Silverbirch Strongbody Clevermind

Linda Hurcombe and Polly Blue, eds

It is Monday.

I am dressed and ready when Wendy comes. I sit on the edge of the hospital bed in my small room. In the past weeks I have often sat here, struggling to eat or being sick. I have dragged myself from bed to bedpan. The smell of urine has been rank in my nostrils. Often I am not in time.

Wendy wheels me out to her car in my chair. She is driving me to see my healer, Matthew Manning. We don't mention our talk of Friday evening . . . 'Jen, this healer you want me to take you to – does he heal in the name of Christ? Is he of God? Or is he something else, something evil?'

For two hours I talked with her. 'His healing feels good. It feels loving. Why should some Christians condemn if he doesn't name Christ?' I was exhausted when she went.

On Saturday I shouted out my anger. I drew a picture of vindictive God. He is the male God who put men in charge of the earth to control and destroy it. For him men killed the witches. For him they fight wars. This God has a malevolent finger. It points at laughter and singing and dancing and freedom. It says No. It says Sin. It says Guilt.

This God does not stop Wendy driving me to Matthew. We leave him behind.

In Matthew's still room his hands send warm messages vibrating through my body. Music flows and ebbs around us.

'That was very good,' I tell him. 'I had a new homoeopathic remedy last week. Tonight Joyce is giving me an osteopathic treatment. Tomorrow I leave hospital. It feels like a time of powerful change.'

I carry his healing back into the hospital. Fresh air and countryside fill me. I will be tired these next few days with these three forms of healing working in me. I am due to leave hospital tomorrow; I go to Gilletts (a rural community in Kent) the day after.

Before I sleep I hear the cries and moans of the women on chemotherapy. 'How can that give them life?' I think. 'I am alive.' I drift into a dream . . .

I am in a log cabin. K. is with me. He strokes my bare skin. I turn and brush my body against him. Every surface of my skin is vibrant with energy as we touch and move against each other. I can feel the life in him. We share this pulse, this rising sap. This is not orgasm or penetration. It is longer and deeper. It carries me outside into the snow. He watches me running. He shouts encouragement. My lungs fill with exhilarating sharpness. People play in the snow. Voices ring out in the stillness. I run through the snow over the red earth under the tall sequoia trees. I run in the valley by the bubbling stream. My body overflows with clear air, sparking water, crumbling earth, tall trees. Life tingles through muscles, bones and cells. Under the sequoia trees I feel the depth of roots. They reach to earth's heart. I feel the great reaching out of branches and greenery into the far distant sky. I feel the strong trunk connecting earth to sky. I am the tree. I reverberate to the thrumming energy. I am alive. I am alive.

I wake in the dim light of my room. Tears stream down my face. I switch on my light. I sit on the side of my bed. Nurse Fran comes in. 'I saw your light. You all right, Jen?'

'Yes, Fran, I'm so happy. I've had an amazing dream. I was so alive in it. I'm sure it's a sign I'm getting better. I'm not going to die, Fran. I'm healing again. Like last year – I was dying then. My bones were full of cancer. I was in terrible pain, and on seven hundred and fifty milligrams of morphine a day. On the summer equinox I got a letter. Somehow it triggered something off. I got better without any drugs. And now it's going to happen again. I know it is.'

'That's marvellous, Jen. Do you want to tell me about this dream?' I tell her. Then she brings me a cup of tea and half a melon. The pink roses in a pink teapot float their fragrance in the room. Wendy gave me these.

Wednesday. I arrive at Gilletts community. I am exhausted. I am very weak. I can scarcely move. I try to sleep in the afternoon. Thoughts race through my head. It is Lammas. This year it coincides with full moon – a powerful conjunction. I can feel its energy in the air.

This morning four of us celebrated Lammas in my room at home. We broke and shared the bread man and drank barley wine, rejoicing for the first fruits of the harvest. Now I lie in bed trying to let go. I hear people talking outside. I feel wide open, exposed. My mind chatters from thought to thought. I relax my limbs. I breathe deep. My body feels heavy. Its weight sinks into the bed. My consciousness sinks too; it falls deeper and deeper. I jerk myself back. I feel I am slipping away. I am losing myself. Is this death? I try to compose myself. I listen to some music. The sounds echo through me. I drown in them. I can't bear it. I try to sleep again. Either tumbling thoughts or vanishing consciousness. I struggle to lift my heavy body to reach for a book. Something light. The words tangle themselves in my head.

Annabelle comes in. 'Are you all right?'

'No. I can't let go. I need to sleep, but every time I let go, I feel like I'm losing myself into unconsciousness. It feels like dying. It's frightening. Please sit with me a while.'

She sits on the bed and holds my hand.

'I need to feel safe. I don't feel safe. That's why I can't let go.'

'What would make you feel safe?'

'Will you be my Mummy? I need a Mummy.'

'Yes, I'll be your Mummy.'

'My Mummy loves me. Tell me my Mummy loves me.'

'Your Mummy loves you.'

'I'm not going to die. My Mummy loves me. I don't have to look after her.'

'You don't have to look after your Mummy. She loves you.'

'Her Mummy looks after her. My Mummy looks after me. I'm safe. She loves me.'

'Yes, she loves you.'

Over and over again I say it, and Annabelle replies. The words live in me, soothing and calming. I fill myself with them; warm gold.

'I come out of my Mummy's tummy. I grow in her body. I am in the dark of her womb, then I am born. I come out into the world. She loves me. She wants me. She's glad I'm here.'

'Your Mummy wants you. She loves you.'

'I gave birth to Shona. I am her Mummy. She came out of my body. I love her. I know how it feels to be born. I know how it feels to give birth. My Mummy came out of her mother. My Mummy was born too.'

For three hours Annabelle guides me through.

My body remembers the feelings of growing in the womb. It remembers forcing out into the world. It remembers through me, through my mother, through my daughter. My body is comforted. My mind is at rest. I am lovingly held in the arms of my own mother love. I am stroked and treasured. I can let go and feel safe. I am reborn. I am a new person. I am a Lammas babe.

'You know what the local country people call a Lammas babe?' said Janet.

'Tell me,' I replied.

'A Lammas babe is very special. It's born to older people on Lammas. Their other children are growing up and this one is a late and unexpected gift, a special child.'

The four ages of woman, daughter, mother, crone and hidden, flow in and out of life spiralling. We live through the depths and heights of each until we know them. We chase through the four seasons. We follow the ever-repeating processes of growth – seeding/blossoming maturity/mellow fruitfulness/into fading and cold death. We live through the four elements. Water expresses emotions and the unconscious; air is mental activity and thought; earth is our bodies, the physical world; fire is self-expression and identity. The hope is that we learn and spiral and transform deeper and higher, wider and more minutely into the magic of the spirit. The spirit breath encompasses all and nestles at its centre.

Numbers. Are they to dance through my life? I shiver in their strong presence. They pluck at fibres where they will pull out their tunes. Some are melodious sweet tones; some wild and joyous as the wind. Others are harsh and clashing. They carry drowning sobs and painful reality. There are many scatterings and gatherings of notes across the scales of human experience. What tunes will they draw out of my poor flesh these days as my life runs – one, two, three, four, five, six, seven, eight, nine, ten – through their life? I let my lungs fill with breath. It washes me through with peace. I am at a beginning. Let its course run through the Great Spirit into me. All will be well.

Today is day one. The day of the ace. I burst into a new beginning of life. It surges and splashes around me in its newness. What does it carry me into? I breathe in the magic of one, the first day of new life. The first day of August. Yes, it carries me into my first ten days. It carries me in and out of ten fingers. It carries me through the ancient mystery of numbers. I will be living the secret of each number with each new day. The secret unfolds itself with the help of the Tarot cards. They wheel around the magic of numbers. They flavour them with fire, water, earth, air. They colour them with the archetypal symbols of life – Magician, High Priestess, Empress, Emperor, Sun, Moon, Death, Judgment . . .

The Ace babies leap out into the world. Fire flames in creative expression. It blazes my role in life. Water bubbles up with the deep secrets of the unconscious. It washes over me with my emotions. Air breathes through the spaces of my mind. Thought flies through the airy spaces. Earth dwells in the clay of my body. I live in its physical being.

One card draws out of the pack to me. It is the Star.

It is Thursday. I wake. I am one day old. I am newborn. I am held safe. A warm shawl of love enfolds me. The smell of a rose floats clear and pink into my awareness. Its soft petals are unfolded before my wide eyes. From my bed I sink into the wonder of it. I reach out a finger to touch its glistening texture.

And who am I? I've yet to find out. Who have I been? I think of the hospital. Withering sickness haunts me, death, dying, screaming corners of the mind, shrinking bodies, answer in my head. I was dying. The thought explodes in me. I nearly died again. Why? Why did I let it happen? I felt alive in hospital. I listened to others fitted to chemotherapy tubes controlled by boxes of lights on stands, mechanical square Christmas trees. I pitied them. I saw them as hopeless. Another thought burst in on me – I was in the same place as them. How dare I be so smug; so arrogant? Their faith was in the doctors and the drugs. To some of them that means recovery. It means life. My path is no more certain than theirs. Lots of perfectly ordinary people get better from cancer. They don't make a fuss about it. They humbly accept what doctors offer them. If it's painful they groan their way through it. For some of them treatment has no side effects. Something inside these people allows only healing and no side effects. I set myself apart as something special because my way has been different. I behaved as though that difference was all my own – unconnected with the hundredfold silver network of giving from other people. My mind ranges over these gifts – healings, prayers, crystals, stones, shells, massage, homoeopathy, osteopathy, reflexology, ritual work, feeding me, driving me places, doing shopping, people having me to stay, practical support, loving letters – yes, the medical support too – drugs that eased pain, steroids stopping my sickness, hormones . . .

I want to be whole and healthy, to feel my body lithe and supple. I feel the memories in my body. Striding out across the ridge. The flowers are clumped and gathered pink, purple, yellow in the grass. The wind buffets my clothes against my skin. My skin feels smooth and firm under the flying cotton. My muscles stretch easily. I am leopard slanting through the high meadows. I am silky cat yawning and stretching in wind-tossed sunshine. Shadows flicker and dance over my movement. My smooth hide flows over my limbs. My legs fill and empty in their loping contact with the soil. My consciousness pours through skin shifting over muscles and bones. Air floods into my lungs. It tingles out through all my tissues. Blood drums through my deep inner darkness. It washes outwards, too. It taps its patterns right through to toes and tail tip and pointed ears. Sun and shadow, I slide through tall trees. Darkness and flame, I leap over fallen trunks. I weave the black and gold of my passage through the tangled bushes. I sink into a coil of slumber in a glade. Warmth and light wash through my dreams. The stream song shimmers under my sleep. I slip into the hidden corners of myself.

I stand in the fairy ring of toadstools and I close my eyes. I see in front of me soft green grass lit by the full moon. Fairies flit on the edges of my vision. The one-eyed face looks at me. I see and I don't see. My one sick eye reminds me I don't have to see anything. Everybody else can see it too if they want to.

> power
> tearing through
> gut despair
> tearing wrenching
> ripping the structures of our
> awareness

Morning. I wake up. I'm awake. What a night. Dreams. Thoughts rushing through my head. A voice in my mind – 'Drink to life'. I laugh. I pour out brandy into a glass. I raise it. 'To life,' I say. I sip the warming amber liquid. 'Here's to life; it's wonderful,' I say. Chuckles bubble out of me. I sit on the side of the bed. The door opens. Janet's head appears. There's a curious look on her face. Pat's head follows after. 'Come in. Here, have some brandy – I've discovered the secret of life. I'm two days old and I'm alive.' They come in. They sit by me. I think – 'They think I've gone crazy. Perhaps I have.' 'Pat, those stories you told me about the drunks, the prostitutes. They know – yes, they know. Everyone thinks they're the dregs. They're not. They see the fairies. That old woman who sat on your knee in the pub for prostitutes and drunks. She knew. She asked you to love her. How proud I've been – I didn't realize.'

'Alasdair is a very fine man.' Pat gazed through the window. Her hands were clasped round her knees. 'Other people didn't see it. I miss him. He meant a lot to me.'

I reached in my memory for Alasdair. In the kitchen, washing up, the first time I came here. His angular body lurched across the kitchen. He had a black eye. 'You one of that lot, come for the weekend?' His voice cut across other conversations.

'Tell me about Alasdair, Pat.'

'He once took me to see the drunks in London. He knows them. "Salt of the earth, they are," he said. "They look after each other." '

'We sat under the arches. A man sat by me to talk to me. He smelt. Alasdair did this to me.' She scratched the back of her grey curly hair with her forefinger. She gave a nod and a wink, mouth downturned. 'Then we went to a pub. He said, "This is known as the worst pub in London. Thieves and prostitutes and vagrants go there. Do you want to come?" I went. I sat at the bar. A little old lady came in. She looked very dirty. She came and sat on my knee. I just sat there. Then do you know what she said? "Will you love me and be my friend? I need a friend. Please will you love me and look after me? Please be my friend." I told her I would.' Pat looked at her hands. A tear lingered on her eyelids. 'Alasdair did this again.' She repeated the forefinger scratch of the head, nod and wink. 'He loved those people.'

'Here, have some brandy.' Pat takes the glass. She sips appreciatively. 'It's very good brandy,' she says. Janet drinks too.

'It's right that you should be here,' I say. 'You two women to share this with me. Janet, you are like the mother goddess to me. Pat, you are for me the crone, the wise older woman goddess. And I am the daughter.'

Janet: I go to see if Jen is awake. I am doing her breakfast today. As I come to the door I hear her shouting and laughing. Pat is just up the corridor. We look at each other. Pat comes hurrying after me. I peep round the door. She is sitting on the edge of her bed. A glass of brandy is in her hand. 'Drink to life,' she calls. 'Is she drunk? Perhaps we shouldn't have got her that brandy. I thought it was meant to help her sleep.' Pat comes into the room behind me. We sit on the bed. Jen is on about life and drunks. She gives us brandy to share. I don't think she is drunk. There's a lot going on for her. I wonder what she wants for breakfast.

Pat: I see Janet going into Jen's room. There is a strange noise coming from Jen's room. I follow Janet. Is Jen all right? She's been so very ill. It seems to be making her act a bit strange. She's drinking brandy, laughing – 'Drink to life.' She's talking about the down-and-outs I met with Alasdair. She's understood about them. She thanks me for telling her about them. I drink the brandy.

'You've got your knickers in a two-and-eight again,' says Janet. She shakes her henna-red hair back.

'What's a two-and-eight?' I ask. She pulls my knickers over my feet.

'Haven't you heard that before? Two-and-eight – state. Cockney slang.' She kneels down and crinkles up my socks to slip them on, then my trousers. She stands up. Her embroidered skirt swishes round her plump figure.

'There, that's better. Now, can you get up all right? Shall I give you a lift?' Before I can reply, she puts her hands under my arms to help me up. I pull up my knickers and trousers.

'Right. All ready to go.'

'Lean on me.' She takes my arm firmly. 'Let's get you back to bed. Do you want a cup of tea?'

'Yes, I'll come to the kitchen.'

Two and eight
STATE
INFINITY
and the DATE
2nd of August

my
2nd day of
being born
knickers
in a twist

strength the card
in the
TAROT

one
two and eight
ad
infinitum

Kees puts his head round the door.

'I'm looking after you now. Do you want to be on your own?'

'I'd like to talk.'

He sets his small body neatly near the bed. The sun catches the silver of his hair. Pixie wisdom sparkles in the blue of his eyes.

'I've just been reading a therapy book. It had some questions you should ask yourself. I was thinking about them.'

'I have questions I ask myself. I have them up on doors in the loo, the bathroom and my bedroom. I try to answer them quickly every time I go through the door. I know. Why don't we play a game. You ask me your questions and I can ask you them. Then we'll ask your questions.'

'All right . . .'

DO YOU KNOW WHO IS LIVING YOU?

It's a secret – the little voice over your shoulder?

DO YOU KNOW WHAT ANYTHING IS?

It's a game.

WHO IS GOD?

I am and you are too if I let you be.

WHAT HAPPENS WHEN WE TOTALLY SURRENDER?

I can make it all into a game and it's easy and it isn't hard.

WHAT WOULD HAPPEN IF I FORGOT EVERYTHING?

I'd invent it all again.

I see clearly a long and happy life ahead of me full of love and other people and fairies and gardens and challenge. This is – or it could be even better – the rest of my life.

My community will be in beautiful country near London. I will be contented enough to want to stay there for the rest of my life as my home. Beautiful house – environment inside house – vegetable garden, flower garden, lawn, pool, trees, stream – people who care about

181

such things and believe, allow, encourage, fairies, Spirit, Goddess, witches, God, Tarot and Tai Chi, living, doing, reading, feminism, liberation, spirituality, theology . . .

Belief in many keys to enlightenment – healing – really good vegetarian cooks – tolerance to meat, tolerance to sex, tolerance to genius – fun kids with good parenting – open to each other in physical sex hugs sister/brother way but not in and out of beds – not open relationships that destroy other people – sensitivity to sound – intruding on others – nice music – meditation room – dancing, lots of different workshops – prepared to spend time together working on things – don't mind losing face, looking a fool, being crazy, daring, having a go.

Passionate concern to help the world clear up some of its muddles but with fun and joy.

People really love and challenge me – I am fit, healthy, alive, full of all my senses, mental, spiritual, physical, alive, cherish myself – really, really happy and enjoying giving and being with other people and the world and being on my own – seeing clearly without fear – always ready to take on something new – outgoing, ready to let go, unafraid, ready to experience – JenJoy, New, New and New, Life expanding newly . . .

The night has been tiring again. The fool wakes me. She dances around the circle which is nothing. Naught, the hole or the whole, the beginning and the completion, emptiness and fullness, centre and circumference. At the centre there is stillness. At the circumference there is the dance, endlessly circling in and out of life. The fool is at the centre and at the same time dances with the whole dance of life. She whirls and dreams, and jokes and sings, and cries through every aspect of it. She is the vital spark of childself. She reaches out to touch everything. She lives intensely through every sense.

In the night she takes yesterday's turbulent up and down of infinity two-and-eight state. She turns it so that the infinity sign, the eight on its side, becomes the circle. I rest in the centre of her circle. I am still in the night darkness. Childself begins to bubble. This is for the third day. Number three. From the union between two is born a third. JenJoy. Childself watches the fool and is gathered into her dance. And there at the centre of the circle is the tree of life; the tree of knowledge. Its apple is a melon, soft and succulent and golden. Fool tastes the melon. She gives it to childself. There is plenty. There is enough for everyone. The golden flesh folds into my mouth, into my flesh. I breathe its sweet flavour. It shimmers through my veins. I want to share it, to give it to other people.

Memories echo. Shadows seize upon pieces of melon. They rush away and hide and hoard. Fearful over-shoulder glances crouch and clutch in hard corners. Hands turn into claws that fight and grab. I watch the golden melon ripped and torn like a tumble of bleeding bodies. Tears break from my eyes. 'No!' I shout. 'It doesn't need to be like that. There is plenty. There is enough for everyone. The source never runs dry.'

I turn back into the circle. I taste the melon. I fool will share it with you fool. I think how I want to share it. I want to draw and sing and walk and dance and be with other people. I want to share with the other people who now sleep around me in the house. I want to draw them out of their selves into a celebration of life and each other. I want to have fun with them.

I draw three magic mushrooms and a circle. I write all the things I want to share all over the paper. Finding, painting, gambolling, seeking, teasing, skipping, singing, hiding, giving, touching, laughing, fun, drawing, writing, tasting, loving, joy, hopping. I call it inspiration. I draw a dancing path round the paper in and out of the words. I write Welcome Today. Are you coming too? It is an invitation to dance with the fool. I will put it on my door in the morning.

The fool dances with the seventy-seven cards of the Tarot. Each card holds its own essence of some life experience. She lifts each in turn, whisks and turns it, vanishes into it and reappears. She pulls out its meaning. She dances on laughing, leaving it to lie waiting for its next revitalization.

It is day three. I wake up. I reach for the invitation to make today a happy fool's day. I am eager to celebrate myself and everyone else. I ask Janet to put my happy fool's day invitation on my door for people to read. She goes out to get my breakfast.

Janet brings porridge with honey and warm honey milk. I flavour the milk with a little brandy. I hear quarrelling voices passing down the corridor out of the front door. It slams. In the garden they are shouting at each other. From the conservatory I hear low intense voices. Another couple are arguing out their differences.

Today is the day of the fool. Today I am three days old. I want to rejoice with all you people. I want you to be happy. The wind hurls a spatter of rain against the window. The early sun has clouded over. Yesterday I stayed in bed. Today I want to get up and move. But I do not. Why? I am afraid that I will not be able to. I fear that I can't walk far. My inner self knows that I can get up, I can walk, I can get upstairs and have a bath. The memory of Wednesday's weakness fills me. It saps my willpower. It weighs heavily in all my limbs. I feel trapped in my bed. Later I say to myself, 'I will get up soon.' I lie back against the pillows, held by inertia. I gaze round the room. The comfortable chairs are so far away across the room. My wheelchair, some four feet away, is across a chasm of effort. The door is three yards away. It takes me through to independence. In mind I go out of it. My mind will not make my body do it.

Today I want a bath. Annabelle comes in. 'I'd like to have a bath. I know I can get upstairs and get in and out of the bath. I've done it recently. But I would feel safer if I had somebody with me as I do it. Would you have time for that this morning?' Her face is still. She does not look at me. 'I don't know. I'll ask the others,' she says in a flat voice. She goes out. I wait for a long time. I hear low voices down the corridor. She returns. 'I think it's better if you wait for the district nurse to come.' Inwardly I fume. What are they afraid of? Their fear is making me afraid. Of course I can get upstairs. Why don't I just go on my own? I think of Barbara. Elderly and arthritic, she does exactly as she wishes. No one stops her. She wouldn't let them. I remember myself being overconcerned on her behalf. She took no notice, just carried on. Nobody would stop her doing as she wished. Other people's fear on my behalf is stopping me doing what I want to do. I am letting them.

The district nurse comes. She sits on the bed and holds my hand. 'They say you want a bath. Well, I've looked at the stairs and they are steep. If you fell I would be legally responsible, and so would they. I can't take the risk. I'm sorry.' I start crying. 'I understand your position. All right, I'll just have a wash.' She washes me in hot water at the wash basin. I can't stop crying. 'I've just realized other people stop me living. I let them, too. When they are afraid for me, when they don't help me stretch myself, they are denying me life. You see, I could walk along the corridor all right. I could easily have got upstairs. But I let their fear prevent me.' She turns her attention from rubbing my back to look at me. 'Yes, I think I understand.' 'It's not just me that condemns me to death – other people do. They think I've got an incurable disease. They won't believe in my healing. They won't allow for the unexpected, the miraculous. I didn't realize people give me healing, but people kill me with their fears and disbelief. And I have let them do it. I have done it myself to other people. People who have given me healing.' 'Yes, I think I know what you are talking about.' She walks with me, clean and fresh and dressed, back to my room. On the way past my door I take down the invitation to share a happy fool's day.

I wake up first thing after last night's strange sleep and some worrying yesterday. I know that I need one affirmation. When I wake today, the voice in my head says 'It's all right, JenJoy' and the affirmation rains softly in the morning light. The rooks cackle off into their day. Janet comes in and I tell her I realize my Mum gave me this affirmation when I was a child. Thank you, Mum. But she also gave me Top of the Class – I've been trying to be Top of the Class – best, first, or a terrible failure – all my life, and winning, and winning. All I need to do is be just average.

Then David comes in to say goodbye from him and Ramadu. He brings me the rest of his father's posh brandy as a gift and a crystal in a little bag too. This is perfect. The crystal can hang round my neck with the affirmation inside. Janet goes to get me a cup of tea. Shona said to me once, 'You don't have to worry, Mum. Things just fall into your hands all the time.' The pattern unfolds, and I'll carry on learning, and maybe perfecting can drive me and failure can balance me.

Margaret asked me what had been the most healing thing for me. Today I realize it is just being average. The Japanese potter will not allow a perfect pot. If it is thought too beautiful they will mark it with a fingerprint lest it offend the deity.

. . . it is scientifically proven that white cells in the blood increase after relaxation. I am allowing mine to. When I shit and pee I shit and pee cancer-illness and let it go, let all the waste go. When I cry the tears take away junk. When I eat, drink, I take in life from the earth, good and wholesome and healing and cleansing, feeding the life cells of my body, regenerating new life. Nothing harms me, everything I take in gives me life. The tablets provoke healing, set a trend of life; the tablets, the chemotherapy, the operations, the radiotherapy and eye stuff, everything from the hospital gives me life. Nothing of the earth can harm me.

Today I am five days old
Count my blessings
Set myself
forward
target regularly
little
and big
Always something
to look forward to

FIVE OF SWORDS
THE POISON
is the
ANSWER
THE
DRUGS
KILL
and
GIVE LIFE
to
PROVOKE
SYNTHESIS
WHOLENESS
FROM CENTRE
IT
STINGS THE MIND
into
ACTION
OR I
can sleep
if I
want to

Six days old. Balance, harmony, victory, pattern, fall into place. Everything and nothing and in between – the opposites, the balance and the synthesis. It's all inside me. I've done it all. I've even died and I can be dead now for a little, and it's all right, I wake up again. Somehow I fell asleep last night. Nothing really did matter. Something about this 'I' that's doing all the living – *I* matter to me now. All the rest is around me, revolves around me; I get pulled out into other people (what they want, think, if I'm hurting them, if they love me, if I offend them, if they reject me). *I*'m doing my living now for me, and my dying. *I* inside the great whole of Beingness. That's all I can do as I live this life . . . For me to dance my dance of life and death and nothing everything – for me to do this happily – I do care about you too. But ultimately it's OK to let go and just be I . . .

Where are my pens? I had three. None of them can I find. I hunt in the bed clothes, under the pillow, on the table, by the side of the bed. And what has become of the papers I've been writing on? They can't possibly have disappeared. Has somebody moved them? I pull my heavy body about trying to find them. Things keep disappearing. The bedding is in a muddle. Where have they gone? I want them. How can they have vanished?

A voice speaks in my head. Calm down, JenJoy. Panicking won't find your pens and papers. Sit still and meditate. When you have been still and calm then the lost things will find themselves easily.

I sit on the edge of the bed. I hear the wind stir in the trees outside. The sun shines warm on my face. I allow stillness and quietness to seep through me. The tensions in my mind and body melt away. An image grows within me. I am a flower. I am the centre of the flower, the tangle of fine filaments, the stamen. I am my consciousness and unconsciousness at the centre of myself. Three petals spread round the centre. One petal is body, another is spirit, the third is mind. They hold my central being in this world. Around the three petals are eight more petals. Four of them are for the goddess, four for the god. They represent the four aspects of the goddess and the god, the four phases of the moon. There is the waxing moon, the daughter, youth and virginity. The full moon is the mother, the mature woman. The waning moon is the crone, the wise old woman. The moon passing through darkness is the hidden aspect, the unknown, the passage from life through death to life again. The petals of the goddess and the god are the cycles of life and death we all move through. Each aspect I know in myself and those around me as we live life as the goddess and the god.

Around the eight petals are the ten sepals, the ten figures, the hands that hold the flower. They are one to ten, the basis of the magic of numerology.

I am my flower. I am centred in it, whole and complete. Around me is a glow of golden light. The great spirit that holds me. Beyond that is the rich darkness of mother earth beneath me, and the vast darkness of the starry universe above me. I offer myself in praise.

Slowly I come back to myself. I feel the weight of my body sitting on the bed. I feel the soles of my feet in contact with the floor. I feel the rough texture of the blanket under the palm of my hands. The wind stirs the whispering trees outside. The sun warms my face.

Of her flower, JenJoy says: 'After many years of searching for my real faith I find this flower. It makes sense for me as my own vision of eternity. My search comes from feeling broken as a woman in my life by a male God and a male-dominated world. I could not find myself in this world. My very woman body seemed to be rejected by it or just not seen, or there to be used or battered. I could not find the voice of faith that I used to know and love and talk and pray to. My search through feminism, feminist theology, politics, liberation theology, has brought me here to this flower. I am still discovering it. I wanted to discover myself as a woman in the world and find a way to understand and love and live with men. I wanted to relate deeply with women. This vision all comes from a process I have been living through the very cells of my body.'

I find one pen under the sheet, another on the floor, the third under the pillow. My papers are there beside the bed. I pull the bed clothes straight. Order is restored.

It is night. The people of the day have gone away. I am on my own for the next few hours whatever they may bring in sleep or wakefulness. I pour myself a little brandy. I sip the amber liquid. It washes warm around my mouth and down my throat. I contemplate the room. I smell the strange sweetness of the cactus flower beside me. Pink petals hold the golden mass of strands in the central cup. The fragile flower stretches out from the fat and solid spiny cactus plant.

I turn off the light and settle down to sleep.

I am in the dark streets of the town. Someone is with me. We hurry along the cobbled road. We go into a shop, a Chinese supermarket. We are buying food. I want to buy pretty things. We are buying vegetables, spinach, chinese leaves, potatoes. I want to spend money on little silk purses and tiny parasols made of paper and small lacquered boxes. I want them to give as gifts for my friends. There is not enough time for this, or enough money.

We are going through a derelict area. The streets are empty. They are littered with rubble. It is dark, only lit by the occasional yellow glare of a street lamp. The buildings are tumbled empty shells. I am in the middle of fallen buildings. I go down some dark stairs into a small dark room under the ground. There is a dank foetid odour. The door is shut. I am alone. I begin to wake. A voice in my head says, 'No, JenJoy, you can't wake up in this terrible place. Carry on dreaming till it comes out better.'

I am under the earth, deep under the sequoia tree at Gilletts. The soft red soil holds my body. A wholesome smell of humus fills me. I feel myself letting go of my flesh. I melt and become one with the earth. My physical being is reabsorbed into the soil. I am releasing freely what has been given to me. My life flows out into the trees, into the plants, into the flowers. I am at one with mother earth.

I am in my body. It feels fresh and new. I am in the house at Gilletts. I am telling people about the vision of my flower. I show it to them, this flower growing amongst grass centred in this place. Someone says, 'Yes, I see it. I understand.' She shows me her flower – it is different. It grows in the wild hills. Another person shows me her flower. It is different again. It grows in the jungle. A third person shows me his flower growing in the desert. I know that there are many

189

different flowers growing in many different places. We share our magic, the flowers of our faith.

I've nearly died – what happened? At the end I was being sick every two hours. I was drinking pints, peeing pints, nearly incontinent and not getting rid of the poisons. I was getting weaker daily.

Here I am now – I've come through. I am alive. Caroline has just come back from the Sudan.

'There were little babies who hadn't eaten for so long they couldn't hold a teaspoon of food down. We had to feed them by the tube until they could eat again.'

And then what happens to them? Thousands of starving children. These are the ones we know about, the ones we hear about.

Lalla visited the free trade zone in Sri Lanka. By special arrangement some of the young girls agreed to talk to her. They earned a tiny amount of money. The working hours were long. The dyes used in the jeans they made were poisonous.

Mary John worked with the very poor in the Philippines. They are so poor and yet they are so happy. They sing and dance and laugh. 'You are so miserable here in Europe.'

My body is healing now. I travel with you starving children, you working girls, you laughing Filipinos. Let us find a way to hear, to live, to laugh together.

Nigel gives us breakfast. Shona here with me sleeping since Sunday. Heather comes in. I tell her about the dream. They are going chopping wood. Would love to go to the woods. But too tired. Pat gives me a back and foot massage. It releases a lot. But I am finding it hard to relax. Why am I so tense? What is happening? Today is seven. Unbalancing factors thrown in. And that is today. Arrival of letters.

I receive Linda's proposal for this book. Sexuality and all the forbidden daring words spring out at me. Do I qualify to write for this book? I ask myself. Am I sexual enough? I feel life tingling and dancing in every cell, but should I be bursting with sexual sensations? Am I? Is what I feel sexual? Perhaps it is. I reflect on the past few months. My body was a painful struggling weight to drag around. It held me in its grip of vomiting and inability to eat, of constant drinking, constant peeing. Increasingly it bound me to the house, to my bed. In those last weeks I held me in a miserable dark hole under the sheets. I could scarcely reach the warm touch of other human beings.

Dying drew me apart from most joyful physical experience. It isolated me from interaction with other people. I was too ill to reach them. Much of what I was experiencing was too alien and disturbing for them to reach me. I still followed the fine silver thread of my faith but it was frail; where it led was uncertain and unknown. Coming back from death is a powerful bursting out from this fading, shrinking self. I rediscover every physical sense in ecstasy. I learn to walk, to eat, to see. Every new physical exertion a victory. People are fascinating flowers, beautiful, exciting, frightening. They are open for my adventures of discovery. My spirit expands like a mist absorbing all sensations, reaches out into every cell of my body. I touch and mingle with other people. I stretch out into trees and grassy earth. I sink without fear into the arms of the starry universe. I rest in the breath of life. Where does sexuality come into this? I haven't had a sexual partner of any sort for months. Do I qualify to talk about sex? I can't separate it off from this whole physical emotional social spiritual experience. I ponder sexual feelings. I sense the touching vivid contact of body with body. I recall the intense spoken and unspoken conversations. I relive the blending of my spirit with another as we unfold into each other's caring. This cannot be confined to one level of intensity or one person. It happens to me in many different levels with many different people. It happens in a shared smile with a stranger on the tube. It happens in tall redwood trees, and the stretching talons of cats. It happens in a talk with women friends. It happens in a moment of laughter after a serious meeting. It happens with secret pools of water with the bank of white daisies tossing in them, where dragon-flies drift, and the mythical dragon who slumbers then spreads her wings to fly through the images of my mind. Sexuality weaves its colours in and out of the whole fabric of my life.

I reread Linda's proposal. I reflect on my experiences with women. So far I'm a failed lesbian. All my successful sexual experience has been with men. Or can I say that? One divorced, one dead, one unwilling to leave Germany to live with me, one with multiple relationships setting woman against woman.

But women who read this now, I don't feel a failure. Please don't blame me if I've had most of my visceral sexual experience with men. Now I hear a pleading in my voice, a slight whining. I'm trying to know what I am sexually. Most of my friends are women. I love

191

women. I love to talk with them, discover them, sleep with them, share massage with them. I am loved by women. They heal me, they give me meals, they wash my sheets, they nurse my sick body. They listen to my anger at men and a broken, male world. They hold me when I cry. I learn and am brought back to life by women.

Letters from home come with Silvia – from my women's writing group. Such love and greetings. They are together in a railway cottage working and sharing – one of them in hospital – wheelchaired – I know what that is like. My bank balance – what a relief. Money has been a muddle. Hard to keep track of when ill. Dan and Silvia – I tell my story of death and rebirth this week. I cry and cry. It's been terrifying. They support me. Shona listens too. All these new factors thrown in today upset the harmony of yesterday, day six.

Day eight. Balance – two-and-eight, late, wait, fate, hate. Into the darkness again to find – *Review* – what has happened in the past year, two years, six years? Why did I nearly die so recently after one year ago I was given life? Why did I so nearly let it go when I chose to return?

1 *Despair*, deep dark despair that I am never going to be able to get out of this, to get better, to share deeply with another person.
2 *Loneliness*; I want to be really close to someone sexually and emotionally as well as enjoy lots of other people.
3 *Unreleased fury* at my environment.

A dream – I am in a bedroom upstairs in a house. There are women around me. They are saying, 'When you have lost a baby you need to mourn it. When you have lost your lover as well, you need to mourn them.'

'I have lost a baby and its father,' I say. 'The baby miscarried – I never saw him. I am divorced from his father. It was my choice, but a piece of my life gone. I have a double mourning to go through.'

I am lying on the bed. The women are all around me. They hold me. 'You're doing fine. You'll be all right.' Groans wave through my body, burst out of my mouth. Grinding energy contracts rhythmically down through my belly. I wake up groaning loudly. Shona is in her bed across the room. She wakes too, and rushes to me. 'Mum, you all right?' 'Yes, yes it's a dream,' I gasp. The sound builds until something lets go. The energy is released between my legs. The pain, the mourning is out into the world. I weep. 'It's all right, Shona, it's

192

good. Such a relief,' I gasp. 'It feels like I've let go of so much. What a strange dream. I hope I didn't wake everyone up, making all that noise.'

Shona hugs me. I let my sobs out until I'm done. 'It was partly about separating from your dad. But it was also about that miscarriage I had some years ago. Do you remember – it was last year [1984] when the bone cancer in my hip and spine bones was very severe and I was dying – Joyce was giving me an osteopathic treatment? She said, "I think that baby you miscarried is still around. I think it's something to do with the illness. You need to deal with it." I didn't know how to. I had dismissed it because it was deformed and cancerous. I was unable to see it as real.

'Earlier this year I had a strange experience in therapy. I felt like a cell before conception. Then the cell was provoked into growth by the invasion of the sperm. It was painful – I was breaking, being broken into a thousand pieces. I was split up from my peaceful unity.

'This concept of conception disturbed me. I told Joyce about it. "Do you remember, a year ago, I told you that miscarried baby was still around?" she asked. This idea was a revelation. "I'll have to find a way to work this one out."

'That night I had a dream. I was behind the curtain on the balcony of a school theatre. Lecky my living son and my other son Stephen were at the school. Stephen was fair haired and plump. He was very sensitive. Lecky understood him. He protected him because he knew he was rather special. Stephen was in the concert. I didn't want him to see me because I was very ill. I didn't want to upset him. Stephen's class was singing an old song about the seasons. He knew what it meant. The real meaning was much deeper than the words. He could see that people didn't see this. He was getting more and more frustrated by their ignorance. On the last verse he could contain himself no longer. He cried and ran off the stage. He was very upset. The staff went to him. Lecky went to him. I went to him. I was aware of what was going on because I live in both worlds.

'I woke up. Stephen is my miscarried child. What should I do for him? Then I knew – I was going to my healer, Matthew Manning, that day. Matthew would be able to help Stephen. He would teach him how to use his gifts. How could I take Stephen to Matthew? I thought of a special stone from Iona. It was white with speckles of the green tears of St Columba in it. It sat comfortably in the palm of my hand. The stone would carry Stephen to Matthew. I would ask

Matthew to keep Stephen in his stone in his healing room. And that is what I did. Stephen stone is still there, learning healing.'

I need to pee again. I am slightly incontinent. Can't quite get to the loo – probably a question of the shelf life of the Desmopressin hormone. I will start a new bottle tomorrow – that one is almost finished. I hope the other bodies are fresh. This all drives me into these questions. I face the possibilities again:

1 I may still die quite soon in a not very nice way. I have already experienced some of the grim possibilities.
2 Again I face my recent fading with death and how unaware I was that it was creeping up on me. The Dark of the Moon, the hidden aspect.
3 I may go on with this up and down for a long time. It may be my work – perhaps it is a way of serving other people, to provoke these questions in their lives, to come close to them in my experiences as I do.
4 I may need Desmopressin always. It may stop working. Or it won't – work out the implications of that.
5 Review my attitude to hospital – the fact is, radiotherapy may be responsible for knocking things out in my pituitary, and has maybe made things worse – don't know. Hard to keep a balance. Need to insist no absolutes are put on me by doctors – no nevers or inevitables; only possibles about anything at all. Must talk to them each time.

I AM A FIGHTER – A WARRIOR – QUEEN BOADICEA – I WILL WIN.

. . . I spend a day of clear-mindedness with Shona and Lecky. Lie in the sun with them as I sense the earth smelling close and sweet. My body came from this. Talk to Shona about the possibility of my death. She knows the fear from when she was a child, afraid of the bomb, fireworks and the world. Talk to Pet, Janet and Sally of emergency – should I get ill here – they feel it's OK. They aren't afraid I'll die. Last thing, we circle dance. I watch – beautiful, healing. Learn to play the Cantankerous Old Bitch some more – shout and yell and laugh at Sally, 'I want the curtains shut. Shut the bloody curtains.' She will not. I yell and demand and yell. She does in the end, laughing too – I feel full of energy and life. I do the same with Silvia and we laugh – I want my hot water bottle – it's lost? So much distress with asking, asking all the time, and now I'm learning to ask positively – and thinking clearly what I want every minute knowing what to ask for.

But I'm a Cantankerous Old Bitch so I know how. Because I am determined to live.

Talking with Janet and Peter about ponding – the life abundant that stirs and fights under the surfaces. The dead mole, soft-furred, little digging claws. Richard comes in and says, 'Come to the conservatory if you want to see the fungus' – I go. Boletus and funnel cap – and another – edible, smells sweetly of funnel cap. I meet Rain – doing surgery, a doctor, psychologist, psychotherapist, training now in osteopathy – extraordinary man – a man of faith with many experiences of miracle and much knowledge of cancer and all the drugs I use. Today I wrote the questions I wanted to ask the doctor – having stipulated the doctor answer me caringly – here is a doctor who knows a lot of what I want to know and is able to give me my answers. This is how my life works. Everything that I need comes to me as I need it. I will live because I choose to live, because others support me in that choice, and because divine grace aids my fight. I will live in joy. It almost seems the current trends of belief affect the belief of the one who's fighting for their life, and they fall from unbelief and thrive on belief. And yet I don't really believe many of us go round expecting anyone will die, so it must be I choosing.

Story from Rain as a young doctor. A man close to death of brittle bone disease. The top three bones of his vertebrae shown completely crumbled on X-Ray. He got dropped when turned – an accident. He cardiac arrested. Then lived! He was technically incapable of it. He was lucid – described the experience as being bathed in golden light. In no pain. Died two days later with his sister by him, in great peace. So, grace? Extraordinary!

I am nine days old. Shona and Lecky are sitting with me in my room. Shona is reading. Lecky doesn't know what to do. I am called to the phone.

As I talk on the phone I hear their voices raised. I try to listen to Lindsay on the phone. I need to talk to her. I hear Shona shouting out. Lecky's voice is loud and heavy. I talk to Lindsay. I will not be drawn away. They are banging around in my room. Shona shoots down the passageway sobbing. Perhaps she has gone to find Silvia.

When I return to my room Lecky is sitting there. He is drawing.

'What happened?' I ask.

'Shona was provoking me. She was singing.'

'Oh, Lecky,' I sigh. 'Come and talk with me.'

'Why? You always blame me. Why should I?'

'Come on.'

'Oh, all right.'

He comes and sits by me. I look at him – this baby son now grown almost six feet into a graceful, strong male body with a deep voice. This young male full of powerful animal energy. I look at him and see his uncertainty, his gentleness. I see the little child who loves life. I see him caught in this male body, in this macho, male world. I see him surrounded by the jibes and jeers of other boys. They compete to show their growing manliness. They try to rival each other being the tough men they see all around them in the adult world.

Poor child. I know he doesn't want to be like that. I reach out to his hands and hold them.

'Lecky, I love you very much,' I say. He looks up at me. 'You know that, don't you?'

Those elfin brown eyes look steadily. I see the scar on his nose from the rugger scrum.

'Yes, Mum, I know you love me.'

'I've always loved you. I wanted to have you. There was love in your making. When you were born you were hungry. You were sticking your fists in your mouth, sucking. I fed you straight away. Your Dad and I rejoiced to see this tiny red thing with a big nose.' He laughs.

'I know it's hard, Lecky. We all get angry sometimes – murderous rage tears through all of us. Times I could have killed. It's part of us all. We can hurt and damage people weaker than ourselves. I remember times when you two were little and I could have shaken you to death. I had to stop myself – run away into the bathroom and hang onto the sink and cry – go and talk it out with my friend Pauline later on.

'Well, you know if the anger gets out of control it only leads to trouble for ourselves – you've had that at school, haven't you?'

'Yes, I've had to learn there. There was one time I was getting into fights all the time. I had no friends. I had to stop myself – pull myself out of it. I managed to do that. I'm much better now. I've got some good mates. I've learnt to manage with the others. But Shona really provokes me. I hate her. She does it on purpose.'

'I used to hate my sister – siblings – it's the hardest one. I suppose in a world where everyone else seems to be putting on us, a sister or brother might be the only one who seems like our equal to fight it out with. That's hard, because a sister or brother could be a friend or ally against all the rest. That would be a lot better.

'Why I find it really hard to take is that you are a boy – almost a man – and Shona is a girl. I can't bear the male violence side of it. I've been damaged and broken myself by it. You know – you've seen it. That's what stirs me up. I know you're trying to deal with this. I value that. Because I love you, I can't bear to see it in you. I am trying to hear your side, now, and listen to how it feels for you.'

'Yes, Mum, I know.'

'I want you to try and find some other ways of dealing with it. Please try if you can – for your own sake. You've seen how it hurt your father to lose control. You've had it yourself at school.'

Mum arrives at five-ish with Ian, who takes Shona and Lecky back. Sit telling stories. Mum talking of her past. Heather, Pat, Silvia coming in and chatting – then Heather and Dan and Sally come in with about five vases of flowers for me – roses, marigolds, phlox. They put them all round the room. And they bring little presents from people in the community – a picture of flowers, a poem that fits perfectly where I am, two little shells, a pine cone, and some leaves from the sequoia tree. Pat gives me a little embroidered bookmark. I am overwhelmed with the love flowing towards me. Dan and Silvia put me to bed – now I am feeling much better – still heavy, but the diarrhoea has stopped and my peeing is under control again, not too much and not too little.

Day ten – I slept wonderfully and wake refreshed. Am feeling a more natural part of the normal world. Powerful sexual dreams last night.

POSTSCRIPT

On Wednesday 12 February 1986, JenJoy became suddenly very weak with a chest infection and was taken into hospital. She died peacefully in the early hours of Friday the 14th, surrounded by a small circle of family and friends. She asked in her Will that her funeral be a celebration, and that we should use the sevenfold Cretan maze whose spiral turnings represented her journey to the still centre where the soul can pass between the worlds. The 14th of February was once a Feast of Love, and survives because, in spite of the commercialization and easy sentiment, we still need a day when the heart is open to give and receive love. Fourteen days after her death, around two hundred people came to say goodbye to JenJoy in a quiet avenue of simple graves on Wanstead Flats, and to celebrate her life. Before we laid her in the earth, we wove a dance of our love around her in three concentric circles, singing the Taizé chant 'Adoramus Te Domine', and watching that still centre into which she passed. We read her own words: 'I dreamt of an avenue of trees up which I must travel. It is cluttered with dead trees and new saplings and brambles. All around me friends are rapidly clearing the avenue, the brambles are cleared, the dead trees are being burned, the saplings replanted in suitable places, the grass is being made clear and wide and soft, the flowers now have more room to grow and bloom freely and fill the air with a wild perfume . . . My avenue is now free to travel along, free and beautiful, an avenue along which to dance and sing to the place where the spring water tastes better than any I have tasted before.'

19

LET YOUR RIGHT BRAIN KNOW

1 Not so long ago
   I heard that science has taken to poetic metaphor
   in describing the human brain.

2 The brain, they declare
   has hemispheric functions,
   has hemispheric bilateral functions
   preconditioned by one's sexual orientation.

3 a Do not despair – this is a poem, not a lesson
      in neurophysiology.
      Poets need to look at, to use
      Big words sometimes
   b (or stroke mute life longings into words of tongued honey)

4 Here below, the Bilateral Functions:

LEFT (MALE) BRAIN	RIGHT (FEMALE) BRAIN
Intellectual	Intuitive
Detailed	Holistic
Logical	Spatial
Controlled	Emotional
Dominant	Passive
Worldly	Spiritual
Active	Receptive
Analytic	Gestalt
Perception of Significant Order	Perception of Abstract Patterns

5 Attempt the following test:

Draw nine circles. Thank you.

Did you draw your circles clockwise?

Or counterclockwise?

Or a combination of the two?

You say you don't remember?
(Which side of the brain forgets?)

If you penned nine clockwise circles you are they say, right brain
dominant –

If counterclockwise, you are left brain dominant.

If you did both you are both. Well done.

And if you believe this you'll believe anything.

On the Common at the Greenham fence
We are in right brain land.
(see list above)
The outside we are on is the right side.
The inside they are in is the left side.

Drill march left right left right.   Halt.

Quite frequently
        we from the outside which is the right side
manage to observe
at close quarters
those on the inside which is the left side.

And we are so serious.
    We move,
    quicksilver
    through the woods
    between the rocks
    around the perimeter
    under the fence
        up the trees
        onto the silos
        through the barriers.
    Beyond the pale.

If there is magic about us,
(read intuitive, holistic, spiritual, gestalt)
It is this: we know what the left brain is doing.
Here, in our right brain Greenham laboratory
is a rejection of illegitimate boundaries,

the centering point for a new equation.

Linda Hurcombe

Photo: Greenham Common. Dancing on the Silos, 1st January 1983. Photo by Raissa Page.

V

FEMINIST THEOLOGY

FROM CASTING A NEW CIRCLE

(jesus
you are in my bones and dreams and memories
i prayed to you when i learned to pray
i learned what god was like by your life
i felt your presence as the presence of god in my life
i touched god in you

jesus . . .

i do not think we are called to elevate him
but to be like him
not to be what he was
but to be what we are
to be like him in that we manifest
the unique sacrament of god/ess that we are
and we are all related . . .

Mykel Johnson

A JEALOUS GOD?
Towards a Feminist Model of Monogamy

Susan Dowell

Marriage and monogamy begin inauspiciously in myth and history, in the overthrow of the Mother and anger of the gods. In the Classic Greek Paradise Lost, Zeus creates the treacherous, beautiful Pandora to punish (male) humanity for receiving the stolen goods of fire – technology and power. Because they would be as gods. A custom-built version of the Mother-goddess, Allgiver and allgiven, Pandora is made over as wife to Epimetheus. Chaos, evil and finitude are loosed on the world through her power and her demotion.

Only after the Fall is Eve acknowledged as powerful and primal in the Judeo-Christian account. She is named 'mother-of-all-that-lives' in that conscious time before she tastes her First Curse and brings forth her children of sorrow out of her desire for Adam and of his rule over her. Here too, it is in her appearance as wife that woman is first the curser and the accursed of man.

Engels's version tells us that the 'origin of monogamy as far as we can trace it among the most civilized and highly developed people of antiquity . . . was not in any way the fruit of individual sex love, with which it had nothing in common. On the contrary it appears as the subjection of one sex by another, as the proclamation of a conflict entirely unknown in pre-historic times.'[1]

Speaking here of marriage and fidelity in biblical terms I am not choosing the story I 'agree with' or even prefer intellectually as the truest reflection of our origins. Only an expanding understanding of women's experience can illuminate these or any other patriarchal texts. 'The past provides us only with a dark mirror on which to throw our images but (Prehistory) yields no developed texts by which to verify our imagination. Better then to claim that imagination as our own.'[2] My preference for the Bible is relative and, of course, culturally conditioned. I can wander here in some ease. But there's something else – emotional, instinctive.

The Hebrew Testament elects to speak our prehistory in human rather than epic language. I like this stubborn particularity. Adam and Eve, watched over by God, share and tend the garden before the Fall, or, in Engels's version, until patriarchy and property rights arise to bring about the descent of Eve and the brutalization of Adam. Eve brings Adam no gifts but her womb, her desire and her thirst for knowledge.

I can, as they say, relate to that. And her desire was with God, from the beginning with the knowing. I need a religion that takes this early me *seriously*, as well as the sullen, confused woman. I want the promised, impossible happy ending, the Quest, armed only with a protective handful of magic apple seeds. The elegant stories of classical mythology don't give me that. Only the men get that, the heroes (they do in Judeo-Christianity too but they aren't *supposed* to. There's a bluff to call somewhere).

Monogamy, the foundational precept of Christian sexual morality, is based in one central explicit teaching of Jesus; that the redeemed order reflects God's original plan in Eden. Woman and man are restored to one another and to God. The two become one flesh and cannot be put asunder. While the church has enthusiastically promoted this teaching it has done so within a totally androcentric anthropology. The influential teachers of the church, seeing men's rule over women as 'natural', have projected it backwards in time to an establishment in the original order of creation. So long as Eve is anchored to the old order by this one thread, all the others – the desire, the sorrow and her children – twist and tangle around it, binding with briars her joys and desires, taking them farther and farther from God. In this tangle of curse and promise lies the grievous confusions and blindness of western model traditions. And so I urge a re-evaluation of monogamy as crucial to a feminist reconstruction of Christianity. Until the unprecedented multidimensional critiques of this century's feminism, it has been impossible to declare a full-blooded feminist interest in monogamy.

Historically, it has been part and parcel of the best deal we can wrest from men. I want in this essay to look at some of the ways in which Christian tradition has misused the biblical concept of 'one flesh' fidelity: betrayed its promise of reconciling men and women and its mystery as a sign of God's covenant with humankind.

I want also to suggest that monogamy has fallen by the wayside of feminist sexual politics. Western feminism has, rightly and determinedly, investigated monogamy as a social construct of patriarchy but paid insufficient attention to its potential as an expression of a universal human need. I say this in fear and trembling. I have been horrified and discouraged, while gathering my thoughts for this chapter, at the plethora of pro-monogamy writings that have appeared in the Rightist press and glossies. Monogamy can be fun, fashionable and you don't get AIDS! Followed by unsavoury tips to spice up a jaded sexual palate. Inseparable, I feel, from other retrenchments, moral and economic, of a dying consumer culture.

Judeo-Christian tradition, and the later secular moral traditions which arose from it, have promoted monogamous marriage as the stable base of a civilized society. While few of the world's people have the time or energy left over from the struggle for existence to make abstract virtue of social necessity, monogamy continues to be upheld in the 'first world' as meeting two essential human needs: that of children for stability and continuity of care, and individuals' primary need for emotional security. As imposed by the church, monogamy claims the threefold authority of scripture, tradition and their combined grace of enriching social values with spiritual meaning. An accumulation of human wisdom. As a feminist I see wisdom and tradition as hijacked by patriarchy. We need to start the journey again, back in the myth with both on board and our own radar controls switched on.

It is often said that the church pays disproportionate attention to sex. I think this criticism is too sweepingly applied. It pays not too much but the wrong kind of attention. Stung, perhaps, by accusations of a prurient obsession with private parts, the dear old church has been cowed into abandoning its central sexual symbolism – and the task of expanding and transforming the symbols – and adopted the infinitely less enlightening idiom of sociology. Unhistorically, therefore dangerously. The sexual and political oppressiveness of the Born-Again Right claims the authority of scripture in its efforts to make the family 'strong again',[3] as if there were a biblical pedigree for the shrunken privatized unit that passes for 'family' today. Neither am I reassured by ernest, liberal ecclesiastical analyses of the changing patterns-of-marriage-today variety. These too are often shallow and shaky, as evidenced by the near universal and totally inaccurate claim that the church has somehow always been 'on the side' of

208

marriage and upheld a single standard of fidelity throughout. The ordering of human sexuality has been the church's most powerful and pervasive means of social control, but it has also shown a contradictory tendency to subvert this 'conformed to the world'-ness. Herein lies its sexual salvation.

Traditional scholarship acknowledges the biblical adoption of stories and symbols from the surrounding Mediterranean and Near Eastern religions, but does not always do justice to the changing sexual perceptions underlying these belief systems. The transition in the first millennium BC from maternal to male-dominated symbol systems is a universal (if mysterious) phenomenon, and one vital to our understanding of the struggles the Hebrew people had with their conquered and conquering neighbours.

Yahwist faith was one which both challenged and reinforced the surrounding cultures. The God of Israel was reputedly the first among his Near Eastern contemporaries to impose monogamy on his chosen people, and we see monogamous marriage, with its attendant double standard, arising in a particular way in Jewish thought, nevertheless on broadly similar sexist lines to the wider pattern.

Woman's journey from 'unfallen' primacy and sexual complementarity, whether seen in terms of a biblical Eden, a Marxist primitive communism or a romantic matricentrism, is one we know only in fragments. But let us imagine a feminist critic today, coming across the Old Testament for the first time. She would no doubt read in that aggressively phallocentric language glimpses of an even earlier male consciousness: one that had newly stumbled on the part played by His seed in the creation of life. In early Old Testament stories, Yahweh himself opens the 'barren' wombs of the patriarchs' long-suffering wives, acting on behalf of their mostly unfaithful husbands. No tricks, no disguises, no furtive visits in showers of gold. *Droit de Seigneur*.

Glimpses of a subversive plurality intrude briefly in Genesis. As pretext and prelude to the Flood, a catastrophe story of Babylonian origins, we hear of the birth of giants from a rape of the 'daughters of men' by the 'sons of God'. Patristic tradition was to change the rape to seduction, thus marking these fair, unfettered daughters as dangerous temptresses. Meanwhile, Yahweh, finding himself on the set of the wrong disaster movie, rages primadonna-ishly at his bit part in these quasi-Olympian antics and calls CUT!

And the Lord said, I will destroy man whom I have created from the face of the earth; both man, and beast, and the creeping thing, and the fowls of the air; for it repenteth me that I have made them.[4]

The 'real life' wives, daughters of the demoted Eve and unnamed in the mythic genealogies, are not promoted to extras. Mrs Noah and her 'sons' wives' are loaded with the beasts and baggage onto the Ark. Mrs N. didn't want to go, say the playwrights, preferring the perilous surge and the singing of her siren sisters. Drowned voices, sea changes. But there was no turning back for her. (Or later, for Mrs Lot!)

The watery chaos recedes and a sharper, clearer image slowly surfaces, as photographers' images do when lifted from their developing fluid.

Now we have real places on a real map – Ararat, Mamre, Jabbok. The first sign of God's covenant is visited on the male body of his people. With Abraham's circumcision God promises the Land of Canaan to Abraham's seed, promises to be on their side forever. No turning back, from the desert patriarch, wrestling man to man with angels and historic destiny, while She waits with more flocks, children and baggage on the riverbanks or eavesdrops at tent doors.

The Lord God of Israel is, on his own admission, a jealous God. He will have no others before him or on the side. He writes these laws in their hearts and on tablets of stone. Thou shalt have no other Gods; thou shalt not commit adultery. Keep taking the tablets. He is neither the husband or lover of any woman but takes to himself a people, a nation for his bride.

Although the patriarchal community was thus collectively imaged as female – a motif used to cloak a multitude of sexist sins to this day – the idea of conjugal fidelity as an image of God's continuing love appears only fragmentarily in early Hebrew consciousness. Rosemary Ruether describes its development as revealing the assimilation of the cultic language of the older Canaanite nature religion:

> Such symbolism . . . reverse the sacred marriage imagery of Sumerian, Babylonian and Canaanite religion. Here the goddess was the dominant divine figure, and the bridegroom (Baal) represented the King, the representative of the human community.[5]

But the patriarchal appropriation and reversal of this sacred marriage did not automatically 'take'. In the popular imagination, it would seem, Yahweh merely replaced Baal as consort to the Great

Mother. This didn't go down too well with the God of Abraham who had returned to this land of milk and honey and ancient cities in conquest. Not for this morganatic marriage had he brought his people out of slavery and the wilderness. The Bride/People Israel are castigated for resisting the exclusive claims of the male god by being depicted as a wayward harlot, as seen in the strange story of the prophet Hosea and Gomer.

Hosea, in an extraordinary amalgam of symbolic and biographical narrative, shows forth God's judgment for spiritual whoredom. Chastened and penitent, the faithless woman is restored to her rightful husband as a sign of God's mercy and supremacy: 'And I said unto her, Thou shalt abide with me many days; thou shalt not play the harlot, and thou shalt not be for another man: so will I also be for thee'.[6]

Sternness and judgment give way to ecstasy and delight in the Song of Songs. This poem, seen by many as the Holy of Holies of scriptural affirmation of human sexuality, owes its contended place in the canon to the fact that bride and lover were interpreted allegorically as Israel and God. This theme is developed in other wisdom literature and in extracanonical Jewish texts.[7] It was taken up by Paul in the New Testament, who taught that human marriage signifies the mystical union between Christ and the church.

But alongside the poetic and prophetic themes of the Old Testament stand the massive legal and historical passages. Feminist biblical scholarship has catalogued and categorized the pervasive denigration and scapegoating of women in the historical narrative. God's pledge to act as a tender faithful husband was not noticeably fulfilled by his creatures. There were few real-life ones! The sexual double standard was enshrined in the Law's countless concessions to male promiscuity, and in the unevenness of punishments for adultery, which was largely seen as a violation of male property rights, and so on and on.[8] I would only ask here which biblical manifestations of a sexual double standard still affect us today – that female virtue is still synonymous with chastity and fidelity? That love is to man a thing apart but woman's whole existence?

Worthy of note in an increasingly militarist/monetarist age is the biblical acceptance of wealth and power as passports to sexual privilege. King David, the Lord's Anointed, was a notorious adulterer, condemned as such when his 'theft' of Bathsheba was compounded by the murder of her husband, Uriah the Hittite.[9] But other such thefts go uncommented on – the unnamed multitudes of women, wives, mothers and daughters, swept off as battle booty. The kings and heroes are disgraced not for rape, cruelty and unfaithfulness, but for their single-minded passion for the dangerous outsider, as in the case of Samson and Delilah.[10] (Have as many as you like but keep them in line.)

The New Testament offers no new sexual ethic. The radical social iconoclasm of Old Testament prophecy is reasserted in Christ's teachings and applied directly to sex and class relations. Jesus, when pressed, tersely condemned adultery. The Mosaic divorce laws, he realistically said, were made for *man's* hardness of heart and the one-flesh promise of Eden is restored in the kingdom. Man and woman, joined by God, cannot be put asunder. Not shouldn't be. Can't be.[11] However, revolutionary new concepts of family and community arise in New Testament teaching. The idea of women being blessed and saved through childbearing is clearly condemned: when hearing the words, 'Blessed is the womb that bare thee and the breasts that gave thee suck,' Jesus answered, 'No, blessed rather is she who hears my words and keeps them.'[12] The primacy of the blood family as a religious and social unit is subverted, both in the words and deeds of Christ and in the ways the new church perceived and organized itself: ' "Who are my mother and brothers?" And looking on those who sat about him, he said, "Here are my mother and my brothers! Whoever does the will of God is my brother and my sister and my mother." '[13] All that believed were together, in a new kind of family, a community of equals in Christ. A woman's right to an autonomous spiritual and social identity was indeed Good News. And her desire shall *not* all be for a husband to rule over her.

Early Christian literature celebrated women as prophets and martyrs, teachers and leaders, married and single. However, a very particular heroism was accorded those women who spurned marital ties, as did Perpetua, martyred with the slave Felicity in North Africa in AD 203,[14] and those who refused to acknowledge pre-contracts and family pressure to marry, even risking their lives as fugitives from state and family authority. For example, Thecla, a young woman from Iconium, ran away to follow Paul.[15]

Sadly, this revolutionary option, along with other signs of female spiritual power and creativity, became circumscribed by the institutional church in the creation of a celibate/ascetic elite. As the celibate option was robbed of its subversive sting, so too was the Way of

Affirmation, indicated in I John 4:12: 'No one has seen God, but as long as we love one another God will live in us and His love will be complete in us.'

As the former way, the *Via Negativa*,[16] became exalted over the second, the once-creative tension between the two collapsed in a virulent sex-negativity and a repatriarchalization of marriage. Saying 'No' to the life of the senses was seen as a denial of its value and power.

So marriage was seen as a way not of receiving the gift of the body but of *submitting* to the flesh, to the curse of Eve and to the existing social order. Absent from biblical and post-biblical texts – a lack which the modern Bible Epic tries to fill in hopelessly idealized but sometimes quite touching ways – is any picture of the impact of incarnational faith on the sexual partnerships of ordinary people. Just *how* did these Christians love one another?

In his history of the holy spirit in the church,[17] Charles Williams refers to a 'lost experiment' which is partially indicated in Paul's first letter to the Corinthians (chapter 5). There had been an explosion of the spirit in the church at Corinth. They were a precocious lot, full of self-esteem, 'puffed up', seeing themselves as an elite. (Unlike many of their neighbour churches they enjoyed the 'glorious liberty of the children of God' in the very real, political sense of freedom from persecution.) Love not Law was the road to union with Christ. It is clear that the notorious burst of fornification condemned by Paul was far from being a backsliding lapse into hedonism. The ecstatic sexual expressions were inseparable from the immediacy and pre-eminence of Love itself and a desire to act upon it. The spirit cut across divisions of sex and property; so, for some marriage was seen both as a hindrance to the mystical union with Christ in the Body and incompatible with the new 'commonism' described in the book of Acts.[18]

Another, quite mysterious element of Williams's 'lost experiment' seems to have been along the lines of Gandhian 'Bramacharya',[19] which Williams sees as an attempt to deinstitutionalize sex undertaken by Christians within the traditional doctrine and morality of the church:

> It seems there was, in the first full rush of the Church, an attempt, encouraged by the Apostles, to 'sublimate'. But the experimenters probably did not call it that. The energy of the effort was in and towards the Crucified and Glorified Redeemer, towards a work of exchange and substitution, a union on earth and in heaven with that Love which was now understood to be capable of loving and of being loved. In some cases it

failed. But we know nothing – most unfortunately – of the cases in which it did not fail, and that there were such cases seems clear from St. Paul's quite simple acceptance of the idea. By . . . the third century the ecclesiastical authorities were much more doubtful . . . The great experiment had to be abandoned because of 'scandal' . . . The Prohibition was natural. Yet it seems a pity that the Church, which realized once that she was founded on a Scandal, not only to the world but to the soul, should be so nervously alive to scandals. It was one of the earliest triumphs of the 'weaker brethren', those innocent sheep who by mere volume of imbecility have trampled over many delicate and attractive flowers of Christendom. It is the loss, so early, of a tradition whose departure left the Church rather overaware of sex, when it might have been creating a polarity with which sex is only partly coincident. It failed, and it must be added that Paul's foresight was justified. The Church abandoned that method in favour of the marriage method, which he had deprecated and eventually lost any really active tradition of marriage as a way of the soul. This we have still to recover; it is, no doubt, practised in a million homes but it can hardly be said to have been diagrammatized or taught by the authorities. Monogamy and meekness have been taught instead.[20]

Instead of what? We cannot clearly tell from Williams's tantalizingly obscure, almost coy account. I have great difficulty in seeing *Bramacharya* – in any faith or century – as more than a spiritualized, phallocentric endurance test. But I'm passionately concerned to seek, here and now, alternatives to the 'meekness' that is assigned to monogamy in our culture. While recognizing the dangers of first-century romanticization, I do see possible parallels between our growing understanding of *female* libido – as diffuse, autonomous, multi-pleasured physicality – and these early Christian attempts to undercut social institutions constructed around male ideas of potency and orgasm.

To be honest, the church has failed, since this time, to attempt anything better. Paul came closest to founding a doctrine of marriage as a 'way of the soul' in his wider command that we glorify God in our bodies. Nowhere in the New Testament is the search for a soulmate suggested as a proper concern for the Christian woman or man. The conflict between the demands of faith and the order of 'the world' is too acute, the appointed time too close. All in all, Paul was far more positive about monogamous marriage as a means of conserving vital energy – hence his deprecatory 'better to marry than burn' – than as a means of meekness or respectability.[21]

In my own life, I go along, all the way, with Paul's energy

conservation policy. I lack the energy (or is it courage? or imagination?) to take on the particular complexities of an adulterous or open marriage. I do fervently believe that for Graham and me a sexually 'open marriage' would militate against too many other things we care about very deeply: other risks worth taking. In making this apologia for my own monogamous lifestyle, I feel it necessary to separate the political significance and consequences of assenting to the *institution* of marriage from our mutually imposed sexual exclusivity. I do not really have too much trouble with the latter. I do not in general believe that a capacity for lovingness is measured by genital activity. I do, however, have trouble with the institution and realize that the two (i.e., marriage and sexual fidelity) make up a visibly conformist package which is potentially oppressive to us, and more importantly to other people in the community. I canot wish away the divide that heterosexual contractual ties place between women. Rejecting these is, for so many of us, central to a feminist identity. Because I live with my children in their father's house, I am protected from the more gruelling punishments a sexist society visits on its dissident women. These I see, less often than is probably good for me, at Greenham Common, when I'm on the streets, alone or politically active. My relationship to the politics I embrace is inevitably altered by my apparent assent to the sexual status quo. All I can do is try to embrace this too: to remember, in penitence, that I am one of those people the 'pro-family' Right upholds. In my name and for my protection, male power, sexual, military and economic, is zealously maintained. Our most violating and alienating social institutions – for housing, child rearing – have evolved to contain our culture's highest values – the sanctity of marriage and the family. Nuke-Leer family.

Mine is a prefeminist marriage. If it had been possible to have celebrated a sacramental marriage in the eyes of God and the church without signing on with the state as well, we would both have thought seriously of doing so. I suppose it would have been too much of a trendy sixty-ish thing to do then, a denial of the current optimism around public politics, but it would make a lot of sense now. 'A sacramental sign in an atheistic age has no value at all. It would be better for all concerned if its contractural nature were a little clearer,' says Germaine Greer.[22] Agreed. Perhaps when the integrity of mutually negotiated bonds between lovers is recognized as such by the community instead of being seen as a licentious second-best to marriage, then the sacramental sign, which is precisely a sign, not a ritual umbrella, might reclaim its own true nature. (I like to think getting married, being married is an odd, rather extreme thing to do. My response to an odd, rare man. I see no reason why any, certainly not why *everybody* else should want to do it too.)

I was brought up on an ideal of love that measured passion's depth and intensity by its exclusive 'foreverness': I'll never look at anybody else, sighed the story-book lovers. Yet I knew that this was not really so. That the 'eternity' we seek and show when we love is qualitative, not fixed in time: that lovingness grown through many different relationships is no less holy or good than lovingness grown through one. By their fruits shall we know them. New Testament teaching emphasizes the 'one flesh' (*henosis*) significance of heterosexual intercourse. Christian tradition as a whole affirms that where the unitive and procreative purposes of human sexuality are joined, the act – however solemnly or not it is undertaken – carries both purposes within itself and is thus indelible and irrevocable.

Behaviour labelled promiscuous in our culture is presumed to deny this radical dimension. This may well hold true for men. Women, however, concerned to transcend male-defined sexuality, see possibilities of non-exclusive sexual expressions which can fearlessly embrace this idea in some form. In a male-structured sexual ethic which sees monogamy as 'natural' *and* beneficial for women this idea is extremely threatening.

But vital for women who so often perceive *henosis* as a life sentence. (How many readers know women, youngish, 'modern', who made doomed marriages 'because I had slept with him, I felt I had to, I belonged to him'?) There is no logical moral connection between *henosis* and the marital vow to 'forsake all others': no moral or spiritual justification for women to forsake their own development.

In *The Female Eunuch* Germaine Greer eloquently defends 'promiscuity', not as hedonism but as a natural outgrowth of a 'self-realising personality' whose 'responses are geared to the present and not to nostalgia or to anticipation. Although they do not serve a religion out of guilt or fear or any sort of compulsion, the religious experience, in Freud's term the *oceanic feeling*, is easier for them to obtain than for the conventionally religious. The essential factor in self-realisation is independence, resistance to enculturation.'[23] In her own life Greer rejects the denial implicit in the pattern of serial monogamy: a new love does not replace the old or diminish them with disloyalty.[24] I think of hers as a circular rather than a linear promiscuity. If we can

216

envisage now a feminist model of sexual plurality, can we not envisage a feminist monogamy? Greer's point about enculturation is well-taken.

Yet there surely is, for some, a *kairos*, a 'Now' which presses lovers to make a commitment 'til death; a knowledge that it will take that long to grow into the present moment. For me that recognition was unmistakable. Surprising, almost shocking. To recognize and act authentically upon this 'Now' needs a grace and community not readily available in a society obsessed with institutionalized security and coupleism.

I am fortunate in being spared many of the perversions of the privatized family. Our household is large and fluid – six Dowells and three/four others. There are all kinds of sexual energy and discussion around with fast-growing children, teenaged and young people. The relationship between my husband and me, though pivotal in some ways (i.e., economic – he's a parish priest and so this vicarage is 'his' house) does not assume the burdensome centrality that it would in more orthodox households. We are not the only people here with the 'right' to explore and express our sexuality. A variety of social and sexual models – plus cuddles – are available to the younger children. I hope this can overturn some of the terminology and 'facts of life' I grew up with: that 'serious' relationships were those which envisioned settled domesticity as their omega point. Traditional patriarchal forms, religious and political, are open to challenges more widely based than the 'generation gap' of the two-tier family. If this sounds all very cosy and correct, it's not meant to. I can be bossy and disapproving but hope, on my better days, that our vintage home-brew adds some good body to the punchbowl – when not too vinegary!

This breathing space, narrow as it is, is useful to all of us, living as we do in the New Right 1980s. Ideologies that uphold marriage and family life tend to deny and devalue all other forms of intimacy, community and love. A bourgeois church that preaches the nuclear family as its paradigm not only shockingly insults the majority of people who do not live in such families but totally reverses the New Testament understanding of the *community* as the basic collective form for carrying God's image and grace.[25] Individualized sex and familial love is contingent on this, only valid so long as it serves the greater good of union with Christ. A clear parallel can be seen in the attack on monogamy by the Left and the women's movement. This is on ideological rather than emotional grounds for narrowing the scope and commitment of other relationships and responsibilities. In a sexist society, women are especially vulnerable to traditional definitions of sexual fidelity. The sexual double standard is compounded by women's social isolation.

But open non-monogamous relationships can be destructively antisocial too, as Sue Cartledge points out in her essay 'On Duty and Desire: Creating a Feminist Morality': 'Even when both partners agree on non-monogamy, the solution which is honourable and realistic for them may be unacceptable to their other lovers.'[26] When interviewed on British television, Simone de Beauvoir described how she and Jean-Paul Sartre agreed at the start of their relationship that each would be the most important person for the other. Their love was 'necessary': but this would not preclude other 'contingent' affairs. And her use of the word 'affairs' for these other lovers is significant.

For it is clear from her autobiographical writings that some other lovers 'resented their automatic second place'.[27] This sexual/emotional hierarchicalism seems to me just as invidious as the Us and Them, backs against the world behaviour found in traditional marriages. (Sue Cartledge seems to feel, as I do, that time and energy are major difficulties militating against the risks and genuine openness that Greer commends.)

As we have seen, Pauline teaching on the sacramental nature of sexual intercourse was soon split off from traditional Judeo-Christian insistence on monogamy. Monogamy came to be seen not as an expression and recognition of sacramentality but as the only and inadequate compromise with the flesh; taught largely in negatives. If you really have to do IT, the least you can do is only do IT with one person. And as little as possible. Only for children, to people heaven. Conjugal sex, way down in the spiritual grace stakes, was constantly subjected to the disciplinarianism of a celibate clergy. Jerome, in the fourth century, said: 'I praise marriage and wedlock, but only because they beget celibates: I gather roses from thorns, gold from the earth, pearls from shells.'[28]

The church's disinvolvement in any creative theology of marriage can be seen in its failure to develop any distinctively Christian marriage liturgy. For several centuries Old Roman ceremonies were followed without alteration. The first traces of Christian rites emerge only in the fourth century; not until the ninth century is there any detailed account of Christian nuptials and even then the order is strikingly akin to that of Imperial Rome. Despite the efforts of reforming Popes to bring free and easy marriage practice under the wing of the church, it was not until the Council of Trent in 1538 that a Christian ceremony was considered essential to a valid marriage. In this climate, it is not surprising that church authorities maintained a *laissez-faire* cynicism towards the openly commercial abuses of feudal marriage, particularly among the upper classes who disposed of their daughters as dynastic breeding stock.

Feminist theology has been quite rightly concerned to undercut the grandiose claims made by Reformation Christianity that it restored marriage – and by implication women themselves – to full spiritual and social dignity. Protestantism failed to overcome either the sexist bias of religious patriarchy or the Christian ascetic's fear and denigration of sexuality. It failed to acknowledge fully, let alone connect, the two. Luther, the champion of marriage, once termed it an 'emergency hospital for the illness of human drives'.[29] A denial of female sexual or spiritual autonomy is evident throughout the Reformer's proclamations: 'A woman is not fully master of herself. God fashioned her body so that she would be with a man.'[30] Desire and ruling shackled again.

While Protestantism elevated woman as the Goodwife, it is to the cults and religious traditions preceding the Reformation that we must look for affirmation of woman as the Beloved. In her fascinating book on the Virgin Mary,[31] Marina Warner describes the ways in which hell-fearing harsh asceticism was softened, in the later middle ages, by sweeter strains of Christian piety, stressing the humanity and self-giving love of Jesus. These intertwined with the secular love lyrics of the troubadors. Courtly love, for all its tortuous ritual and elitism, stressed the desirability of *emotional* parity in sexual relationships: an idea which ultimately discredited its *raison d'être*, the marriage of convenience and the need to pursue passion outside. The Cult of Romance was transmuted into the ideal of True Love, with monogamous marriage as its honourable end.

Feminist consciousness, too, contributed to the changing values of the Renaissance and Reformation. The learned Christine de Pisane, in the fifteenth century, campaigned vigorously for women's education, against medieval misogyny, while extolling the goodness and delight of the marriage bed: a theme taken up in the popular literature of the next two centuries.

The Reformers made it stick, giving it biblical and liturgical affirmation. The major contribution of Protestantism was to open up an awareness, developed over succeeding centuries, that sexual intercourse had a value quite independent of procreation. Without this perspective, we cannot fruitfully explore the idea of monogamy in a Christian liberationist context.

Many feminists see romantic love as a modern western smokescreen against the imbalances of the real world. It yields the same results as arranged marriage – compulsory heterosexuality and motherhood for most of the female population, now accompanied by the dangerous delusion of choice and a destructive guilt and grief when love fades. A kind of psychic trip wire placed across a feminist sexual politics. But 'falling in love' is part of the air we breathe. Rather than deny or ignore this powerful, inescapable reality, we have to blend the personal and political in new powerful ways to stop both from falling on their faces – or backs! 'So how should we deal with it from a perspective of feminism?' asks Lucy Goodison.[32] 'Should we struggle against these tendencies and feelings in ourselves as counter-productive? I don't think so. Rather, I feel we should take that power and vitality and work with them. If we were not damaged and empty, if our life experiences had been different, perhaps our loving would not be shot through with need, pain and obsession. But we are as we are and we have to start from there. Rather than denigrating falling in love, we could see it as a healthy response to a crazy world and perhaps one of the stratagems our organism uses to survive. It can act as a beam of light which can cut through the crap, which reveals the mediocrity, hypocrisy and banality of so much of our society.'[33]

The banality is most evident in the moulds our society offers to pour our love experiences into – both the long-term structures of the nuclear family and the ephemeral language and ritual of courtship. Graham and I fled to Africa to work and live, but partly to avoid the conventional middle-class wedding; only to find that a few friendly expatriates had thoughtfully laid on some of the more monstrous accoutrements, including, I still remember with actue embarrassment, a snowy crinoline of a cake, complete with bride and groom luridly grinning on top. I'd hoped to avoid *such* a stark contrast to the liturgy itself which still moves me as much for its earthy realism as for its daunting solemnity.

Solemn vows are not the preserve of the conventionally wedded. To explore this question of monogamy more deeply, we do well to learn from those people for whom society offers no pre-formed moulds to pour their loving into – gay people in particular. Monogamy is widely thought of as the saving grace of these and other unorthodox relationships. Whether this *should* be so is another question, but not a simple one of a heterosexist society imposing its own rules and blueprints to bring dissidents into line. It is the permanent commitment made to one another that many gay people wish to be affirmed by society. For gay Christians, this includes the church and liturgical forms of celebration. Many gay people are insulted and wounded by liberals who idealize the 'freedom' of gay people from institutional forms.

In feminist writing and thinking, gay and heterosexual, the vexed question of monogamy arises most clearly and insistently alongside the recognition of the spiritual dimensions of our sexuality:

> As an ineffable, intense, other-worldly experience, being in love has been compared to religious ecstasy. It has also been suggested that sexual relationships more often have spiritual overtones for women than for men . . . Perhaps the strong link which occurs when we fall in love can open us up to these wider connections. Perhaps it is an experience which opens the 'lines' between ourselves and the world. In a culture which denies spirituality outside the confines of established religion, falling in love may have become unusually important as one of our few routes to an experience of the transcendent. It has been understood as a distortion of a deep urge to love the world which through social pressure gets funnelled into one person.[34]

Delete the negatives (of 'social pressure' and 'distortion') from this last sentence and you have a classic apologia for incarnational Christianity. Scandalous particularity.

These questions and connections have, recently and rarely, been incorporated into mainstream theological thinking. James Nelson's *Embodiment* is a good gift to the churches as well as being a useful context for women who wish to work within the traditional language and imagery of Christianity. Nelson traces the sources and history of Christian sex-negativity and the consequent failure of the church to develop a real sexual theology on which to project its ethical teaching:

> Few would doubt that this is a time of transition in our understanding of human sexuality. The confusion about sexual mores is the more obvious evidence of this. But there is something else. For too long the bulk of Christian reflection about sexuality has asked an essentially one-directional question: what does Christian faith have to say about our lives as sexual beings? Now we are beginning to realize that the enterprise must be a genuinely two-directional affair. The first question is essential and we

221

must continue unfailingly to press it. But at the same time it must be joined by, indeed interwoven with, a companion query: What does our experience as sexual human beings mean for the way in which we understand and attempt to live out the faith? What does it mean that we as body-selves are invited to participate in the reality of God?[35]

In a lecture to the Gay Christian Movement in 1984, the black feminist theologian Sheila Briggs spelled this theme and methodology to the traditional doctrine of the Trinity. In the belief that human sexuality is made in and corresponds to the reality we call God, Briggs proposed we envision God, in the first person of the Trinity, as a parable of heterosexuality: God the creator, who calls a different reality into existence and loves it. The relationship is expressed in the beloved 'otherness' of creator and creation. But, if we stop there, as heterosexist pragmatists would have us do, if we limit our naming and loving to this alone, we lose the wholeness of God's word made flesh. We become, in Briggs's words, 'sexual Unitarians'. God continues, as redeemer and sanctifier (Daughter/Son and Holy Spirit) to make and keep the world. Redemption through sameness is the heart of the Christian revelation. Gay people have a particular way of showing forth this part of the Three-in-One. 'God so loved the world that God gave His/Her Own.' In sisterhood, women say, 'I have a shared past with you, as daughter, as a woman.' Or as the popular Christmas carol has it, 'Day by day like us He grew.' Gay sexuality underlines the libido's function of knowledge.

As Christ was in his earthly life so too are gay people vulnerable to rejection by the 'world'. (Sheila Briggs warned of the dangers of pressing the 'despised and rejected' metaphor too far.) The lecture tantalizingly left us to explore the significance of the third person of the Trinity for ourselves. The Spirit/Sanctifier which flows around and between, connecting the poles of human sexuality is the inspiration for this book. The spirit blows where it lists, through sisterhood, celibacy. The oceanic dimension.

Christian mystics of earlier ages were not afraid to participate in the sexual reality of God. They sought and named God-as-lover in fiercely passionate, ecstatic language; experienced the body as the site of divine revelations that were often explicitly sexual/genital in character. Men and women. The pre-formed mould for these experiences is almost universally a monastic one. Christianity's spiritualistic dualism has ensured that these visions remain safely distanced from the strivings of more mundane God-seekers. They have either been venerated as the fruits of a soul uncontaminated by the flesh, therefore not *really* sexual or, more recently, analysed as 'interesting' sublimations.

So what is it we ask of God? That (S)He loves us, uniquely, wholeheartedly, and will never turn away. My God is not a harem master of a Great Mother Mistress of Heaven with a cyclical order of favourites, a jealous God who will never let us go. Can we not begin to think of monogamy, sexual exclusivity, not as prudent conformity – doing what God, the church or society tells us – but as a way of knowing and being known in this fierce singularity of Creator and Redeemer? *A* way, not *the* way, of being-in-God:

> The unknownness of my needs frightens me, . . . I miss God. I miss the company of somebody utterly loyal. I still don't think of God as my betrayer. The servants of God, yes, but servants by their very nature betray. I miss God who was my friend. I don't even know if God exists, but I do know that if God is your emotional role model, very few human relationships will match up to it. I have an idea that someday it may be possible. I thought once it had become possible, and that glimpse has set me wandering, trying to find the balance between earth and sky. As it is I can't settle. I want someone who is fierce and will love me until death, and be on my side for ever and ever. I want someone who will destroy and be destroyed by me. There are many forms of love and affection, some people can spend their whole lives without knowing each other's names. But on the wild nights who calls you home? Only the one who knows your name.[36]

'And Jacob was left alone; and there wrestled a man with him until the breaking of the day . . . And he said, Let me go for the day breaketh. And he said I will not let thee go, except thou bless me. And he said unto him, What is thy name . . .'[37] Betrayal, jealousy, not letting go. Coming to adulthood, Christianity (and Jean-Paul Sartre!) in the 'sexual revolution', I picked up the 1960s disapproval, even taboo around these feelings. Jealousy was indistinguishable from stifling possessiveness – bourgeois, petty, destructive. Immature. Only the insecure wanted to be called home on the wild nights. Home? A jealous God was a primitivist concept in a century where Man (*sic*) had Come of Age and was reaching for the heavens. Feminist social theory was quick to discern the phallocentric pragmatism of the sexual revolution, to articulate our 'ambiguity about sexual freedom at the expense of sexual protection'.[38] Only by combining the God truths and Body truths that we are discovering in ourselves and one another can we declare a liberated woman's 'interest' in monogamy. Both have been hard-won. Beatrix Campbell analyses the difficulties of maintaining a 'feminist sexual politics as an optimistic feature of the women's liberation movement: The books [of the sexual revolution] seemed to pre-empt women's disappointment with "it" when they counselled patience in the face of failure and frigidity. Frigidity we knew was a female condition, but having embraced sex nothing could be worse than having to own up to yourself being part of the female condition . . . Instead we lurched rather unselfconsciously into feminism with a mysterious sense of sexual disappointment, or with a strong yet untheorized sense of the mismatch between the natural order of heterosexual practice and the nature of women's desire.'[39]

Traditional Christian moralists saw that female wellbeing was not well served by sexual permissiveness: but their patronizing protectiveness did not address the age-old mismatch between patriarchal morality and 'the nature of women's desire'. Having had such great difficulty in seeing the holiness of their own desires, the possibility of God's nature being more completely shown forth in ours is only conceded with enormous ambiguity. It always was, which is why the idea is so suppressed in religious forms and language. We can remind ourselves of the more blatant rationales of 'ruled' female desire with an example from our old sexist 'protector' C.S. Lewis, who asserts that:

> Women are more naturally monogamous than men. It is a biological necessity. Where promiscuity prevails, they will always be more often the victims than the culprits. Also domestic happiness is more necessary to them than to us, and the quality by which they most easily hold a man, their beauty, decreases every year after they come to maturity.[40]

Now, we do not need a return to chivalry or more cults in Praise of the Older Woman to be rescued from victimization (or cant like this!). We need the precious but more accessible strengths of self-knowledge, a combined political and spiritual awareness. Lewis's statement sums up the blackmail and distortion that have clung around Christian thinking on this issue – and around the images of women perpetuated by this thinking. It has allowed faithfulness to be seen as a gift of godly upright men to women.

If monogamous marriage is the vocation the church claims it to be, then it is clearly not 'natural' for either sex. It requires discipline, humour, forbearance and trust. Particular virtues. Virtue is not 'natural'. It is godly, of God. Women bear the image and grace of

God, as do men. God cannot be labelled and parcelled out in the service of some tired sexual status quo or tamed in 'domestic happiness'. God's restless curiosity and creativity belong to us too, as much as the sturdy, homely dependability and changelessness that men would assign to us for their safekeeping. Perhaps we *are* able to hold the one-ness of God, in our bodies and in community, more completely than men. Perhaps we are more 'naturally monogamous' because we can. I do not know.

But I do know this. A feminist future scorns the Janus face of Libertine/Ascetic in patriarchal sexuality. A feminist future will banish the spectre of the better-preserved gent who leaves or threatens to leave a woman who will not 'hold' him by placing his pride at the centre of her existence rather than the challenges to growth in a shared life. Nor will a woman so abandoned see her sexual self as obliterated in his rejection.

NOTES

All biblical quotes are from the Authorized (King James) version.
1   Friedrich Engels, *The Origin and History of the Family, Private Property and the State*, Zurich, 1884, in Karl Marx and Friedrich Engels, *Selected Works* (3 vols), Progress Publishers, Moscow, 1970, vol.3, p.233.
2   Rosemary Radford Ruether, *Womanguides: Readings towards a Feminist Theology*, Boston, Beacon Press, 1985, p.x.
3   For a fuller analysis of this claim see Ruether, *Church and Family*, English Dominicans (eds), Oxford, New Blackfriars, n.d.
4   Genesis 6:7.
5   Ruether, *Womanguides*, op. cit., p.158.
6   Hosea 3:3: The narrative begins 'And the Lord said to Hosea, "Go take thee a wife of whoredoms and children of whoredoms": for the land committed great whoredom, departing from the Lord. So he went and took Gomer the daughter of Dibliam' (Hosea 1:1-3).
7   An important book on this submerged tradition is Raphael Patai's *The Hebrew Goddess*, Chicago, McGraw-Hill, 1966.
8   Phyllis Bird, 'Images of Women in the Old Testament', in Ruether (ed.), *Religion and Sexism*, New York, Simon & Schuster, 1974, pp.41-88.
9   II Samuel 11.
10 Judges 16.
11 Matthew 19:9; Mark 10:2-9; Luke 16:18.
12 Luke 11:27-28.

13 Mark 3:31–35.

14 *The Passion of Saints Perpetua and Felicity* (trans. W.H. Shewring), London, Sheed & Ward, 1931, pp.24–38.

15 Hennecke and Schneemelcher, *New Testament Apocrypha*, vol. II, Philadelphia, Westminster, 1965, pp.322–90. The Acts of Paul and Thecla is a popular second-century writing devoted to the story of Thecla, a woman missionary. This collection mentions many other women prophets and teachers, and is seen as an authoritative mandate for female leadership.

16 Literally translated, 'Way of Negation'. A concept which stresses that God cannot be known or named in human material reality. This not-knownness is pursued by nonattachment to the things of this world, through celibacy and asceticism. The tension between the Way of Negation and the Way of Affirmation can be seen in a different but not unconnected form in the Iconoclastic controversy which arose in the Greek Church in the sixth and seventh centuries, which contributed to the split between Eastern and Western Christendom. The Iconoclasts accused the Iconists of idolatry – in the East a major obstacle to the conversion of Jews and Moslems (both anti-'graven image'). The Western (Roman) Church was rich in artistic depictions of biblical stories. The theological assumptions undergirding this book and women's spirituality in general are iconic, i.e., we need more inclusive images of God. But few would deny a creative, non-dualistic tension: 'This Thou, yet this is not Thou' (Dionysius). God is within yet beyond the image.

17 Charles Williams, *The Descent of the Dove: a Short History of the Holy Spirit in the Church*, London, Faber Religious Book Club, 1939.

18 Acts 2:44–46: 'And all that believed were together, and had all things common. And sold their possessions and goods, and parted them to all men, as every man had need.'

19 Means simply 'way of the monk'. The word is widely associated with Gandhi's teaching and practice of the importance of sexual abstinence. Gandhi exposed himself to temptation in order to test his self-control, first with his wife Kasturbai and later with much younger women. His justification of this practice is interesting: 'I am amazed that my experiment implied any assumption of woman's inferiority. She would be, if I looked upon her with lust, with or without her consent. I have believed in woman's perfect equality with man. My wife was "Inferior" when she was the instrument of my lust. She ceased to be that when she lay with me naked as my sister . . . the contact raised both of us. Should there be a difference if it is not my wife, as she once was, but some other sister?'. Cf. Andrews, *Mahatma Gandhi: His Own Story*, vol. I, London, 1930, pp. 94–5, quoted in Arthur Koestler, 'Mahatma Gandhi: A Revaluation', *Bricks to Babel*, London, Hutchinson, 1980, pp.595–621.

20 Williams, op. cit., pp.12–14. The women who shared this experiment were known as 'subintroductae', living with men in spiritual marriage. The emphasis by rare accounts is far less self-conscious than Gandhi's. The practice was probably practical as well as defiantly 'alternative', and has been repeated throughout the church's history, from mixed monastic communities in early times and in more modern secular projects.

21 Ruether cites (in *Church and Family*, op. cit.) the 'Household lists' of Paul (exhorting sober and upright behaviour) as illustrating Paul's concern to modify the confrontation between church and family in New Testament times, a concern neither wholehearted nor wholly successful. She suggests Paul's heart was with the radical claims of faith against family and state.

22 Germaine Greer, *The Female Eunuch*, London, Paladin, 1971, p.242.

23 *Ibid.*, p.145.

24 Chairing a television broadcast (*Choices*), 15 August 1985. The focus of the discussion was on two gay Christian men, defending their relationship (one had been pressured to resign from his job as clergyman) on the grounds of its permanence and its pledge to growth and service in their local community. Greer challenged this 'justification', claiming her own integrity as a 'promiscuous' woman (Greer's own word, not mine).

25 For an example of this reversal, see Jack Dominion, *Cycles of Affirmation: Psychological Essays in Christian Living*, London, Darton, Longman & Todd, 1975, p.169: 'How are we to experience the fullness of Christ in his Church? The sacraments are one means. And within them (and here is the distinguishing mark of Catholicism) one of them, marriage, which is embraced by the overwhelming majority of human beings, brings the Church into their life . . . every marriage becomes a "little church" in which the affirmation of its members shares and participates in the affirmation of Christ for the Church. Marriage remains central in the original revelation of God to man in creation and in it confirmation in the life and death of his only Son.'

26 Sue Cartledge and Joanna Ryan (eds), *Sex and Love: New Thoughts on Old Contradictions*, London, The Women's Press, 1983, pp.167–80.

27 Quoted in James Nelson, *Embodiment: An Approach to Sexuality and Christian Theology*, London, SPCK, 1979, p.52.

28 *Ibid.*, p.55.

29 Quoted in Julia O'Faolain and Lauro Martinez, *Not in God's Image: Women in History*, London, Virago, 1979.

30 *Ibid.*

31 Marina Warner, *Alone of all her Sex: The Myth and Cult of the Virgin Mary*, London, Quartet Books, 1978, pp.144 ff.

32 Lucy Goodison, 'Really Being in Love Means Wanting to Live in a

Different World', from Cartledge and Ryan, op. cit., pp.63 and 50.

33 *Ibid.*
34 *Ibid.*, p.62.
35 Nelson, op. cit., p.8.
36 Jeanette Winterson, *Oranges are not the Only Fruit*, London, Pandora Press (Routledge & Kegan Paul), 1985, p.170.
37 Genesis 32:24–27.
38 Beatrix Campbell, 'A Feminist Sexual Politics: Now You See it, Now you Don't', in *Feminist Review*, no. 5, London, 1980, pp.1–18. Also in Mary Evans (ed.), *The Woman Question: Readings on the Subordination of Women*, Oxford, OUP/Fontana, 1982, p.125.
39 *Ibid.*, p.127.
40 C.S. Lewis, 'We have no Right to Happiness', in *Saturday Evening Post*, vol. CCXXXVI, Dec. 1963 (posthumous), pp.10–12. (From C.S. Lewis, *God in the Dock: Essays on Theology*, Collins, Fount Paperbacks, 1979, pp.107–8.

22

ASCETICISM AND FEMINISM: STRANGE BEDMATES?

Rosemary Radford Ruether

Asceticism does not have a good press in the twentieth century. Heirs of the Protestant rejection of monasticism and celibacy, and of the increasing turn from other-worldliness to this-worldliness or the Renaissance, the Enlightenment and the contemporary celebration of embodiment, modern Western people generally see asceticism as the epitome of a sex-phobic, body-hating world view. Liberation theologians have called us to a new integration of the religious and the social, overcoming the traditional split between the sacred and the secular. The Gay Rights Movement affirms the goodness of sexual pleasure in itself, and not simply as a means of procreation within marriage. Feminists have seen the interconnection of the traditions of rejection of the body and physical nature and the culture of misogyny that inferiorizes women by identifying them with despised sexuality and material existence.

These negative tendencies have indeed been part of some aspects of asceticism. But to reduce asceticism to hostility to women, body, and nature fails to do justice to the complexity of the ascetic tradition in Christianity and in human culture generally. Why have major religious movements such as Christianity focused much of their best energy for more than a millennium and a half on ascetic practices? Why has asceticism been a major part of other world religions, such as Buddhism? The importance of asceticism in major periods of human culture indicates that it has been a popular mass movement, not simply an expression of repression imposed by sadistic authorities from above. It also has attracted women as much as men. Nor has this popularity of asceticism disappeared today as a discredited impulse. Rather we need to recognize our own analogues to ascetic practices by which we today attempt to solve similar problems to those which beset our ancestors.

The modern post-Christian rejection of asceticism and other-worldliness often constructs a 'romantic' picture of the 'happy pagan' as a 'child of nature' who is innocent of any conflict of instinct and consciouness and happily enjoys bodily pleasures. But any examination of those sort of tribal cultures usually imagined to be characteristic of the 'happy native' will reveal a different picture, in which endurance of deprivation and even self-torture was an integral part either of rites of passage (generally male rites of passage) or special quests for visionary empowerment as shamans. Fasting, sexual abstinence, deprivation of sleep, endurance of pain inflicted on oneself or by others, solitude, conquering the fear of wilderness places, exercises of concentration of breathing and thought, and prolonged ceremonial dancing all have been aspects of the sort of 'ascesis' (exercises) by which early cultures have signaled the passage from one state of life to another, sought heightened experience and reconciliation of conflicting forces in the human and cosmic community.

I will give two examples of such ascetic practices in American Indian culture in its quest for spiritual empowerment and cosmic reconciliation. The 'vision quest' was a process by which most American Indian cultures sought special visionary experiences, both for those who sought to set themselves apart as shamans, and for ordinary men and women, as a part of their developing spiritual power and identity.[1] This typically involved strenuous fasting. Algonkians began to prepare their children by the age of seven for the ability to endure prolonged fasting by having them go without food for a day. In addition to fasting, the ordeal of the vision quest involved going out into the wilderness and dwelling alone for some days, enduring the fear of loneliness and the buffeting of 'ghosts' or spirits. Cutting off a finger joint, or some other expression of physical self-sacrifice, might be an extreme form of the quest. The ordeal continued until it was rewarded with a vision which served to reorient the seekers' consciousness, and to give them a new sense of identity and guidance, either for the whole of their lives or for a particular project which they sought to undertake.

The sun dance was another Indian ceremony involving ritual asceticism. The sun dance developed around 1800, among the Plains Indians, with the advent of the horse which allowed for large ceremonial gatherings of tribes. It centered in a Pledger who vowed to carry out the ceremony. The Pledger (a male) prepared for the ceremony by fasting and sexual abstinence. His wife also fasted and both were regarded as holy. They were instructed by past Pledgers and their wives. The Pledgers thus became a holy brotherhood, somewhat like the Spanish *flagellantes* (who had brought their customs to the American Southwest in the seventeenth century).

Once the Indians had gathered, intense preparations by creating the ritual tipis and dance space took place, each step demanding a careful ceremony. Sun dance itself was carried out over two to four days, with the dancers dancing continually without food or water. A special elite engaged in further rites of self-mutilation. This ritual of physical endurance was seen as benefiting not only the Pledger and the inner circle of dancers and self-torturers, but the whole community. Through their self-sacrifice and endurance, communion was restored with the sun, the earth, the spirits, and the winds. Like the even more bloody human sacrifices of the Mesoamerican Indians, in which a throbbing heart was cut from the chest of the victim and offered to the sun, the sun dance was essentially a fertility rite.[2]

Ritual asceticism is, by its very nature, occasional. Fasting, sexual abstinence, pain, and physical endurance happen in times set apart from the rest of life to achieve heightened consciousness and individual and communal empowerment. This power then flows back to enhance everyday life. In the process a shamanistic elite may be set apart by their prowess in these rites, but in order to make themselves conduits of this power for the whole community.

Such Indian ritual asceticism seems far removed from Christian asceticism. But, once one removes differences of terminology, early Christian ascetics, particularly the desert hermits such as St Anthony, have far more in common with shamanistic holy men (and women), or what Indians would call 'medicine men' (and women), than we have realized. Like the shamans in search of their vision quest, the Christian hermits went out into the wilderness outside of human habitation to engage in an ordeal of physical, mental and spiritual endurance. He or she fasted and prayed, but, above all, endured the buffetings of the demonic spirits that inhabited these wilderness places. The demonic powers tortured the holy hermit physically and mentally in what is typically described as a combat and struggle.

The end of the contest is a gradual transformation in which the ascetic achieves inner calm, peace, wisdom and even physical renewal. Thus after twenty years of fasting and demon combat, Anthony is described by Athanasius in his classic hagiography as emerging, not only filled with spiritual radiance, but physically healthy, 'neither fat nor thin.'[3] The ascetic goal is not destruction of the body for the sake of the soul, but a destruction of the turmoil of conflicting thoughts and feelings that make the person a battleground. The goal is psycho-somatic spiritual integration, a redeemed soul in a resurrected body.

Contrary to what has tended to be supposed by a post-Reformation scholarship hostile to asceticism, the desert holy one is seen as bringing great benefits on the whole community, and not as one who turned his or her back on the community. The holy one was, above all, a spiritual director for others, particularly other seekers of holiness who came into the desert to become his or her disciples. But the ascetic also gave advice and counsel to others who did not seek to join this way of life on a regular basis. Indeed the accounts of the desert monks of the fourth century sound as if the fame of these saints quickly turned the desert into a highway, with streams of people making the pilgrimage to visit and gain the benefit of contact with these holy persons. The ascetic was also a healer, casting out demons and curing illnesses. Their benefits were not just individual. Their very presence brought benefit to the city and surrounding neighbourhood of their habitations. They appeared at critical moments in the urban scene to arbitrate disputes and even to protect the city against the wrath of the emperor in political conflicts. In short the ascetic becomes a conduit of divine blessing for the whole community.[4]

However, this shamanistic asceticism of the desert hermits was gradually transformed by the Christian church into communal forms of monastic life, formed into religious orders under the supervision of bishops. Its individualism and exhibitionism was curbed and domesticated by the rules of St Basil in the East and St Benedict in the West. A steady but moderate simplicity of life was valued over the flamboyant ordeal, and the wandering individualist taught to bend his or her will to the discipline of community life.[5] Above all, the more magical world view of demon combat and holy desert animals who care for the saints is replaced by the intellectual theory of an ascetic theology that synthesized Christianity and Platonism. It is this intellectual theory of ascetic theology that needs to be examined to see how it both shapes and changes the earlier impulses of popular Christian asceticism. I will look particularly at the understanding of sexuality in the economy of holiness and how this affects changing attitudes toward women.

Early Christian asceticism operated within a spiritual world of late antiquity preoccupied with the mortality and corruptibility of material reality. It looked to ascetic disciplines as the way of withdrawing one's energies from the death-tending directions of existence and centering them on 'eternal life'; i.e., on that secure foundation of authentic being that transcended and could sustain human spiritual life and meaning beyond not only death itself, but all the death-aspects of present life. These fears of mortality and the ascetic quest for abundant life was typical of late antique culture in all of its religious manifestations, whether we look at pagan piety in Neo-Platonism or Hellenistic and apocalyptic types of Judaism in the Dead Sea Scroll Sect or in the writings of Philo the Alexandrian, or Christianity or eclectic wisdom movements, such as gnosticism.

Modern Protestant scholarship has wished to heap the 'blame' for asceticism on its favourite scapegoat, gnosticism, or 'acute hellenism,' and to exempt Judaism from any ascetic tendencies. Judaism is proclaimed to have a 'robust', this-worldly point of view hostile to asceticism.[6] The purpose of such marginalizing of asceticism is, of course, to repudiate the legitimacy of its credentials as an expression of Christianity. Jesus and the New Testament are proclaimed to be free of it. This view greatly under-estimates the extent to which an ascetic element had become a part of the sectarian forms of Judaism which were the immediate roots of Christianity and also how central asceticism was to the interpretation of the earliest Christian world view, as found in the New Testament itself.

Seeing themselves as living in the crisis of the present world systems of family and state and anticipating a new messianic order, early Christians saw themselves as prefiguring, by lifestyles of detachment and resistance to the systems by which the present world order was maintained, the new age to come. Rejection of marriage, not simply in the sense of pleasure denial, but in the sense of resistance to worldly preoccupations, was one central way of symbolizing the anticipation of that age when there would be 'neither marrying or giving in marriage.'

Paul writes, in his first letter to the Corinthians, that while it is good for everyone to be married and to render to their spouse their conjugal rights, rather than to fall into immorality (sex outside of marriage), it would be still better to abstain from sex for seasons of prayer. As the passage continues, it becomes clear that Paul regards celibacy as the higher Christian ethic and wishes that 'all were as he is,' but does not feel mandated to impose this as a commandment (as some other more ascetic Christian groups probably did).[7] Paul equates not marrying, or being released from marriage by the death of a spouse, with freedom from worldly concerns for full devotion to relationship to Christ. He specifically equates singleness for women with the emancipation of a slave from slavery. Both the woman and the slave are thereby released from bondage to the masters to which they were bound by worldly law and become free and autonomous persons able to order their own lives. He hints that he recognizes that marriage is not entirely desirable for a woman, precisely because of this bondage, when he says:

> A wife is bound to her husband as long as she lives. If the husband dies, she is free to be married to whom she wishes, only in the Lord (i.e., to a fellow Christian). But in my judgment she is happier if she remains as she is. And I think that I have the Spirit of God. (I Corinthians 7:39–40)

Paul accepted the general assumption of his religious culture that patriarchal hierarchy was part of the 'order of nature.' This hierarchy included the subordination of slaves to masters, wives to husbands and children to parents. This hierarchy also reflects a hierarchy of relation to God in which the male is the normative image of God and the woman falls beneath his sway and is related to God through him (I Corinthians 11:7). But he is distinctly troubled by the contradiction between this order of nature, established in the original creation of woman from man, and the tradition that he received from the early church that baptism into Christ overcomes the separation of male and female, Jews and Greeks, slave and free (Galatians 3:28).[8] He lamely tries to suggest that, while woman might have been made from man originally, subsequently all males are born from women, and so a kind of rough 'mutuality' has been established in practice:

> Nevertheless, in the Lord, woman is not independent of man nor man from woman, for as woman was made from man, so man is now born of woman. And all things are from God. (I Corinthians 11:11)

When this uneasiness about women's subordination in creation is taken together with Paul's assumption that the Christian is emancipated from the orders of creation through Christ and lives already in anticipation of a new order, one ends with a strong suggestion of a conflict between creational subordination and eschatological emancipation of women which Paul himself could not resolve systematically. His basic social bias was against radical changes in present social arrangements, but this was largely because he saw such social arrangements as ephemeral, soon to be dissolved and replaced by the coming order of the Kingdom of Heaven:

> I think in view of the impending distress it is well for a person to remain as he (or she) is. Are you bound to a wife? Do not seek to be free. Are you free from a wife? Do not seek marriage. But if you marry you do not sin, and if a girl marries, she does not sin. Yet those who marry will have worldly troubles, and I would spare you that. I mean, brothers and sisters, the appointed time has grown very short; from now on, let those who have wives live as though they had none, and those who mourn as though they were not mourning and those who rejoice as though they were not rejoicing and those who buy as though they had no goods and those who deal with the world as though they had no dealings with it. For the form of this world is passing away. (I Corinthians 7:25–31)

For Paul the present 'form' of this world was precisely its mortality and corruptibility. This was what was passing away. The form of the world to come would be incorruptible and everlasting. The saints, raised from the dead in glorious, spiritual, and imperishable bodies, would be fitted to this new 'form of the world.' Reproduction would no longer be necessary because there would be no more mortality; i.e., both birth and death would disappear. Hence marriage and sexual intercourse would likewise be unnecessary.

This view shows how closely Paul, in common with religious and philosophical thinkers of antiquity, linked sexual intercourse, marriage, procreation and mortality. The only legitimate purpose of sexual intercourse was procreation. One produced babies only because humans die and need to be replaced by new humans in a temporal system of birthing and dying. These thinkers also saw the subordination of women as necessitated by this structure of reproduction. The woman was not so much spiritually or intellectually unequal with men, as made socially unequal by her role as childbearer within the family system of male headship. They could not imagine any other kind of family system or way of ordering sex, reproduction, childraising, kinship relations, and inheritance of property into the political order of family life which was, for them, closely linked with the state, or the collective political order of society.

For thinkers in antiquity, this patriarchal organization of reproduction was an unchangeable part of the present 'cosmic order.' They could imagine a radical transformation of this social order of state and family life only when the maintenance of the whole cosmic temporal order of birthing, planting and reaping, buying and spending, sleeping and waking, eating and elimination had been overcome by a higher order of immortal life that had shucked off this 'perishable shell' of the mortal body. It was in this new system of immortal life that the subordination of women would no longer be necessary, and their spiritual equality could be fully vindicated. To remain unmarried, or to be released from marital bondage, was to anticipate that new order of female autonomy and equality.

These contradictions in the teachings of the historical Paul between his patriarchal understanding of the order of creation, and his suggestions that spiritual equivalence of women with men might be anticipated through rejection of marriage, led to sharp conflicts in second-generation Pauline churches. On the one hand, the more conservative, and probably more traditionally rabbinic elements, of the second generation Pauline community reasserted the normative character of the patriarchal family for the Christian church. Leadership was explicitly said to be modeled after exemplary patriarchal heads of family who have proven their ability to rule over their wives, children, and slaves. This role of exemplary male household management is the primary qualification for a bishop or a presbyter:

> A bishop must be above reproach, married only once, temperate, sensible, dignified, hospitable, an apt teacher, no drunkard, not violent, but gentle, not quarrelsome, and no lover of money. He must manage his own household well, keeping his children submissive and respectful in every way, for if a man does not know how to manage his own household, how can he care for God's church? (I Timothy 3:2–5)

Gone is the world of the historical Paul with its preference for charismatic and itinerant, rather than local and institutional, ministry and also Paul's preference for the unmarried state as anticipation of an impending eschatological order. The Pastoral Epistles particularly are concerned to stress that the subordination of women, established in the order of creation, is still in force in the Christian church. Woman not only was created second, but sinned first, and this establishes, not only her secondary, but also her suppressed role as a sinner 'put back in her place.' Her place must be that of silence and submissiveness and of childbearing:

> Let a woman learn in silence with all submissiveness. I permit no woman to teach or to have authority over men. She is to keep silent. For Adam was

formed first and then Eve. And Adam was not deceived, but the woman was deceived and became a transgressor. Yet woman will be saved through bearing children. (I Timothy 2:11)

This language in I Timothy, which was to become normative in Christianity for interpreting women's role, was far from normative in early Pauline churches when it was first written. Rather it was part of a head-on collision between reactionary, patriarchal Christians, who sought to reassert the patriarchal order with its functions of marriage and procreation as the framework for defining the Christian community, and those Christians, who saw themselves equally as disciples of Paul, who opted for a celibate life in anticipation of the new age. For this second group of Pauline Christians celibacy signaled the dissolution of the constraints upon woman. Childbearing was no longer a necessary task because the old aeon of birthing and dying was coming to an end. Women, released from marriage and procreation by Christian chastity, were also emancipated from patriarchal subordination. Their spiritual equality was not only affirmed in theory, but expressed in their right to autonomy. They need no longer keep silence, but were mandated to preach, teach and evangelize, like their brothers.

This alternative world of Pauline Christians is reflected in the *Acts of Paul and Thecla*. The *Acts* were probably written in their present form in the late second century AD. But Dennis R. MacDonald has argued that the basic legend behind the *Acts* was already a part of Christian oral tradition at the time of the authorship of I Timothy, and that I Timothy was written specifically to counteract that view of Paul found in the story of Paul and Thecla.[9] Whether it can be proven that the author of I Timothy had the legend of Thecla specifically in mind when he wrote, it should be evident that the legend of Thecla represents Paul in exactly the opposite stance from that attributed to him in I Timothy.

In I Timothy Paul enjoins a married congregational ministry of bishops, presbyters and deacons. Such a ministry is ignored in the legend, which favours an itinerant charismatic ministry of which the apostles are themselves the prototype.[10] The Paul of I Timothy tells women they will be saved by bearing children. The Paul of the legend identified conversion to Christ with chastity and rejection of marriage. The Paul of I Timothy tells women to be silent and submissive and have no authority over men. The Paul of legend not only authorizes Thecla's rejection of her marital promise and her travels as an itinerant, ascetic teacher dressed in male garb, but appears on the scene at the end of the story to bless her adventures by commissioning her to return to her hometown to evangelize:

> And Paul took her by the hand, led her into the house of Hermias and heard everything from her, so that he was much amazed and those who heard were confirmed and prayed for Tryphaena. Thecla rose and said to Paul, 'I go to Iconium.' And Paul said, 'Go and teach the word of God.' . . . And when she had witnessed to these things she departed for Seleucia and when she had enlightened many people with the word of God, she slept with a good sleep.[11]

This conflict between eschatological, egalitarian Paulinism and patriarchal Paulinism continues to shape second- and third-century Christianity, although the radical expressions of eschatological Christianity come to be defined as 'heretical.' The egalitarian ideal continued to be enunciated in popular Christian writings, such as the passions of the martyrs and popular apocryphal *Acts*. But the fact that it is the Paul of I Timothy that becomes the canonical Paul means that patriarchal Christianity has established itself as the orthodox line for interpreting both the New Testament and subsequent Christian theology on the subject of gender relations.

Gnostics and Montanists represent alternative lines of Christianity that are marginalized and condemned by established orthodoxy in the late second century. Both movements are strongly ascetic, although Montanist asceticism is based on the revival of primitive Christian apocalypticism with its belief in an imminent end of the world and in the direct authority of the Holy Spirit indwelling in prophets and prophetesses. The fact that two of its three prophet-leaders were female was a major cause of orthodox objection to it. The heresy-hunter, Epiphanius, condemns Montanists because they claim that the sister of Moses was a prophetess and allowed women to serve as bishops.

Among the charges against the Montanists is that they dissolved marriages and allowed women to leave their husbands. This is interpreted by their critics as a mandate for loose living and insubordination of women. In the popular apocryphal *Acts*, however, we see a Christianity probably similar to that of Montanism which believed that conversion to chastity freed a woman from subordination to her betrothed or her husband and allowed her to become an itinerant teacher. For the Montanists the present form of this world is passing away. So the historical shape of the patriarchal family could be put aside in anticipation of that new age soon to come where there would be no more marrying or giving in marriage and where the saints would reign according to their holiness, not according to their social status in the 'world.'

Although gnosticism also thinks of the form of this present world as ripe for dissolution, its spirituality is one of mystical withdrawal from the world 'below,' rather than political confrontation with authorities of state and family. Gnostic asceticism is based on a philosophical dualism which divides reality between a higher androgynous spiritual world and a lower world of material oppression, which is typically seen as ruled over by the patriarchal God of creation whom the gnostics demote into being a fallen 'archon' or demonic power. Sophia, or the mother power of the spiritual world, is seen as being both involved in the fall of the higher spiritual world into bondage, but also the means of inspiration who enlightens humanity and awakens them to their true spiritual nature and to the falsity of the present material world and its evil gods.

Thus in the gnostic creation story, the *Hypostasis of the Archons*, Sophia communicates through the snake, as the representative of wisdom and new life, to Eve who is the first to be enlightened because she is closer to Wisdom. Eve, in turn, enlightens Adam, and their eyes are opened to their naked condition; i.e., their lack of spiritual power. Sabaoth, the Creator of the material world, who orders the primal couple not to eat of the fruit of the tree of knowledge (gnosis), is interpreted as trying to keep them in ignorance and bondage to material existence. His expulsion of the couple is understood as an effort to throw them into such distraction with daily toil that they will be unable to follow up this insight into the higher spiritual world:

> They threw humanity into great distraction and into a life of toil so that their humanity might be occupied by worldly affairs and might not have the opportunity of being devoted to the Holy Spirit.[12]

In the fragmentary gnostic Christian gospel, the *Gospel of Mary*, we see a conscious defense of women's apostolic authority over against a patriarchal Christianity, which gnostics identified particularly with Peter (for the orthodox, the founder of episcopal hierarchy). In this gospel the risen Lord specifically instructs the disciples to live out of an internal power of the Spirit and not to create institutional structures:

> For the Son of Man is within you. Follow after him! Those who seek him

239

will find him. Go then and preach the gospel of the kingdom. Do not lay down any rules beyond what I appointed for you and do not give a law like a lawgiver lest you be constrained by it.[13]

With these words the Savior departs, leaving the assembled disciples in consternation. The disciples include Mary of Magdala and probably several other women. The gnostics here follow the early Christian tradition that identified the women around Jesus as part of the Pentecostal community. The disciples are seen as lacking the power of the Spirit and to be in fear of persecution from their enemies. Seeking the spiritual power of faith, they turn to Mary Magdala as one closest to the Savior:

> Peter said to Mary, 'Sister, we know the Savior loved you more than the rest of women. Tell us the words of the Savior which you remember, which you know, but we do not nor have we heard them.'[14]

Mary proceeds to proclaim the power of salvation in a visionary discourse. After her discourse a dispute breaks out among the male disciples about her authority to be thus endowed with higher spiritual knowledge beyond that possessed by the male disciples. Andrew declares his disbelief in Mary's teaching and this is followed by Peter:

> Peter answered and spoke concerning these same things. He questioned them about the Savior. 'Did he really speak privately with a woman and not openly to us? Are we to turn about and listen to her? Did he prefer her to us?'

Levi rebukes Peter for his hostility to Mary and his inability to accept her authority:

> Levi answered and said to Peter, 'Peter, you have always been hot-tempered. Now I see you contending against the woman like the adversaries. But if the Savior made her worthy, who are you indeed to reject her? Surely the Savior knows her very well. That is why he loved her more than us. Rather let us be ashamed and put on the perfect humanness and separate as he commanded us and preach the gospel, not laying down any rule or other law beyond what the Savior said.'[15]

With these words the disciples are endowed with the power of faith they previously lacked and 'they began to go forth and proclaim and to preach.'

These texts make clear that the debate over women's power to preach and teach was conscious and explicit in second-century Christianity. It was the 'separatist' types of Christians, who saw themselves as departing both from the world, in the sense of existing social structures of family and state, and from a fallen material universe, who championed women's spiritual equality as the principle that should define social relations in the community of redemption.

Patriarchal Christians, by contrast, rejected this separatism, increasingly believed in integrating into the existing social structures of society. They defended marriage, the family and the goodness of creation, but did so in such a way as to identify the 'order of creation' with patriarchal hierarchy. This hierarchy they believed to be still intact and to define the social order, not only of the world, but of the church as well. Although spiritual equality might be the order of heaven, this was not to be seen as mandating social equality of women with men in church society. On the contrary, woman would attain holiness by recognizing her sinfulness as the one who brought sin into the world in the first place and by making atonement by redoubled submission to her subordinate role in the family and also in the church.

By the fourth century we see a new synthesis being created between patriarchal pro-family and ascetic anti-family types of Christianity. In this new synthesis it is taken for granted that only men may have public leadership roles in the church. Marriage and childbearing are to be defended, but they are seen as the lowest rung of holiness in the church, tolerated and given the minimal blessings by God, but secondary to the higher blessings of virginity and chaste widowhood. The end of the world is near, so reproduction, while still allowed, is no longer necessary. Those who would seek the higher holiness of Christ should renounce sexuality, marriage and reproduction for chastity. These now become a spiritual elite, but within, not against, the ecclesiastical order which, in turn, is taking its place as a new governing order of Christian society.[16]

Women ascetics, while spiritually equal with men, gain no official public authority thereby. Indeed they prove their true holiness by their spirit of submission and humility to every male authority, especially the bishop. During this period we see a marked effort to fuse ascetic charismatic power with episcopal ecclesiastical power. Bishops and, if possible, priests should renounce sexual relations with their wives and live in chastity. At the same time the sexuality of the laity, especially that of women, comes under great suspicion.[17] Women, even ascetic women, are seen as dangerous temptresses who must be carefully veiled and segregated lest their presence contaminate the holiness of the clergy.

This clericalization of asceticism shifts the psychology of asceticism decisively. Instead of a radical ethic which dissolved worldly authority and freed women to act with spiritual authority, sexual abstinence now became linked with a magical concept of the holiness of the sacramental priesthood. The sacred and the secular become divided into the two spheres of the celibate clergy and the sexual laity, with women as the epitome of the anti-sacred or that which 'pollutes' the sacred.

As one moves into the early Middle Ages, from the fifth to the ninth century, there is an increasing appropriation of the purity taboos of Levitical law and their application to the Christian priesthood. Menstruating women, and couples who have recently had sexual intercourse, are regarded as too impure to receive the sacrament. Females must be kept out of sanctuary. This idea exercised a decisive role in eliminating certain ministerial roles, such as deaconesses, which women had continued to exercise from early Christianity. The mere touch of female hands was regarded as contaminating, and so women were instructed to cover their hands when receiving the sacred vessels for cleaning.[18]

Medieval Christianity does not entirely lose remnants of ascetic egalitarianism. Female religious orders up to the twelfth century preserve ideas that the monastic vocation liberates women from family authority and that holy women not only have prophetic and healing authority whereby they can rebuke and instruct the church, but also are self-governing and have pastoral authority within their own realm.[19] But the later Middle Ages and the Counter-Reformation see an increasing effort to undermine the autonomy of nuns and to subject them to clerical rule.[20] Clerical celibacy mandates a continual barrage of sermonic hostility to women as the antithesis of all that is godly.[21]

On the other hand, radical groups, both popular prophetic sects like the Waldensians and neo-gnostics such as the Manichaeans, rediscover a Christianity in radical opposition to the power structures of society, including that identified with the ecclesiastical hierarchy. In the process they also rediscover an egalitarian concept of the community of redemption. Thus Waldensians in the twelfth century allowed women to preach on the grounds that preaching was a prophetic office given by the Holy Spirit, poured out on 'the menservants and the maidservants.'[22] And Manichaeans in southern France numbered powerful women among the 'Perfecti' who, through adopting the radical ascetic discipline of fasting and sexual abstinence, were regarded as the spiritual leaders of the sect.[23]

The Reformation saw this conflict between radical ascetic and ecclesiastical Christianity restated. The magisterial Reformation (Lutheran, Anglican, Calvinist) swept away the whole structure of patristic and medieval clerical celibacy and monasticism. The married life was declared normative for all Christians. All were to pursue their Christian vocation in everyday life, not in a separated world of higher holiness as a celibate elite. But, on the other hand, the Reformation made the patriarchal household codes normative for Christian family life and for the social order generally. 'Wives obey your husbands, children obey your parents, servants obey your masters' rang out from the Puritan pulpit as the epitome of the Christian order, understood as the order of Creation restored from sinful insubordination.[24] Thus the elimination of monasticism also eliminated the accepted place for an ascetic counter-culture in Christian society.

However, very quickly, the Reformation developed its own left-wing radicals who rediscovered the direct, unmediated inspiration of the Holy Spirit and saw this spiritual power as poured out on charismatic woman and men alike. Thus Baptists in the Puritan Civil War upheld women as preachers.[25] Quakers, imbued with the power of the inner light, believed that Christ restored women to their created equality in the image of God. For Quakers, this restoration of women to spiritual equality meant that women may both preach and teach as evangelists and share in church government through the 'women's meetings.'[26]

This sectarian wing of Protestantism reinvented Christian celibacy in the eighteenth and nineteenth centuries, associating it not with a clerical order but with the converted spiritual community as a whole. Thus the Shakers, a radical English spiritualist group of the late eighteenth and nineteenth centuries, believed that sin originated with sexuality. This fall into sexuality also plunged women into oppressive childbearing and domination by the husband. Conversion to Christ is identified with conversion to chastity, in anticipation of the heavenly order when there will be no marrying or giving in marriage. In the millennial community of Christ's Second Appearing, women have been restored to complete equality with men. This means that women and men exercise parallel and equal authority of government within the church.

The Shakers link this egalitarianism with an androgynous concept of God and of Christ. God is both mother and father, and so humanity, made in the image of God as male and female, reflects this androgynous or dual nature of God. Christ, in turn, must come both in male and in female form in order to complete the revelation of God in history. The Shakers, who saw themselves as arising from the second appearing of Christ in female form (as Mother Ann Lee, the foundress of the community), thus represent the fulfillment of God's revelation. They are the millennial community where women's spiritual equality is realized.[27] Similar, although somewhat less radical, concepts of divine androgyny and spiritual equality of men and women are found in other priest sects in nineteenth-century Germany and America. Transcendentalism and Christian Science also affirm the 'female' aspect of the divine. Notions that the female represented the higher spiritual power, and that this female spirituality was now being revealed as a transformative power that would create a higher and more moral social order, were widespread in nineteenth-century millennialism. Some kind of asceticism, in the sense of a spiritual transcendence of sexuality and 'materiality,' was a typical correlate of this revelation of the 'feminine.'[28]

Thus the history of Christian asceticism presents us with a marked contradiction. While a clericalized celibacy has typically been linked with misogyny and suppression of women in society and especially in the church, a counter-cultural egalitarian Christianity not only existed as the earliest form of Christian asceticism, but has been continually renewed in sectarian, millennialist movements from Montanism down to nineteenth-century groups such as Shakers. This counter-cultural asceticism links withdrawal from sexuality and reproduction with dissolution of the patriarchal family and social order and sees the church as a community of spiritual equality. What are feminists today to make of these contradictory understandings of asceticism and gender relations and, particularly, can feminists appropriate this counter-cultural wing of Christianity into their own efforts to reintegrate sexuality and spirituality?

The basic mistake shared by patriarchal and counter-cultural Christianity alike in this tradition was to identify sexuality and reproduction with a patriarchal understanding of society as the 'natural order.' Thus women's spiritual equality could only be established on a basis transcendent to nature, referring back to a spiritual 'creation' before the 'fall' of humanity into sexuality, on the one hand, and referring forward to a heavenly order beyond nature on the other. Counter-cultural, ascetic Christians differed from patriarchal Christians only in believing that this millennial order was already injected into history, displacing the creational structures of patriarchy and raising up a redemptive community of spiritual equals who anticipated the heavenly order by transcending sexuality and reproduction.

Patriarchal Christians, on the other hand, believed that the patriarchal order of the family continued to be normative for history, mandating the subordination of women in the family in the lower orders of the laity and the governing power of males in the ecclesiastical order. Holy women will be equal in heaven, but they will earn this equality by humble submission to the created order restored in the church. Thus patriarchal and counter-cultural Christianity both saw patriarchy as the order of creation and linked it with male domination, reproduction and mortality. But they differed radically on how they connected the historical church as community of redemption to this patriarchal order of creation and society.

Feminism, by contrast, takes its origins from modern post-Enlightenment views that regard 'original nature' as egalitarian. All humans are 'created equal' and 'endowed by their Creator with the same inalienable rights.' This is the basic creation-based theology of modern liberalism. Hierarchical privilege of class, race, or gender groups does not derive from the original order of nature, but from a distortion of nature into systems of domination and oppression. Sin is not a fall into sexuality, but a fall into oppression and injustice. Salvation is not a flight from the body, nature, and history, but a reordering of the social systems by which we live our embodied historical lives so that the full value and dignity of all persons can be realized.[29]

Thus, while feminists would reject the idea that sexual intercourse and reproduction 'naturally' subject women to a state of inferiority, they also recognize that the social ordering of these functions into heterosexual sexuality and the patriarchal family does indeed do so. In practice, we find it almost as difficult in the twentieth century as our ancestors did in the second or twelfth or sixteenth centuries for women to marry and have children and, at the same time, appropriate the intellectual self-development and public social self-expression

associated with full human potential (as that has been developed by
and for males). The choice between marriage and career continues to
be a very real one for most women. Radical feminists suspect that any
capitulation to social or sexual relations with males is a capitulation
to subordinate status, and so they reject, not sexuality, but heterosexuality. Only women bonding together against the patriarchal order of
family and society can create the social basis of liberation of women.

Some lesbian feminists would want to integrate childbearing or
childraising into this community of women, either through artificial
insemination or adoption of children. The desire to appropriate
motherhood as central to women's creative power is affirmed, but the
ambivalence remains. Is women's creativity to be 'reduced' to
motherhood, or is all female creativity to be seen as an extension of
motherhood? For many this sounds too much like the biological
reductionism by which male culture has sought to confine women to
their reproductive functions. Moreover, no matter how much a
women's community seeks to raise a child equally, there still remains
a strong social disposition to see the biological mother as primarily
responsible for parenting. *Vis-à-vis* a male social order, where male
freedom is based on female childraising, even two women raising a
child together are disadvantaged. Two female incomes may barely
equal one male income, and one still has all the problems of childcare
of 'working mothers' in a society constructed for female auxiliary
status in a public world of male wage labor and male ownership of
income-producing institutions. The female-bonding community remains a small, marginal 'sect' *vis-à-vis* a largely unchanged patriarchal world.

It seems to this author that an effort to totalize the lesbian
separatist community as the normative feminist solution is untenable
and will result in marginalizing and discrediting feminist questions
for all men and most women. This, however, does not mean that such
communities cannot be enormously creative 'ginger' groups that raise
the important questions, provide some alternatives for some women
and are fonts of new culture. But one needs to find ways to integrate
these insights both into a new human culture and a new social order.

In imagining a new culture, feminism cannot totally repudiate the
recognition of tension between spirituality and sexuality, intellectual
creativity and bodily appetites, which is the basis of the ascetic
tradition. One cannot assume that once oppressive social structures
are thrown off, a wholistic energy that harmonizes all things will arise

like magic from a world of reclaimed natural spontaneity. The utopian, separatist community still finds itself with the basic human problems of mortality and finitude, of organizing work and adjudicating relationships between people. Substance abuse, whether of food, alcohol or drugs, is not conducive to the best use of our minds and spirits.

The counter-cultural community today is filled with 'new ascetics,' who through meditation, diet, rigorous physical exercise and psychological 'therapy' seek to integrate their physical, mental and emotional energies into a whole. One difference between these modern ascetics and the ancient ones is that the ancient ascetic spent most of his or her effort on cultivating the spirit, while limiting the demands of the body, while the modern ascetic comes at the control of feelings primarily through the control of the body. Often this takes the form of manipulating the body by trickery, such as 'non-caloric foods' and diet pills which seek to avoid disciplining of the appetites. Spiritual life and relation to the divine is neglected, while one looks for solutions to inner harmony through ingesting the right chemistry.

I believe that we should think of the human being, not as a dualism of mind and body, but as one psycho-physical organism (the hyphen itself indicates how lacking our language is in a wholistic language for this). Nevertheless the various energies of the self are not easily integrated, especially in a society shaped by rising expectations and expanding poverty. In the midst of this barrage of socially-fed contradictions, we too need to develop some basic 'ascesis' (the word means simply 'discipline' and was originally drawn from the Greek word for the regime of the athlete). Our *ascesis* is not to be aimed at rejecting one part of our energy for another, but at integrating the spiritual, the emotional, the sexual, and the artistic.[30] This involves not only certain disciplines aimed at the unifying of one's self, such as diet, exercise, and conscious focusing of mental energy in meditation, but also an *ascesis* toward the demands of society; limiting the demands of consumerism, refusing to work all day and every day, staying in one place more, creating more unified and intentional communities. All this seems to be very necessary for a new *ascesis* that aims at helping people today to overcome fragmentation and burn out and to achieve sufficient inner calm and efficacy to be centers of new culture.

Secondly, we need to design a new social order that expresses this relationality of people, women and women, women and men, men and men, in genuine mutuality. This is a global historical project, but we cannot wait for a total revolution of the world system to happen. One needs to find ways to begin in the communities of primary bonding in which we live our daily lives and then reach out from there to neighbourhoods, local communities, and regional governments, seeking policies that can overcome oppressive duality and encourage mutuality. This is not the place to spell out this project even in such minimum detail as one can begin to imagine, for we are far from imagining how these local efforts can add up to transformation of the larger national and international systems of power. Suffice it to say that some combination of 'ascesis,' or discipline aiming at personal harmonization of creative energies, and the transformation of the world, or 'salvation,' is still our agenda as human beings. But we need to do that by reintegrating the sexual and the spiritual, the personal and the social, rather than by seeking one side of this tension by rejection and flight from the other.

NOTES

1 Jacqueline Peterson and Mary Druke, 'American Indian Women and Religion,' in *Women and Religion in America: The Colonial and Revolutionary Periods*, Rosemary S. Keller and Rosemary R. Ruether (eds), San Francisco, Harper & Row, 1983, pp.6–7, and documents 6–9.

2 Ruth Underhill, *Red Man's Religion*, Chicago, University of Chicago Press, 1972, pp.146–52.

3 After twenty years of pursuit of severe ascetic discipline alone in a desert fortress, Anthony is described as emerging 'as though from some shrine, having been led into divine mysteries and inspired by God.' Those who beheld him 'were amazed to see that his body has maintained its former condition, neither fat from lack of exercise, nor emaciated from fasting and combat with demons, but just as they had known him prior to his withdrawal.' The chief effect of his combat was the achievement of complete mental calm and balance. Athanasius, *Life of Anthony*, sec. 14. Translation Robert Gregg.

4 Peter Brown, *The Making of Late Antiquity*, Cambridge, Mass., Harvard University Press, 1978.

5 Owen Chadwick, *Western Asceticism*, Philadelphia, Westminster, 1958.

6 The idea that the ascetic impulse in Christianity came primarily from Platonism and Greek philosophy and was alien to the Jewish sources of Christianity was developed particularly by the German Church historian Adolf Harnack in his *Lehrbuch der Dogmengeschichte* (3 vols), 1886–9.

7   Syriac Christianity seems to have been highly ascetic from its earliest development and some groups required celibacy as a condition of baptism: see Arthur Vööbus, *Celibacy as a Requirement for Admission to Baptism in the Early Syriac Church*, Stockholm, 1951.

8   Galatians 3:28 is generally thought to be a baptismal formula that pre-existed the Pauline churches and reflects a conscious rejection of the Hellenistic and Jewish formulas which thanked God to have been born male and not female, free and n. See Elisabeth S. Fiorenza, *In Memory of Her: A Feminist Theological Reconstruction of Christian Origins*, New York, Crossroads Press, 1983, pp.208–26.

9   Dennis R. Macdonald, *The Legend and the Apostle: The Battle for Paul in Story and Canon*, Philadelphia, Westminster Press, 1983.

10 Steven Davies, *The Revolt of the Widows: The Social World of the Apocryphal Acts*, Southern Illinois University Press, 1980.

11 *The Acts of Paul and Thecla*, vol. 8 in *Ante-Nicene Fathers*, Alexander Roberts and James Donaldson (eds), New York, Scribner's, 1885–97, pp.487ff.

12 *The Hypostasis of the Archons*, in *The Nag Hammadi Library in English*, New York, Harper & Row, 1977, p.156.

13 *The Gospel of Mary*, in *The Nag Hammadi Library in English*, p.472.

14 *Ibid.*

15 *Ibid.*, pp.473–4.

16 This understanding of asceticism emerges particularly with ascetic bishops, such as St Augustine in the late fourth century. See Rosemary Ruether, 'Misogynism and Virginal Feminism in the Fathers of the Church,' in *Religion and Sexism: Images of Women in the Jewish and Christian Traditions*, Rosemary R. Ruether (ed.), New York, Harper & Row, pp.156–68.

17 This connection of clerical celibacy and hostility to women's sexuality is found particularly in the canons of the Council of Elvira; see Samuel Laeuchli, *Power and Sexuality: The Emergence of Canon Law at the Council of Elvira*, Philadelphia, Temple University Press, 1972.

18 This theme has been developed particularly in the book by Susan Wemple, *Women in Frankish Society: Marriage and the Cloister, 500–900 A.D.*, Philadelphia, University of Pennsylvania Press, 1983.

19 The power and autonomy of early medieval nuns is shown in the classical study by Lina Eckerstein, *Women Under Monasticism. Saint Lore and Convent Life*, Cambridge, Cambridge University Press, 1896.

20 The constriction of women's autonomy in religious orders in the Council of Trent and the efforts of women to resist this constriction is developed in Ruth Liebowitz, 'Virgins in the Service of Christ: The Dispute over the Active Apostolate for Women During the Counter-Reformation,' in *Women of Spirit: Female Leadership in the Jewish and Christian Traditions*, Rosemary Ruether and Eleanor McLaughlin (eds), New York, Simon & Schuster, 1979, pp.132–52.

21 Pulpit hostility to women was commonplace in the later Middle Ages and was a prime source of the popular diatribe against women that also passed into secular literature in the late Medieval and Renaissance worlds; see G. C. Coulton, *Medieval Panorama: The English Scene from Conquest to Reformation*, New York, Meridian, 1955, p.622.

22 I owe this information on medieval Waldensians to the president of the Waldensian Church, Georgia Bouchard. See also Shulamith Shahar, *The Fourth Estate: A History of Women in the Middle Ages*, New York, Methuen, 1983, pp.254–8.

23 *Ibid.*, pp.259–68.

24 See, for example, William Perkins, *Christian Oeconomie*, London, 1590.

25 See Rosemary Ruether, 'Women in Sectarian and Utopian Groups,' in *Women and Religion in America: The Colonial and Revolutionary War Periods*, R. Ruether and R. Keller (eds), pp.261–2, 278–88.

26 *Ibid.*, pp.266–8, 305–12.

27 Rosemary Ruether, 'Women in Utopian Movements,' *Women and Religion in America: The Nineteenth Century*, San Francisco, Harper & Row, 1981, pp.48–9, 83–7.

28 *Ibid.*, p.48.

29 The connection of the liberal doctrine of original nature with the Biblical understanding of creation in the image of God, male and female, is the foundational presupposition of nineteenth-century American Christian feminism. See, for example, Sarah Grimke, *Letters on the Equality of the Sexes and the Condition of Women*, 1837, in *Feminism: Essential Historical Writings*, Miriam Schneir (ed.), New York, Vintage, 1972, pp.36–43.

30 Margaret Miles, *Fullness of Life: Historical Foundations for a New Asceticism* (Philadelphia, Westminster, 1981) is a major effort to reclaim asceticism for feminism and for modern wholistic thought, but it suffers from an underplaying of the misogynist tradition in asceticism and also a failure to recognize the social element in asceticism in the conflict between Christian counter-culture and clericalization.

23

SEXUAL JUSTICE AND THE 'RIGHTEOUSNESS OF GOD'

Sheila Briggs

> Our sexuality is our desire to participate in making love, making justice, in the world; our drive toward one another; our movement in love; our expression of being bonded together in life and death. Sexuality is expressed not only between lovers in personal relationship, but also in the work of an artist who loves her painting or poetry, a father who loves his children, a revolutionary who loves her people. (Carter Heyward)[1]

The Christian tradition has said much about justice. Many feminists, remaining in the Christian churches, explain their commitment to institutions which are patriarchal in their organization and often misogynistic in their teaching, by their belief in a thirsting after the righteousness of God's rule as being central to the Christian gospel. The feminist vision of Christianity is an empowerment of believers as doers of justice. In consequence, feminists feel alienated from those parts of the Christian tradition which seem either indifferent to the concrete needs of people for justice in their daily lives or happily acquiescent in systems of social injustice. This sense of alienation is heightened by the fact that feminists, like Marxists, are aware that injustice is not only a maldistribution of material goods and the abandonment of human beings to horrible physical wants, but also a crippling of the spirit and the production of 'false consciousness'.

Our sexuality embodies the injustice of our society. There is no reservation of our personal lives, where the freedom and fulfillment denied us in our public and formal relations with others in our society is compensated by the free play of sensuality and the achievement of intimacy. The most well-known slogan of the women's movement, 'The personal is political', grew out of the painful realization of women, gathering together in groups during the 1960s and 1970s, that their common experiences revealed a socially conditioned shallowness of passion. Women discovered that we are not happy because we are not just; justice is neither done to us nor by us.

The following essay looks at how the Christian understanding of justice emerged within the mental patterns of the slaveholding household of the ancient Graeco-Roman world. It will argue that the power relations of this society moulded the understanding of God and the righteousness of God in the texts of the New Testament. Early Christianity asserted the control of women's sexuality through the sanction of patriarchal marriage as the only acceptable sexual lifestyle and the accompanying condemnation of lesbian sexual relations. This ethic was intertwined with Christianity's view of God's justice and its social context of slavery. The possibility of a critique of patriarchal society on the basis of the righteousness of God will be contrasted with feminist theory and praxis of justice.

LOVE AND SLAVERY IN THE CHRISTIAN HOUSEHOLD

The language in which Christian theology has traditionally discussed justice was framed around the social interactions in pre-modern, hierarchically organized and often slave-holding societies. Thus, in the *Letter to the Colossians*, attributed to the apostle Paul but probably written by a follower, we find rules of conduct for the Christian slave and the Christian slaveowner, which never question the institution of slavery itself. On the contrary, slaveowners are exhorted in Colossians 4:1 to treat their slaves with justice within the institution of slavery, because they themselves stand in the same relationship to God, the 'master in heaven', as their slaves do to them. In this passage and elsewhere in the New Testament we find a play on words between the title 'Lord' given by Christians to Christ and the common usage of 'lords' to designate those who were masters of slaves. Christianity, even in its earliest period, supported the exploitation of the slave's labour.

In every slave-holding society, including that of the ancient Graeco-Roman world, the sexual exploitation of slaves has been intrinsic to the institution of slavery. Male and female slaves were subject to the sexual use and abuse of their owners in the social world of early Christianity. On the other side, both women and men were slaveholders and, in some cases, women also had sexual access to slaves.[2] None the less, the dominant form of sexual exploitation was that by male slaveowner of female slave. Sexual exploitation of female slaves had a twofold purpose. It had an obvious economic value: the master owned the slave's body including its reproductive capacities. In ancient Rome it was said that a female slave had earned her freedom when she had borne her master four children (who would remain his property).[3]

Secondly, there was the psychological value of rape as a means of social control of slaves. In the Roman Empire during the two centuries immediately prior to the emergence of Christianity the slave markets had been swelled by those who had been enslaved as a result of Roman conquest. Amongst these slaves there was a preponderance of women. It is normally assumed that women were more likely to be enslaved because they were more manageable. But what made women more manageable and what was the form of management? It was hardly physical weakness that made women more malleable in the process of enslavement since female slaves carried out heavy labour.

Orlando Patterson has shown in his major comparative study of slavery that the social psychology of a slaveholding society hinges on a strong conception of honour. Patterson departed from previous discussions on slavery by describing it not in terms of legal status but as a relation of domination. This relation of domination is marked by natal alienation and the opposition of honour and degradation. By natal alienation Patterson means that the slave loses or never possesses rights, privileges or status as member of a kinship group, tribe, etc. He or she only exists through his or her master. The slaveowner's status and the status of all free individuals is symbolized in their community by its contrast to the dishonour of slaves: 'The dishonour of the slave sprang . . . from that raw, human sense of debasement inherent in having no being except as an expression of another's being.'[4]

Patterson sees the honour/dishonour polarity as universal to the condition of slavery and also recognizes the ubiquity of the sexual use and abuse of slave women by their masters, but does not perceive the connection between these two facets of slavery. The social degradation of the slave was most complete in the sexual abuse of the female slave. Her honour was the control of her sexuality by her kinsmen. In the state of slavery she was kinless and without the protection of her honour. The invasion of her body was the re-enactment of the dishonouring of her enslavement. Thus, the rape of slave women was not the arbitrary expression of the sexual lusts of their owners, it was the everyday symbolic re-assertion of the institution of slavery. For the woman, enslaved by conquest or born into slavery, and for the male and female slaves around her rape was the reminder that they were persons without honour.

Christianity probably left unchallenged the sexual subjection of slave to master. There is no explicit prohibition of sexual relations between slaveowner and slave in the New Testament. The apostle Paul in the *First Letter to the Corinthians* warns Christians to avoid illicit sexual activity (*porneia*). It has been hotly debated what sexual relations Paul included under *porneia*, but Paul's own definition of the 'fornicator' (*ho porneuôn*) as one who 'sins against his own body' (1 Corinthians 6:18) would not have been held by the typical ancient slaveowner to have included the sexual exploitation of his slave. Paul is speaking here specifically – though not necessarily exclusively – of sexual intercourse with prostitutes, who were also commonly slaves but someone else's. The apostle sees such action in terms of ritual impurity: the desecration of the 'temple of the Holy Spirit' in the body of the Christian. Contact with an externally unclean object results in the pollution of the fornicator. The level of impurity is in this case especially severe because sexual intercourse in Paul's interpretation of Genesis 2:24 results in the man and woman becoming one flesh. Since the slave woman in her master's household was inside his body and not external to it she could not contaminate it. She was already part of his flesh through the socially parasitic relationship of slavery. Her dishonour and sexual abasement did not degrade her master but enhanced his honour.

The image of God as a heavenly slaveowner is interrelated to the notion of Christians being included within the body of Christ. Christians, like earthly slaves, are extensions of the body of their master. The slaveownver is very frequently a husband and his body, like his household, includes a wife as well as slaves. Although the wife had a clearly distinct legal status from the slave in antiquity, yet there was a continuity between her own and the slave's absorption into the body of the male head of the household. Outside of his body the recognition of the wife's existence was limited, in the case of the slave, denied. Wives were legally inferior persons; slaves were non-persons.

This reality of Christian marriage within a slave-owning society is captured in another letter written by a follower of Paul, *The Letter to the Ephesians*. The author of Ephesians is careful to make a distinction between the wife and the slave in the words chosen to describe their respective status under the authority of the male head of household. Wives are required to be subordinate to their husbands (*hypotasses-thai*). The subordination of wife to husband in Ephesians 5:23f. seems to be a particular case of the more general and mutual 'giving way to one another in the fear of Christ' (the same verb *hypotassesthai* is also used) in the immediately preceding passage, Ephesians 5:21. From children and slaves it is demanded that they obey (*hypakouein*) their parents or masters respectively.

This difference in terminology has led some Christian apologists to claim that the relationship of husband and wife, envisaged in Ephesians, recognizes the worth and dignity of women. They ignore the fact that by the same argument the worth and dignity of slave women is denied! A more plausible explanation of the care taken by the author of Ephesians to differentiate the status of wife from that of slave is that the scope and content of the subjection of the wife to the husband seems to vary little from the master–slave relationship.[5]

There is no limitation put on the subordination of wives to husbands. They are to be submissive to their husbands in everything, and in this they will reflect the perfect submission of the church to Christ (v.24). Most intriguing is the reason, given by the author, for why husbands should love their wives. Husbands should love their wives 'as their own bodies' (v.28). The wife is as much an extension of the husband's body as the slave, however different their status may be. The theological warrant for this statement is provided in this passage primarily by an analogy to the relationship of Christ to the church. Christ loves and cares for the church as his body.

The love of husband for wife and Christ for the church is expressed in Ephesians by the verb *agapan*. The author of Ephesians did not place upon this word the same theological freight that modern theologians have, seeing *agape* as a distinctively Christian love. Nevertheless, Ephesians endows the love of husband for wife with theological meaning by comparing it to Christ's love for the church. Love is characterized as a constituent element of a relationship of domination. The dominant reciprocates the submissiveness of the dominated with love.

The difference between the relationship of husband to wife and master to slave lies for Ephesians not in the extent of domination, but in the appropriate forms of reciprocity. The husband can expect from his wife a subordination that is no less complete in its subjection than the obedience of the slave. But the wife is a free person, she possesses honour, and the relationship of domination must reflect that status. Her subordination is not at the cost of her honour because her husband 'does not hate his own flesh' (v.29).

In the case of slaves the body metaphor for their inclusion under the authority of the male head of household disappears, not because they are conceded an existence independent of him, but because Ephesians has reserved this metaphor for the form of domination existing between persons of honour. Masters are not exhorted to love their slaves, but to 'cease from threatening'. Indeed threats are redundant in the relationship between Christian master and Christian slave as slaves have been previously commanded to obey their masters 'with fear and trembling' (Ephesians 6:5). Wives are not expected to exhibit the tokens of abject fear in their relationship to their husbands. What makes 'fear and trembling' necessary to the recognition by the slave of the authority of the male head of household over her or him, when this is not so for the wife? I suggest that 'fear and trembling' represents the slave's acceptance of her or his state of dishonour, that she or he is a non-person.

If Ephesians had chosen to expand the body metaphor to the master–slave relationship, then it would have been unlikely to have adopted the parallel to the care of the body with which it chose to describe the husband–wife relation (5:29). A very probable candidate for an analogy to the master–slave relationship would have been the discipline of the body. Ancient notions of the body reflected societal relationships. On the one hand, the body was tended so that in its physical appearance it might give expression to the honour and status of the person: on the other, it was an instrument to be trained, even with harshness, to submit to the will of the person.

The second understanding of the body occurs indirectly in Ephesians' prescriptions for slaves. Just as wives' subordination to their husbands had been predicted upon the relationship of subordination of the body of the church to its head Christ, so slaves are reminded that their status is common to all who are part of the body of Christ. They are commanded to 'do as slaves of Christ the will of God from the heart and with zeal . . . seeing that everyone who does good, will receive recompense for this from the Lord, whether slave or free' (6:7 f.). The reference to slaves of earthly masters as 'slaves of Christ' implies that to be a member of the body of Christ, the church, is to be subject to the will of God disciplining the body of Christ. In terms of enslavement within the body of Christ the socially free and the socially enslaved share the same status, which allows Ephesians to universalize its exhortation to slaves. In the words addressed by Ephesians to masters one finds the same warning as in Colossians that they should behave in the light of the fact they have a 'master in heaven'. There is a notable expansion. This master in heaven is described as not showing preference (*prosôpolêpsia*) to anyone. This should not be interpreted in an apologetic sense – the claim that Ephesians intends with this remark to relativize the social distinction of master and slave. Rather, it is the logical consequence of the inclusion of masters within the body of Christ: as slaves of Christ too they have no honour before God which would differentiate them from their earthly slaves.

The 'love patriarchalism' (as biblical scholars refer to the rules of conduct for wives and husbands in Ephesians and Colossians) is part of a pattern of domination, which rests upon the dishonouring of Christians as part of their enslavement within the body of Christ. The distinction between the honour of the wife and the dishonour of the slave, the care of the body and the discipline of the body, provides the basis in material reality and social meaning for the theological dialectics of justification. The person who is justified in Christ goes through a process of dishonouring and receiving back honour. Translated into the terms of the social reality of the ancient world, the Christian soul is a woman who, enslaved by Christ, is made his concubine and then elevated to his wife. The reversal of the woman's/soul's status is totally dependent upon the will of her master and husband.

JUSTIFICATION AS ENSLAVEMENT AND MARRIAGE

Most New Testament scholars see the use of the language of justification in Colossians 4 as peripheral to the central statement of justification by Paul in his letters to the Romans and to the Galatians. In part, this judgment is based upon the attribution of Colossians not to Paul himself but to a follower. To a greater extent, however, a methodological premise is at work here which sharply distinguishes, on the one hand, between the Christian theological understanding of justice and, on the other, the ethical idea of justice and its social undergirdings present in the Graeco-Roman environment. At the same time, it is realized that the Colossians text contains the social metaphors in which Paul's doctrine of justification is framed. One scholar admits that 'Paul's idea of the Christian life as a transfer of masters is reflected' in the admonition to slaveowners that they treat their slaves justly and fairly since they have a master in heaven.[6]

A closer look at the text of Colossians 4:1 shows that the socio-ethical description of the earthly master's behaviour is a precise parallel to Paul's understanding of God's activity in making the sinner just, at least as later Christian theologians and exegetes, particularly but not exclusively those in the tradition of the Protestant Reformation, have interpreted the authentic theological meaning of Paul. Slaveowners are exhorted to *parachesthai to dikaion kai tên isotêta* to their slaves, which can be literally translated as 'grant justice and fairness'. The verb *parachesthai* clearly denotes that justice and fairness in the relationship between master and slave is in the gift of the master. The preceding rules of conduct for slaves in Colossians 3:22–25 do not suggest that the slave has any claim on justice or fairness from her or his master. They resemble closely and even share the same phraseology as their counterpart in Ephesians.

It is the slaveowner who establishes justice in his relationship to the slave in much the same way as it is God who establishes justice in relationship to the sinner. The distinction between the 'active justice' of God and the 'passive justice' of the justified sinner, so underscored by the Protestant Reformation, has its social roots in the institution of slavery. Human beings in general, just as the slave in particular, are totally dependent for justice on their master. Human beings have an intrinsic incapacity to create justice. This general anthropological insight had in the world of antiquity a social correlate in the inability of the slave to participate in social relationships of justice of their own accord. A slave's testimony in court could only be given under torture. The slave as a dishonoured person lacked the capacity to be involved in the process of establishing justice except under coercion. The passivity of the slave, even to the extent of undergoing torture, was her or his fundamental connection to justice. Activity in creating justice was the prerogative of the master.

Turning to Paul's *Letter to the Romans* we find the structural correspondence between the social vocabulary of slavery and the theological language of justification confirmed. The theme of God as the slaveowner of the Christian, which the later followers of Paul applied to the social relation of master and slave, was used by Paul himself to explore the drastic reversal of a human being's status before God. In Romans 6:20–22 the justified sinners are portrayed as being formerly 'the slaves of sin' but now 'in bondage to God'. The transition of the Christian from the domination of sin into the realm of God's authority is seen as an exchange of masters.

Paul then proceeds to make marriage a simile of the justification event. Justification as freedom from the law is placed in a rather tortured analogy to the situation of a woman who is *hypandros*, 'under the power of a man', i.e., married to him. While her husband lives she is an adulteress if she gives herself to another man; if her husband dies she becomes free to give herself to another man. Christians, says Paul, are like the woman 'under the power of a man'. They have been made dead to the law through the body of Christ and now belong to another, namely Christ (Rom. 7:2–5). As in the later *Letter to the Ephesians* marriage and incorporation within the husband's body, whether human or Christ's, are juxtaposed. How does the body of Christ nullify the bond of human beings to the law? Because it breaks the marriage ties between human beings and the law by making them part of a new husband's body.

The comparison of the justification of Christians and the re-marriage of a widow is followed by reflections upon the helplessness of the human condition without the intervention of God. For Paul, of course, the law and sin are in no way identical. Sin derives its power from the law because human beings under sin are powerless to fulfill the law and thus fall ever deeper under the sway of sin. The powerlessness of the human being is expressed in terms of the slave's lack of freedom. Paul exclaims of his former condition that he is 'sold under sin' (7:14). Sin is seen as owning Paul's flesh.

Paul's concept of 'flesh' is exceedingly complex and no simple synonym of body. But the portrayal of being owned by sin moves within the same mental boundaries as the experience of social slavery:

I do not know what I do. For I do that which I do not want to do, but that which I hate I do ... It is no longer I that do it but the sin that dwells within me. For I know that no goodness resides in me, that is, in my flesh, (Romans 7:15–17)

The fundamental experience of slavery is the lack of control over the self. This lack of control extends further than the total subjection of the body to the power of another. Certainly, the self as an embodied self under slavery is vulnerable to enormous physical sufferings – beatings, rape, mutilation, death under torture. Nevertheless, even where the most inhumane treatment of the slave is absent, the slave is none the less 'socially dead' in Orlando Patterson's terminology. The master parasitically lives the life of the slave. The slave has no life of her or his own, because possessing no honour there is no demarcation line between the slave's and master's existence. The slave has been entirely absorbed into the master's will.

Sin for Paul is the theological twin of the slave's dishonour. Indeed, Paul's remark that under sin no goodness resides in him also runs parallel to the comon Graeco-Roman image of the slave as morally inferior. Aristotle had argued that some human beings were naturally slaves because their character was base.[7] One need not retroject later Christian doctrines of original sin onto Paul to see that he believed that sin, if not an innate quality, was none the less a permanent and ineradicable constituent of the human condition. The basic meaning of 'flesh' in Paul is the totality of the human self in its subjection to sin. The involuntary nature of the actions of the human being 'in the flesh', like those of the slave, arises out of the condition of being morally unfit to live according to one's own will.

D.W. Lucas has shown that Paul's notion of a human being, committing an action which she or he knows to be wrong and takes place through the overriding of her or his will by a force external to it, is not original.[8] Lucas refers to the passage in Euripides' play *Medea* where Medea says, 'I know that which I am about to do is evil, but passion is stronger than my will' (1078–9). According to the Greek myth retold by Euripides Medea falls in love with Jason when he and the Argonauts come to her father's kingdom in search of the Golden Fleece. She betrays her father, murders her brother, helps Jason steal the fleece and leaves with him. She becomes his wife and bears him children. But she shares the vulnerability of the enslaved woman, who without status and protection through male kin in a foreign community, is helpless against any abuse she might suffer from the hands of the man in whose household she dwells. Jason treats Medea like a concubine; he abandons her to marry the daughter of the ruler of the city, a woman who unambiguously possesses honour in the community. Medea becomes fully aware of her social marginalization; she is not only to be cast off by her husband but also deprived of her children. Medea's powerlessness is complete. She resists Jason's will not through the assertion of any will or rights of her own but through succumbing to the dictates of fate, which she feels as the dreadful impulse to kill her children.

Euripides and Paul both conceived of the human condition as fundamental powerlessness in relation to forces external to the human will but internally controlling human nature. The particular social reality of women and slaves was a metonymy for the human predicament. Euripides in a later play, *The Trojan Women*, went on to explore the link between the gender inferiority of women and the process of enslavement. Paul in chapters 6 and 7 of Romans intermingled slavery and marriage as social metaphors for the Christian experience of justification.

Paul does not use slavery and marriage identically in analogies to the justification event. Subjection to the law and marriage are compared on the one hand, and slavery and bondage to sin on the other. The distinction between a relation of domination which allows the honour of the inferior participant and a relation of domination which dishonours the one held in subjection seems to have concerned the apostle as much as his later follower, the author of Ephesians. For Paul subjection to the law does not equal the bondage of human beings to sin. The law does not strip the human being of all honour before God but the sinner. The social parallel in slaveholding patriarchy would be the effect of sexual intercourse. Sexual intercourse does not dishonour the woman but the slave. The total identity of the human being with the sinner is universal for Paul but no more necessary than the coincidence of enslaved status and female sex. The later doctrine of original sin has confused the universal fact of human sin in the apostle's eyes with its absolute necessity.

Sin for Paul is quite a different matter. He asserts a dialectic of dishonour/honour in which human beings are faced with a strange paradox. The alternatives are not slavery or freedom. We are either slaves of sin and free from righteousness, or we are free from sin and slaves of God. One is both slave and free, justified and a sinner. The righteousness of God is a freedom that enslaves.

Despite the careful differentiation of sin and law and their respective social metaphors of slavery and marriage there occurs just as much a convergence in theological discourse as in social reality. The bondage to sin and the sovereignty of the law do not differ in the degree of subjection that they impose upon a human being. Christ is the end of the law (Romans 10:4) but not the end of human subjection, no more than the woman, whose first husband is dead, is free from subordination to her new husband. Human domination by the law is replaced by human domination by love through which Christians fulfill the demands of the law (Romans 13:8). 'Love patriarchalism' is not only the Christian arrangement of marriage, as we find it in Ephesians, but also the underlying framework for Paul's understanding of the righteousness of God.

THE RIGHTEOUSNESS OF GOD AND SEXUALITY IN ROMANS

Paul's *Letter to the Romans* contains its own explicit working out of the theme of the righteousness of God as it bears upon human sexuality. In chapter 1 of Romans Paul proclaims that salvation is available in the gospel through its revelation of the righteousness of God. He then proceeds to demonstrate that the righteousness of God and the salvation it brings can only be obtained through faith in Jesus Christ. Paul contrasts the righteousness of God with the 'wrath of God'. The wrath of God befalls all those, who ignorant of the true nature of God, are incapable of doing good. Paul is directing his polemic against the Non-Jews of the ancient world, whose religions were from his Jewish perspective idolatry. The results of non-Jewish religious practices were dire in Paul's eyes:

> Therefore God gave them up in the lusts of their hearts to impurity, to the dishonouring of their bodies among themselves, because they exchanged the truth about God for a lie and worshipped and served the creature rather than the Creator, who is blessed forever! Amen. For this reason God gave them up to dishonourable passions. Their women exchanged natural relations for unnatural, and the men likewise gave up natural relations with women and were consumed with passion for one another, men committing shameless acts with men and receiving in their own persons the due penalty for their error. (Romans 1:24–27).

In recent years this passage of Romans has come under increased scrutiny as lesbians and gay men have pointed out how the Christian church has been a leading force in the persecution of gay people in the West. In addition, the Christian churches themselves have debated whether homosexuality is sinful or not and whether lesbians and gay men can be members or hold positions of responsibility in Christian congregations. There has been a similar apologetic response to the moral indictment of Christianity by gay people as there was to the charges of the patriarchal nature of the church made by feminists. Paul, we are told, has been misunderstood, and he was condemning sexual behaviour very different from that of today's lesbians and gay men.

John Boswell in his influential book *Christianity, Social Tolerance, and Homosexuality* contends that Paul's condemnation does not refer to gay people but to heterosexual persons who participate in homosexual acts.[9] His argument is based on a rather strained interpretation of the phrase *para phusin* which means 'against nature' and is frequently translated as unnatural. Boswell thinks that Paul is speaking of heterosexuals defying their own *personal* nature and not of homosexuals transgressing *universal* standards of natural morality. One is left wondering by Boswell's interpretation why Paul does not attack homosexuals who commit heterosexual acts. In chapter 1 of Romans Paul places women and men who have relations with their own sex side by side in his description of the objects of God's wrath, not homosexuals and heterosexuals who act contrary to their own sexual orientation.

Another example of the apologetic approach to Romans 1 is to be found in Robin Scroggs's argument that under the social conditions and from the cultural perspective of the ancient world pederasty between adult males and youths was the only form of homosexuality which was perceived or recognized. Hence, Paul shared the cultural blinkers of his contemporaries and his statements in Romans *ipso facto* touch only the homosexual form of pederasty, as it was known in the ancient world.[10] Scroggs draws attention to the social construction of sexuality but fails to make a convincing case that the ancient world and Paul equated homosexuality solely and fully with pederasty. Boswell and others have provided ample evidence of same-sex relations in antiquity which were not pederastic.

Both of these authors concentrate almost exclusively on male homosexuality. In contrast Bernadette Brooten insists that 'it is methodologically questionable· to subsume love relations between women under male homosexuality.'[11] She sees the condemnation of men loving men related to but not parallel to that of women loving women in this passage of Romans. Although ancient attitudes to male homosexuality were varied, the response to lesbian relations was almost universally negative and sometimes expressed in violent scorn. Brooten has demonstrated that the abhorrence of lesbian relations both in ancient writers in general and in Paul in particular was based on their view that such bonds between women subverted gender hierarchy. Gender hierarchy depended on the acceptance of the social and sexual roles of male activity and female passivity. Within the ancient understanding of sexuality one of the women in a lesbian relation must be usurping the active male role.

What to a modern reader of Paul's *First Letter to the Corinthians* may seem a trivial concern with hairstyles in chapter 11 was by no means an eccentricity in his social world. Brooten points out the link between the adoption of the outward appearance of the opposite sex, homosexuality and the confusion of gender roles in the ancient discussions of lesbian and gay male sexuality. Hence Paul's demands in 1 Corinthians 11 that women subordinate themselves to men and wear a headdress appropriate to their sex both reinforce each other and are on the same mental continuum with his condemnation of same-sex love relations. Disorder in the gender hierarchy is fundamental to Paul's description of the malaise both of the homosexual pagans of the Graeco-Roman world and of the hairstyles of the Corinthian congregation.

Most important for the present essay is Brooten's discussion of Paul's belief that same-sex relations incur for the pagans the 'dishonouring of their bodies among themselves' (Romans 1:24).[12] She explores this notion of dishonour through the anthropological category of impurity, as it has been established by Mary Douglas. Distinctions between pure and impure can be expressed in a variety of forms such as dietary laws and codes of sexual behaviour. The division of objects or actions into pure and impure shapes a symbolic system through which the world is given order and hierarchy.

The explanation of Paul's use of the terminology of dishonour through the anthropological category of impurity is not identical but also not incompatible with Patterson's theory of slavery as a system, based on a dichotomy of honour and dishonour. The slave's dishonour, unlike that of the woman who resists heterosexual subordination, does not disrupt the social hierarchy and its symbolic universe because the slave has no longer honour to lose. The homosexual pagans of Romans 1 are on account of the dishonouring of their bodies among the 'slaves of sin', whose fate later passages of the letter describe. The horror of sin for Paul is that, although sin occurs against human nature in the denial of the moral law inscribed in the human heart (Romans 2:15), it becomes human nature when it is the universal condition of all humanity. The moral freedom of human nature under the divine law has been polluted by the moral slavery of sin. Those who should possess honour have lost it through idolatry and its consequences of homosexuality. Christ's death, which has restored the honour of at least part of humanity, provides sure spiritual foundations for a world of order and hierarchy.

The righteousness of God for Paul is revealed in human sexuality. Admittedly, human sexuality is not an instrument of God's justice; the righteousness of God is not revealed *through* it. Yet, sexual expression marks the boundaries between the righteousness of God and the wrath of God, between the preservation of hierarchy and order and its confusion. Ironically, homosexuality plays a crucial role for Paul in the economy of divine justice since it signifies this through being in opposition to it as the cause of the wrath of God. The same dependence on contradiction is shared by the concepts of honour and freedom. A sense of honour develops in counterpoint to the recognition of how degradation is felt; the idea of freedom was born in the experience of slavery. It is not a matter of coincidence that it was the slaveholding ancient Greeks and modern Americans who gave the West its primary models of democracy.

The homosexual pagans are necessary to Paul's theological scheme for without them the knowledge of God's justice and its implications for human social order would be deprived of their source of life in the antonym. The cognitive parasitism of the righteousness of God is required by its character of a relationship of domination. The sovereignty of God and God's honour (which pagan worship is seen as disrespecting) rests upon God's power of violent coercion. It is assumed that human beings desire, even if not with their rational will, to be pagans, to be lesbians and unveiled women casting off divine authority. God's power is displayed not in the elimination of these but in their 'theologically dead' existence as a contrary and subjugated reality. Paul's insistence that all have sinned is not matched by a conviction that all will be saved. God's salvation does not demand the eradication of sin from the world, but that the distinction between righteousness and sin be restored. The slavery and dishonour of sin will remain, but God has separated some human beings from this state and chosen them for honour and righteousness:

> Has not the potter the authority to make out of his clay one pot for *honour* and another for *dishonour*? So what if God wished to show his anger and to make known his power by sustaining with great forbearance the vessels of wrath, he had made for damnation, so that he might show the riches of his

glory on the vessels of mercy, which he had prepared beforehand for glory. (Romans 9:21–23; emphases mine)

The binary division of pure and impure, honourable and dishonourable, found in the cultural codes of hierarchically ordered reality, is reduplicated in Paul's theological discourse on the righteousness of God which makes a human being just.

Paul's understanding of women loving women and men loving men as simultaneously an assault on gender hierarchy and a process of enslavement leaves no doubt as to the relation of the righteousness of God to sexuality in his mind. The righteousness of God demands the sexual subordination of women to men. Honouring our body for a woman means subjecting it to the sexual control of a man. For a man honouring his body prohibits that he take a passive effeminate role (the view of male homosexuality among Paul and many of his contemporaries). Instead a man must take an active and superordinate role in his social and sexual relations to women. For a woman or man to step outside the gender hierarchy reduces them to a condition of moral slavery.

THE RIGHTEOUSNESS OF GOD AS A CRITIQUE OF HUMAN MORALITY

Paul and especially his *Letter to the Romans* has provided the framework for the theological debate over justice within western Christianity. The Protestant Reformation of the sixteenth century emphasized Paul's teaching of justification by faith alone. Indeed, Luther gave the doctrine of justification through faith alone a clarity which is not apparent in the text of Romans.

Luther understood Paul to be claiming the impossibility of human beings to do good without the prior intervention of God's grace. There was nothing, no 'good works', through which a human being could earn God's grace. Indeed, the human attempt to be righteous, before God had imparted justice to a human being, was itself the fundamental nature of sin. For Luther the human condition was inherently in opposition to God. It was characterized by being turned in upon oneself (*incurvitas in se*). This self-directedness of human beings was reflected in all dimensions of human life, in the religious as much as in the social and political. Human beings contrived moral codes and religious practices to enshrine their own sense of righteousness, a righteousness inevitably at odds with the righteousness of God. Luther asserted a radical disjunction between the standards of human morality – even of Christian morality – and the righteousness which was valid in God's sight.

Luther was writing in a world without pagans, in an early modern Europe, where Christianity still permeated every area of political and cultural life. His attack upon the Christianity of his day was predicted on Paul's polemic against the Jews, rather than on the apostle's polemic against the pagans. Luther equated the Catholicism of his day with the non-Christian Judaism of Paul's time. Paul had warned his fellow-Jews that salvation was not obtainable through the Law. In chapter 10 of Romans the righteousness of God, revealed in Jesus Christ, is seen as 'the end of Law'. Luther believed that Paul's insistence on the inefficacy of the Law for salvation applied not only to the Jewish Torah but equally to Christian codes of moral behaviour. Paul had believed that the Jewish Torah had become ineffective for salvation because Jews as a matter of fact had not fulfilled it. Luther took Paul's critique of the Law to a radical conclusion by converting the non-fulfillment of the law from a fact into a necessity.

Human standards of morality are at worst deflections from the righteousness of God. At best they play an ambiguous role; incapable of promoting human goodness they may, when backed by the coercive power of the state, inhibit human wickedness. Their major function, however, is to drive a human being to despair, to the realization that his or her conceptions and practice of justice are hostile to the righteousness of God.[13] Luther clung to the belief that human standards of morality derived from the will of God, when they were equivalent to a universal natural law. But in their form of moral prescription they obscured the true nature of practical justice which was the spontaneous doing of good as a result of faith.

The righteousness of God had implications for human sexuality. Luther did not believe that a particular sexual lifestyle was the high road to salvation. Luther was an ardent critic of the Catholic practice of celibacy. In medieval Catholicism celibacy was counted among *the counsels of perfection*, that is, it was considered a meritorious way of life which allowed a fuller reception of God's grace. Celibacy was, of course, mandatory for the clergy and those in monastic orders. It was seen as distinguishing them from the laity, and their lack of sexual activity was seen as a mark of their belonging to a spiritual élite. Luther rejected this division of the church into first-class and second-class

Christians on the basis of sexual lifestyle. Moreover, the understanding of celibacy as a vehicle of spiritual perfection ran counter to
the core of his theology: justification through faith alone. Luther
reformulated the egalitarian baptismal formula which the apostle
Paul quoted in his *Letter to the Galatians* and yet departed from in so
many places of his later letters. Luther writes: 'In Christ there is
neither male nor female, thus neither celibate nor spouse.'[14]

The doctrine of justification through faith alone provided a theological framework for social criticism. Yet, Luther himself muted the
radical implications of his teaching, most notoriously in his vitriolic
opposition to the peasants' rebellion against their oppression, a revolt
which had been inspired by the Reformation teaching about justice.
Luther was willing to allow social and political institutions – such as
the feudal state and serfdom – to remain in place, even to see them
mandated by God, but denied them any capacity to make human
beings good or righteous.

In his struggle against élitist celibacy he extolled marriage. The
institution of marriage, which Luther knew from his parents' and his
own marriage to an ex-nun in the context of the German city of the
sixteenth-century, was certainly patriarchal. He was willing to leave
the patriarchal institution intact, and yet he wanted egalitarian
reforms in the sphere of the spiritual function of the household. This
was the religious instruction of children and servants. Luther recognized an 'office of the mother' alongside the 'office of the father' in the
patriarchal household, through which wives shared in the spiritual
authority of their husbands over the household's members. He also
pleaded for the education of girls, albeit with a training in the duties of
wives and mothers.[15] Marriage among German burghers of the
sixteenth century did not preclude the economic activity of wives. The
household was also a unit of economic production. Thus, women's
work in the household often gave them a standing not incompatible
with the spiritual authority Luther allotted them.

Luther's solution to the social implications of the righteousness of
God was an uneasy compromise. He affirmed social hierarchies, yet
gave them far weaker theological warrants than Paul and his followers. His theology provided a basis for social criticism, and yet his
acceptance of the existing social institutions as the best possible in a
sinful world undercut Reformation teaching as a vehicle for social
change. Luther was not unaware of social injustices and believed it
was the Christian's task to correct them. Yet, since Luther's view of

the law was negative in the sense that he saw it as forming a bulwark against human wickedness and not as a means of creating justice and the conditions for the flourishing of goodness among human beings, he most often commended passive resistance to Christians in the face of injustice.

Luther had taken over from Paul wholesale the apostle's definition and critique of the Jewish Torah. The lack of pagans in Luther's world prevented him from adopting Paul's polemic against the homosexuality of the pagans. Jews, however, were present. Luther at first hoped to convert them to Christianity, believing that the impure teaching of the gospel was the reason for Jewish rejection of it. When Jews failed to be won over to the Christianity of the Protestant Reformation Luther's attitude hardened into vituperative attack on the Jews and the acceptance of their persecution. Luther thus perpetuated Paul's antisemitism which was to have such devastating effects, especially in his own country.

Luther's inability to appreciate the Jewish Torah was linked to his lack of insight into the *social* relativity of such institutions as princely government and the patriarchal household. He could not see law as the means by which a community could positively shape and change their collective life in response to the righteousness of God because he saw social and political institutions as part of a permanent changeless natural substratum to human sinful life. The relativity of social institutions only became part of western consciousness when industrialization and political revolution overturned and re-shaped them, giving rise, among other things, to the modern family and the modern state. One cannot fault Luther for living in a pre-modern age and hence within the intellectual boundaries of its social theory. But one can ask in what ways can Luther's theological heritage be legitimately claimed for the possibilities of human liberation – and of human oppression – which the modern period has disclosed.

The failure of Luther's social criticism to promote social change was due not only to his narrow concept of human law but also to his dualistic idea of human love. It was not Luther – nor Paul – who introduced into Christianity the notion of two loves. That dubious distinction belongs to the fifth-century church father, Augustine. None the less, Luther integrated Augustine's thinking on love into his renewal of Paul's teaching of justification through faith alone. Luther distinguished Christian love from the self-love of the individual turned in on him – or herself. Yet, this dichotomy of love in Luther's thought was thoroughly secondary to his dualistic separation of love from faith.

The Christian possessed both faith and love, but experienced them in diverse spheres in diverse ways. Luther in the *Freedom of a Christian* expressed this distinction in a famous paradox: 'A Christian is a perfectly free lord of all, subject to none. A Christian is a perfectly dutiful servant (*Knecht*)[16] of all, subject to all.'[17] The reconciliation of these contrary statements lies for Luther in the two distinct results of the grace and righteousness of God operating on a human being to make that person just. The direct result of the righteousness of God is to make the sinner the just. The justified sinner is also free; this freedom consists in a faith that exempts the Christian from the requirements of the Law, all human standards of morality. Yet, the fruit of faith is love and thus the indirect but necessary consequence of the righteousness of God justifying the sinner.[18]

The love of the Christian is fundamentally other-directed and void of self-directedness. This is the logical consequence of Luther's belief that the human condition and human sin is self-directedness. The turning outwards of the human being towards God through justification is the turning away from the self. What has occurred in the sphere of faith is retained as the anthropological structure of the Christian in the sphere of love. Although Christians are free from being judged and judging themselves according to human standards of morality they, nevertheless, accept wholeheartedly their subjection to the social institutions and restrictions that human morality underpins. Christians are not concerned for their own welfare but solely for that of their neighbour. The only cases in which Luther allows an active resistance to oppression is when the welfare of the neighbour is at risk. Through love Christians submit themselves spontaneously to social authority and hierarchy and not because they are required by moral prescriptions, the threat of legal penalty, or self-interest. Christian love is the foundation for a relationship of domination by the neighbour, especially when that neighbour has the authority of a feudal prince or husband.

THE RIGHTEOUSNESS OF GOD AND FEMINIST JUSTICE

What the theological discourse of the righteousness of God has in common with feminist conceptions of justice is that it locates the roots of justice – and injustice – within human experience. Both the righteousness of God and feminist justice are peculiar understandings of justice. They have little to do with the theories of justice found in western legal or political science. They do not reject ideas of distributive justice, of equity, or of careful restraints on the pursuit of self-interest, but deem these inadequate for just relations between human beings. The righteousness of God and feminist justice seek the complete transformation of the structures of the human self and experience. When feminist ethicists claim that women's experience is normative for feminist ethics, they understand women's experience to include the core of women's personhood, the relationship of women's selves to female social roles and most importantly feminist praxis as a means of change for women's lives in their personal and political dimensions, the private and public spheres, and beyond these divisions.

Feminist justice is seen as reflexive of women's selves. In this it most closely resembles the Aristotelian virtue concept of justice in the ethical tradition. Yet this similarity is bounded by a fundamental antithesis. Feminists do not see different human virtues as the source and ground of differing social roles and statuses in a hierarchically ordered society. They do not see their political praxis as an affirmation of the existing political order as the necessary framework for the social and cultural expression of women. The unity of a person's life, which is virtue for Aristotle, is disrupted in women's experience. Feminists recognize the incongruence between women's selves and female social roles. Justice as a virtue, as part of the integrity of women's lives and the societies they live in is not a given of the moral order of the universe but requires a praxis transformative of the self and its individual and communal contexts.

The righteousness of God shares the suspicion of feminist justice that natural justice is the naturalization of injustice in a system of moral values that cloaks power relations. However, the result of a person's justification by God is not to abolish the earthly conditions of domination and self-alienation but to relativize these through the ultimate power-over relationship of God's total claim on the Christian's life and through the thorough alienation of the person from any self which is not absorbed into this relationship with God. God's righteousness becomes our own by remaining fully alien to us. The capacity for justice is therefore external and transcendent to the

271

human self. The justice which occurs 'outside of us', in the phrase of the Protestant Reformation, defines the love between us. God's self-sacrificing love in the death of Christ is held to be the model for the exercise of power over dependents. Love does not eradicate but changes the modes of domination; no longer self-love but love for others is applauded as the motive for domination.

Sexuality in a relationship of domination is either the exercise of or the submission to power. Christian sexual attitudes absorbed the negative evaluations of the body and passion in its early mental environment of Hellenistic philosophy. This process was inevitable because of a prior theological decision to understand the God–human relationship in continuity with the power relations of slaveholding patriarchy. Passion means to be in a state of passivity where one is subject to the rule of external forces. The body is the instrument for mastery over the person and passion, which finds its seat within it, makes the body permeable to control.

Lesbian sexuality disrupted the symbolism of power. It subverted sexual intercourse as the representation of male activity and authority and of female passivity and subservience. Passivity was the necessary attribute of those whom nature fitted to be dominated by others. In denying the passivity of women lesbian sexuality challenged the order of a universe, where it is natural for some to dominate and others to be dominated. It undercut the ideological base for the sexual abuse of women in marriage and under slavery. Although Paul and early Christianity cared little for the continued material existence of this world which was 'passing away', they had a vast stake in its symbolism of power because they had chosen to express the nature of God and God's relationship to human beings in its terms.

Can one love someone over whom one holds power? The sexual subjection of all women in slaveholding patriarchy places the marriage of the freeborn woman and the mistress of the household on a continuum with the rape of the slave woman. The institution of slavery both in ancient and modern societies must be studied in its interweaving with the structure of the household. The condition of women in slaveholding patriarchy can only be understood in its connection to the institution of slavery and the sexual exploitation of women under slavery.

The same holds true today. The sexual exploitation of women and the control of their sexuality is not located in an isolated patriarchal aspect of society. The feminist vision of justice must contain analysis of the interconnections of gender oppression to all forms of oppression in our society. This endeavour should not be reductionist; it should refrain from asserting that patriarchy is the root of all evil. Interlocking relationships of domination create a world in which human bodies are instruments of productive as well as reproductive labour and material and symbolic commodities of exchange in the transactions of the powerful. Women's bodies have been especially vulnerable to the process of domination because of the economic value of their reproductive functions and their susceptibility to control through rape.

Christianity, unwilling to criticize the sexual exploitation of women within marriage or under slavery, has projected the malaise of the social institution onto sexuality itself. Theologians have fled from the ambiguity of love by asserting its duality. In this century the Danish theologian Nygren's typology of *agape* and *eros* has re-asserted that there are two loves: eros which is self-seeking, and agape which is other-directed. Agape is God's love for us and the love with which we reciprocate God's love. The cultural maimings of the heart can be thus laid at the door of imperfect human love, eros. The human heart itself can take refuge in the love of God and in an undefiled, because 'unerotic', love of neighbour.

With the differentiation of gender roles in modern society, the division of home from workplace and the separation of public and private, an economy of the two loves has developed which assigns women the social roles of agape and self-sacrifice and men the social roles of eros and self-assertion. The two loves, like the two sexes, are seen not simply in opposition to one another but also complementary to each other. The 'battle of the sexes' is also reflected in the struggle of the two loves, and both are essential to the stability and growth of patriarchal culture. Admittedly, the theologians are more censorious of the prevalence of self-love but are none the less reconciled to its permanence as part of the human condition.

Self-sacrificing love is the virtue of the home and private life. Its viability in the public sphere of governmental and business policy is limited. Yet without domestic and private agape the aggressive, 'masculine' pursuit of self-interest in the public domain would be impossible. The social reproduction of the family, which is in modern society as crucial as its biological reproduction, nurtures and socializes its members into the roles approved by culture and society. Agape reproduces eros. For instance the present debate within American feminism over racism in the women's movement needs to be viewed against the social construction of the heart in a racist post-slavery society of the modern west. In understanding the failure of white women to combat racism one has to examine their intimate connection to white men. Where do white men learn to assert themselves at the cost of sacrifice to others? At their mother's knee and in their wife's or lover's arms.

The fusion of self-love with love of others is a pre-requisite for feminist justice. Such an integrated love will be at its very core erotic. Erotic love seeks self-fulfillment through relation to the other; it is simultaneously self- and other-directed. As such it shares the structure of compassion, for compassion is not disinterested love nor love without a self-reference. Compassion is an act of empathy in which one is moved to connect the sufferings of another to one's own feelings, to link the material and emotional needs of another to one's own desire for happiness. The inclusion of the self, in the justice which we seek for others, arises out of the realization that eros and compassion together constitute what Carter Heyward has so aptly called 'our passion for justice'.

Feminist justice is faced with the moral ambiguity of human existence even when it overcomes the dualism of patriarchal love. Women's experience is no less socially constructed than the word of God, and hence feminist justice like the righteousness of God is practised and understood within the boundaries of a given culture and society. Yet, human beings can never be reduced to the sum of social variables which configure their existence. There is a surplus of experience, not independent nor separable from the social construction of reality, but not contained entirely within its limits. To move into this surplus of experience is to enter the realm of ambiguity, where the ethical guides of one's society may lose their prescriptive force but not their capacity to torment conscience.

Despair at the efficacy of the ethical norms to promote justice does not banish guilt at their transgression. But we must act in the midst of ambiguity even when we do not have a vision of the righteous self with which we want to replace our present existence of insufficient justice. It was passage into the surplus of human experience which made the theological discourse of the righteousness of God necessary. Both Paul and Luther underwent the profound disorientation of awakening to the fracture between the socially constructed self and the self on the edge of reality. Luther understood the movement into the surplus of experience and the imperative to action as the demand on the

Christian to live outside of him- or herself 'in Christ through faith, in his neighbour through love'.[19]

Feminists will reject the grounding of the surplus of experience in a transcendent other. Yet, the contrary position, favoured by many feminists, that the ultimate source of our lives is to be found within ourselves is equally erroneous because it takes as little account of the social construction of experience as Luther. There is no depth of women's experience unsullied by patriarchy. The spatial metaphors of inside/outside and the corresponding philosophical concepts of immanence and transcendence are inadequate to describe the structure of experience. When I as a woman enter my surplus of experience I encounter a self of mine outside of my self. This self outside the self can be equally well described as a movement within as beyond the self.

Living towards myself outside myself I feel ambiguity most keenly in the area of sexuality. Luther as a monk discovered that the righteousness of God had a greater moral affinity with his sexual lusts than with the supposed spirituality of celibacy. Despite his enthusiasm for marriage Luther would certainly have been distressed by present-day Christians' proclamation of the salvific effects of marriage and the family. When Christian truth is collapsed into the identification with a particular sexual lifestyle then one is confronted with what Luther called 'justification through works' and condemned as contrary to Christian faith and trust in the righteousness of God.

Feminist justice must oppose compulsory heterosexuality[20] as fiercely as Luther did the exaltation of celibacy. The discrimination and persecution of lesbians suppresses an alternative to heterosexual marriage and male control of women's sexuality. It, therefore, reinforces patriarchal society's construction of *all* women's experience. At the same time, it attempts to cut every woman off from her surplus of experience, whether lesbian or not, because it confines the expanse of a woman's passion to the narrow limits of patriarchal morality. It removes her from the source of her sense of justice in its connection to the erotic affirmation of herself as a woman.

Our sexuality may disclose to us the God who sustains the feminist quest for justice, a God that dwells in our ambiguity as we stretch our experience beyond that legitimated by our social and cultural institutions. The justice of such a God would be the critical affirmation of women's selves as they become aware of their complicity in their own oppression and the oppression of others, and would impassion them to become the righteous selves they are not. Can there be such a thing as a feminist righteousness of God?

NOTES

Several modern versions of the New Testament were used in translating the biblical quotations directly from the Greek text which, therefore, do not depend on any one English translation.

1 *Our Passion for Justice*, New York, Pilgrim Press, 1984, p.86.
2 Sexual liaisons between free women and slaves did occur, but were frowned upon. Clement of Alexandria, writing as a church father at the turn of the second century, castigates women for bathing naked in the presence of their slaves because this provides opportunity for sexual excitement and activity (*Paedagogus*, III,5,8–13). For an English translation see *The Writings of Clement of Alexandria*, Ante-Nicene Christian Library, vol. 6, trans. William Wilson, Edinburgh, T. & T. Clark, 1867, p.297. The first Christian emperor Constantine specified capital punishment for a free woman who had sexual intercourse with a slave; see Sarah B. Pomeroy, *Goddesses, Whores, Wives, and Slaves. Women in Classical Antiquity*, New York, Shocken, 1975, p.160.
3 Pomeroy, op. cit., p.196.
4 Orlando Patterson, *Slavery and Social Death* (Cambridge, Ma.: Harvard University Press, 1982), p.78.
5 See G.E.M. de Ste Croix, *The Class Struggle in the Ancient World*, Ithaca, Cornell University Press, 1981, pp.104f., 419. He notes, for example, that the word *hypotassesthai*, used for the subjection of wives to husbands in Ephesians 5 is used of the master–slave relation in other New Testament writings (Titus 2:9, 1 Peter 2:18).
6 John Reumann, *Righteousness in the New Testament*, Philadelphia: Fortress/ New York: Paulist Press, 1982, p.91.
7 Aristotle, *Politics*, I.5.1254b, 1255a-b. The stereotype of the morally inferior slave was also shared by Christian writers. See Salvian, *The Governance of God*, 8.3, quoted in Thomas Wiedemann, *Greek and Roman Slavery*, London, Croom Helm, 1981, pp.61f.
8 D.W. Lucas, *The Greek Tragic Poets*, 2nd rev. edn, London, Cohen & West, 1959, p.180.
9 John Boswell, *Christianity, Social Tolerance, and Homosexuality. Gay People in Western Europe from the Beginning of the Christian Era to the Fourteenth Century*, Chicago, University of Chicago Press, 1980, pp.109–12.
10 Robin Scroggs, *The New Testament and Homosexuality*, Philadelphia, Fortress, 1983.
11 Bernadette Brooten, 'Paul's Views on the Nature of Women and Female

Homoeroticism' in *Immaculate and Powerful. The Female in Sacred Image and Social Reality*, ed. Clarissa W. Atkinson, Constance H. Buchanan and Margaret Miles, Boston, Beacon Press, 1985, p.78.

12 *Ibid.*, pp.72–5.

13 *Lectures on Galatians* (1535), Luther's Works, vol. 26, trans. J. Pelikan, St Louis, Concordia, 1963, pp.308–10.

14 Weimarer Ausgabe, 8, 652, 'In Christo autem neque masculus neque femina, ita neque virgo neque uxor.' Cf. Galatians 3:28, 'There is neither Jew nor Greek, slave nor free, male nor female; for you are all one in Christ Jesus.'

15 See Gerta Scarffenorth, *Freunde in Christus. Die Beziehung von Mann und Frau bei Luther im Rahmen seines Kirchenverständnisses*, Studien und Problemberichte aus dem Projekt des Deutschen Nationalkomitees des Lutherischen Weltbundes, vol. 1, Gelnhausen, Burckhardthaus-Verlag, 1977, pp.243–62.

16 *Knecht* was the translation chosen by Luther for the Greek word *doulos* (slave) in the New Testament. *Knecht* in Luther's own society designated a serf. Serfdom represents an intermediate stage of bondage between slavery and freedom. Its conditions can be harsh and the severity of their exploitation had induced the German peasants to revolt in the years 1524 and 1525.

17 *The Freedom of a Christian*, Luther's Works, vol. 31, Philadelphia, Muhlenberg Press, 1957, p.344.

18 *Ibid.*, pp.358–60.

19 *The Freedom of a Christian*, p.371.

20 The phrase 'compulsory heterosexuality' is, of course, borrowed from Adrienne Rich's article 'Compulsory Heterosexuality and Lesbian Existence' in *Signs*, vol. 5 (1980), pp.631–60.

24

PRAYER FOR CONTINUATION

1

There is a record
I wish to make here.
A life.
And not this life alone
but the thread
which keeps shining
like gold floss woven into cloth
which catches your eyes
and you are won over.

Kyrie Eleison
Baruch atah
Hosana   adonai
Omne Padme   Gloria
Nam Myo-Ho
Renge Kyo
Galan
galancillo.
Do you love
this world?

Where is the point I can enter?
Where is the place I can touch?

Let me tell you
I am so serious
and taking aim
like a woman with a bow
eyes looking silently
at each space between the trees
for movement.

2

I cannot begin now.
I do not wish to write these numbers
on this page here.
224 warheads destroy
every Soviet city with a population
over 100,000.
But once I begin writing
the figures do not stop.
A 20 megaton
bomb, a firestorm rages over
3,000 acres.
A 1,000 megaton bomb
destroys
California
Nevada, Utah, Oregon,
Puget Sound.
Destroys
California.

3

Thirty-seven days from my
fortieth birthday. I have
gone up and down this coast
so many times I could trace
the shape of it for you
with my hands, up
into the high cold trees, down
to warm water and
the sprawling city
where I was
born, 1943.
In that year
while I slept
not entirely wanted
in a still room
behind venetian blinds
somewhere in a foreign language
babies were set on fire.
Their cries did not wake me.
Only I breathed in the dust
of their deaths.

4

It is my love I hold back
hide
not wanting to be seen
scrawl of hand
writing
don't guess
don't guess at my
passion
a wholly wild and raging
love for this world.

5

(Home)
If you look in this block
in the North of California
you will find a house
perhaps a century old
with the original wood shingles
dark from years of sun
and fine old joints, the men
who made them are dead, the attic
made into a bedroom now, the
linoleum added in 1955.
Twenty years ago
I lived there, a student
studying the history of
Western Civilization, reading John Milton,
looking out the attic window
at a cement sidewalk
which was before just a
dirt path
and Spanish, and was before
perhaps, a forest or a
meadow, a field,
belonging to the Ohlone
who have all
even their children
even all traces of who they were
perished.

6

This is the world I was born into.
Very young I learned
my mother and my father
had a terrible sorrow.
And very young
I learned this sorrow from them.

7

The mind is vast
what we know small.
Do you think we are not all
sewn together?
I still argue with her
grit my teeth trying to feel
the pain that riddled her body
the day they told her
she would never walk.
I try to enter her mind
the night she took her own life.

Cells have memory!
I shout to her.
Science gave you
an unnecessary despair.

8

Nor do they argue
nor do they understand
nor do they know
but still it is so.
And there are structures of
unknowing
we call disbelief.

9

Every American city
with a population above
25,000
targeted.
A bomb with the
explosive power
of 20 million tons of TNT.
80 per cent of all cancers.
How is it,
this woman asks,
the brilliant efforts of
American scientists
have been put
to such destructive uses?

10

It is not real, they tell us,
this home we long for
but a dream of a place
that never
existed.
But it is so familiar!
And the longing in us is
ourselves

11

This is the world I was born into.
I saw the wave and its white curl.
I saw branches coming from trees
like streams from rivers.
And the water poisoned
and the land.
I saw the whale leap out of the water
I saw my child's eyes come out of me
                              her first cry.
And the air, the rain acid.

Kyrie Eleison

Baruch atah
Hosana
Adonai
Do you love the world?

12

Suppose she lay down her bow.
And went into
that place
stepping so slowly
so surely

13

This is what I wanted to tell you.
This is what I wanted to say.
Words come late and dark
near sleep.
She said to me
my head was eating my heart.
And what is good?
What is bad?
The delicacy of transmission.
Old alliances fracture
like the cold branches of a
winter tree.
This is the closest I can get.
The world is washed in space.
It is the words she used
precisely those
and I could not remember them.
Only my conviction.
There was badness and goodness.
One was bad.
The other suffered.
And I wanted to
I wanted to mend her.
She told me the whole story
and I told her what was
good and what was bad,

and this was not what she needed.
You think I am trying
to throw away morality
but I am not.
I am not trying to
throw away caring.
In a dream
I see myself
a handsome man
walking without feeling
into a desert.
I am not like him
yet this dream comes to me
and I feel grief.
Out at the edge of this territory
is a missile.
I know for certain
this weapon is bad.
I do not try to mend her
and this makes me weep
for what she has suffered.

14

(The Enemy)
I wanted you to be good.
I wanted your judgements.
But all your rules became ash.
Your goodness was like an island.
(Your sainthood *was* the sin.)
Now that you have fallen
I cross the water
wrestle with you
charge you to bless me
watch as you
appear and disappear
become me.

15

The mind is vast.
A whale blows.

Shall we pitch ourselves into terror?
Shall we come home?
Enter darkness, weep
know the dimension
of absence, the unreachable deep.

16

How far can they go?
This is my speech
an American speech of whalers
and farmers what my
people did
plain, simple, honed
to the point
how far will they go?
Is there a stopping point?
Everyone knows there is not.

17

What can we make of this?
Two children held hostage together
in a van
for ten months.
What kind of man?
A girl, born three years ago
in California,
a boy who was born in
and survived Vietnam.
How far?
The children were continually beaten
with a rubber hose
and forced into sexual acts
in exchange for being fed.
I am a woman
who reads this story
in a newspaper.

18

(Bone Cancer)
You must not let terror overtake you.
It is a bone breaking in the middle of the night.
It is a misspelled word.
It is everything you thought you knew
becoming unknown, the leaves
stripped from the tree,
all the greenness orange and dry,
it is pain past bearable, you must not.
Down the street in the darkness someone young
is dying. The soil, perhaps, under your feet
is poison, the water you drink.
What is this? Be reasonable. Disaster
is always predicted and look
we exist. Humanity had a day of birth,
slow, unreasoned, surprising. Now,
is it possible, is it possible
could this be?

19

Do we not want
this place
to find it
the body again
hearth, heart.
How is it I can say this
so that you will
see too what I have seen.
After the fires
(after the unspeakable)
there will be no home.
And what of us
will remain in memory?
Nothing?

20

At least we think of them.
The six million.
We long for them.
Want them to be like they were
before
want the music
their mothers and fathers sang
to pass from our lips.
And we ask
How is it they did not know?

21

Do you think it is right
to despair?
No, no, it is not about
right and wrong.
It is the thread
shining.

22

Kyrie Eleison
Baruch atah   adonai
Omne Padme
New rules
take the place of old.
Be Here Now
is the lesson.
But I do not want to be.
I am one hundred years away
into the future.
My heart aches wondering.
Will this old tree grow even bigger?
Will its roots threaten the foundation of
                        this house?
Will there be a daughter of a
        daughter of a daughter
        a son? And what is the

look in their eyes? Tell me
what you see there. And
do you like to watch
them as they walk across
fields.

Fields?

Susan Griffin

INDEX

Compiled by Jean Ottley, Linda Hurcombe, Tom Hurcombe and Trish Johnson.

Francis of Assisi
Cartledge, Susan, 218
Catherine of Sienna, Ste, 126–7
Casting a new circle . . . (excerpt), 205
celebration of children, 89
celibacy, 4, 72ff; and autonomy, 61,
  236; as a choice of sexual lifestyle,
  72, 81; in the church, 58, 242; and
  dualism, 76, 79; as high ethic, 233;
  non-historical, 78; Protestant
  rejection of, 229; 'religious', 73;
  and solitude, 79; as vocation, 76,
  241; women-identified, 62, 236
celibate elite, 212
Chadwick, Owen, 232
chameleon mode, 110, 119
chastity, 56, 72; as highest calling,
  241; as spiritual elite, 241; and
  fear, 59; *see also* celibacy
childbirth, 99–100, 147ff, 153, 157
choice, between marriage and
  career, 246
Christ, as bridegroom, 133
christianity: conversion to, 234
  complete equality between male
  and female, 234, 243–4; counter-
  cultural, 245; Medieval, 242; and
  platonism, 232; and suffering, 130
*Christianity, Social Tolerance and
  Homosexuality, see* Boswell, John
post-Christianity, and rejection of
  asceticism, 230
Christian Science, 244
Church, 31; as mother, 133ff
Color Purple, The, 2
'coming out', 109ff, 113, 118
community, 181–2; 'counter-cultural'
  contemporary, and 'new ascetics',
  247; Divine, 53; as female, 210;
  and *Kairos,* 217; life as nun, 96; of
  love, 138; of rational thought, 92;
  religious, 73; school, 104; separatist,
  75, 241; separatist lesbian, marginalization of, 246; of women, 131
concubine, 257, 260
consumerism, 247
contrasexual, 22
control, 98

Corinthians, 213
'counter-cultural': Christianity, 245;
  community, contemporary, and
  'new ascetics', 247
coupledom, *see* pair bond
creationism, 1
Cretan maze, 197
Cruise missiles, 45
cults, 129, 219
Curb, Rosemary, with Monahan,
  Nancy, 82

Dahl, Bryony, 45
Daly, Mary, 61, 114
David, King, *see* Bathsheba
Davies, Steven, 249
Dead Sea Scrolls, 233
death, 100–2; and dying, 191, 194;
  mini-death, 100; mortality, 233,
  235
Delilah, 212
democracy, models of, 265
demons, 231
desire: expressed, 134; sexual, 6
Dickson, Anne, 80–1
Diman, Muriel, 114
discipline: as an appropriate feminist
  agenda, 248; and integration with
  world transformation, 248
discrimination: against lesbians,
  111; *see also* oppression
domesticity, 2
Doonesbury, 62
Douglas, Mary, 264
Dowell, Susan, 206ff
dreams, 174, 178, 189, 193, 198
dress codes, male/female, 264
Druke, Mary, with Peterson,
  Jacqueline, 230
dualism, 8, 129ff, 222, 266, 270

ecstacy, 79, 102; sexual, 211, 213
Ego, 32
embodiment, turn from other
  worldliness, 229
*Embodiment: An Approach to Sexuality
  and Christian Theology, see* Nelson,
  James